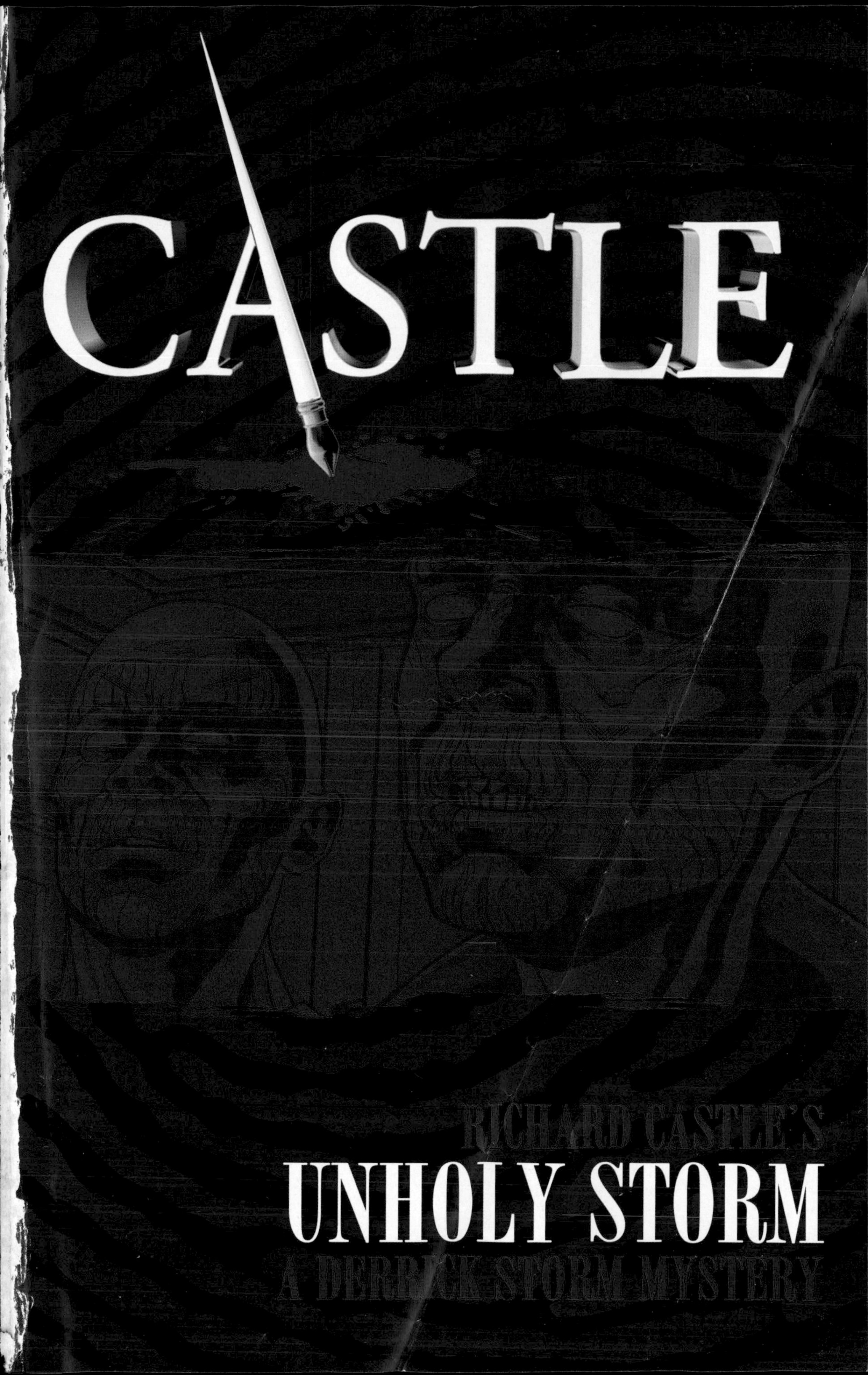
CASTLE
RICHARD CASTLE'S
UNHOLY STORM
A DERRICK STORM MYSTERY

WRITER
CULLEN BUNN

PENCILS
ROBERT ATKINS,
WILL SLINEY &
ANDREA MUTTI

INKS
SCOTT HANNA, WILL SLINEY
& ANDREA MUTTI

COLORS
SOTOCOLOR

LETTERER
VIRTUAL CALLIGRAPHY'S CORY PETIT

COVER ART
CARLO PAGULAYAN
WITH **SCOTT HANNA & PAUL MOUNTS**

EDITOR
EMILY SHAW

Special Thanks to
Andrew Marlowe, Lisa Schomas, Cooper McMains,
and Rosalie Villapando

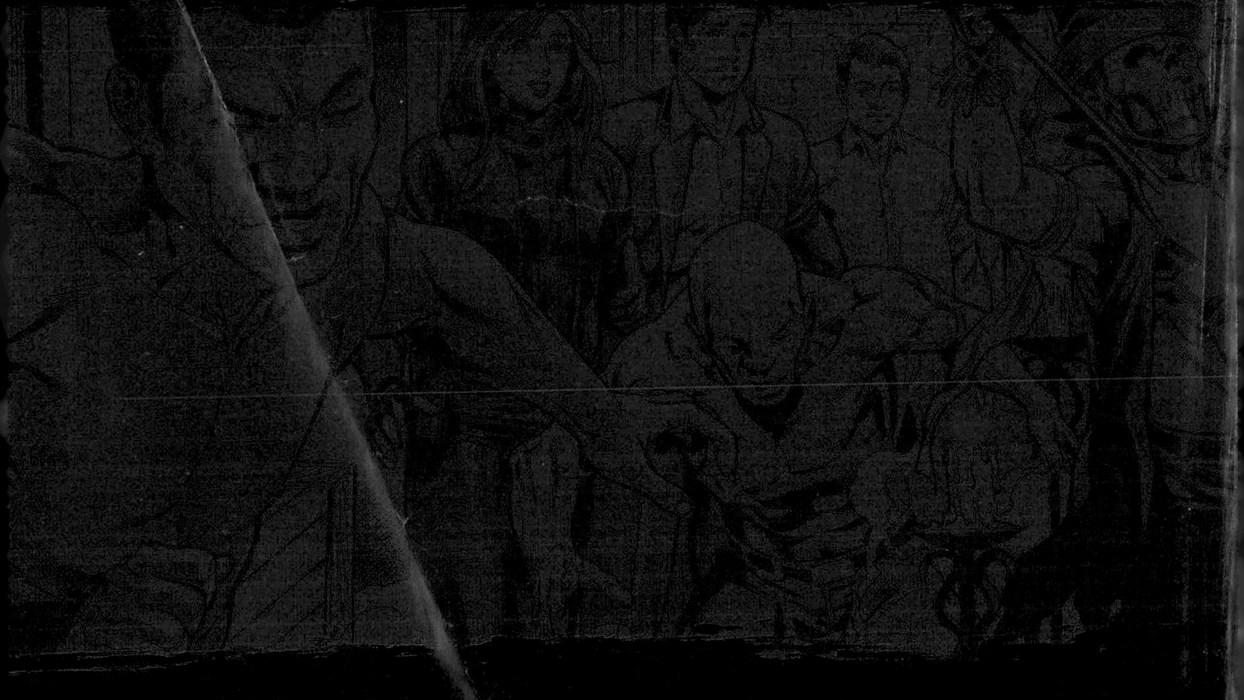

Collection Editor Jennifer Grünwald Associate Managing Editor Alex Starbuck Editor, Special Projects Mark D. Beazley
Senior Editor, Special Projects Jeff Youngquist SVP Print, Sales & Marketing David Gabriel Book Design Jeff Powell
Editor in Chief Axel Alonso Chief Creative Officer Joe Quesada Publisher Dan Buckley

CASTLE

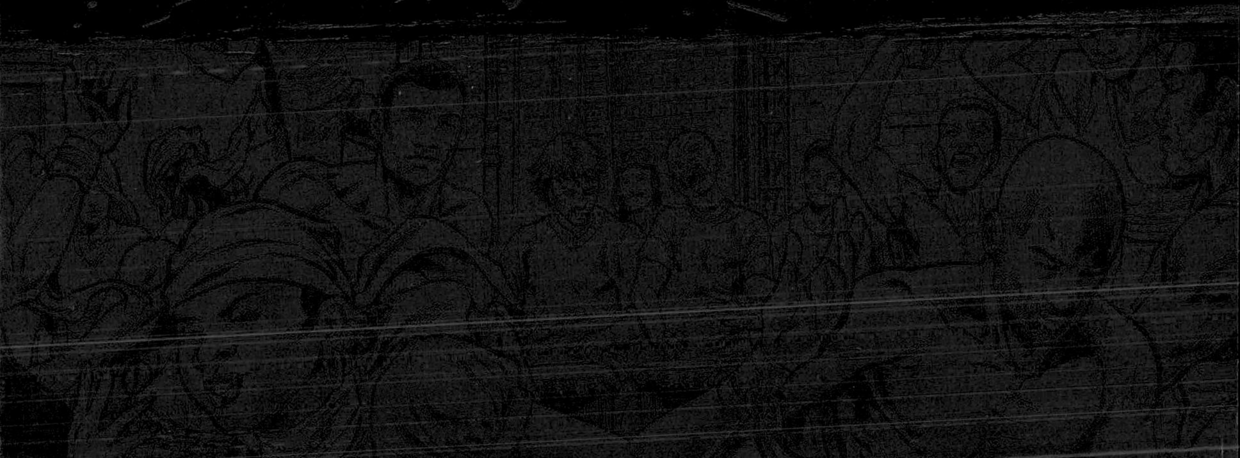

RICHARD CASTLE'S

UNHOLY STORM

A DERRICK STORM MYSTERY

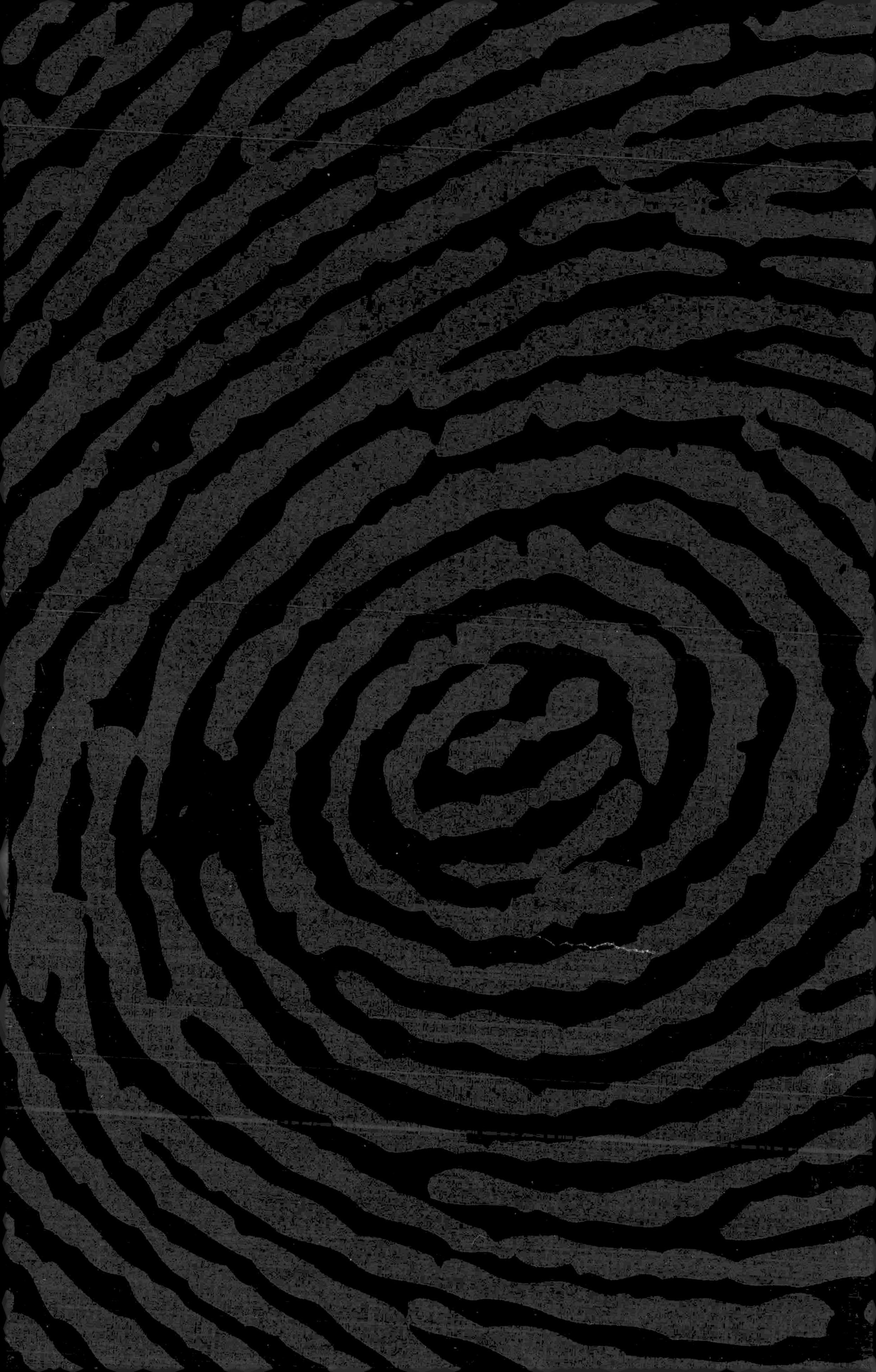

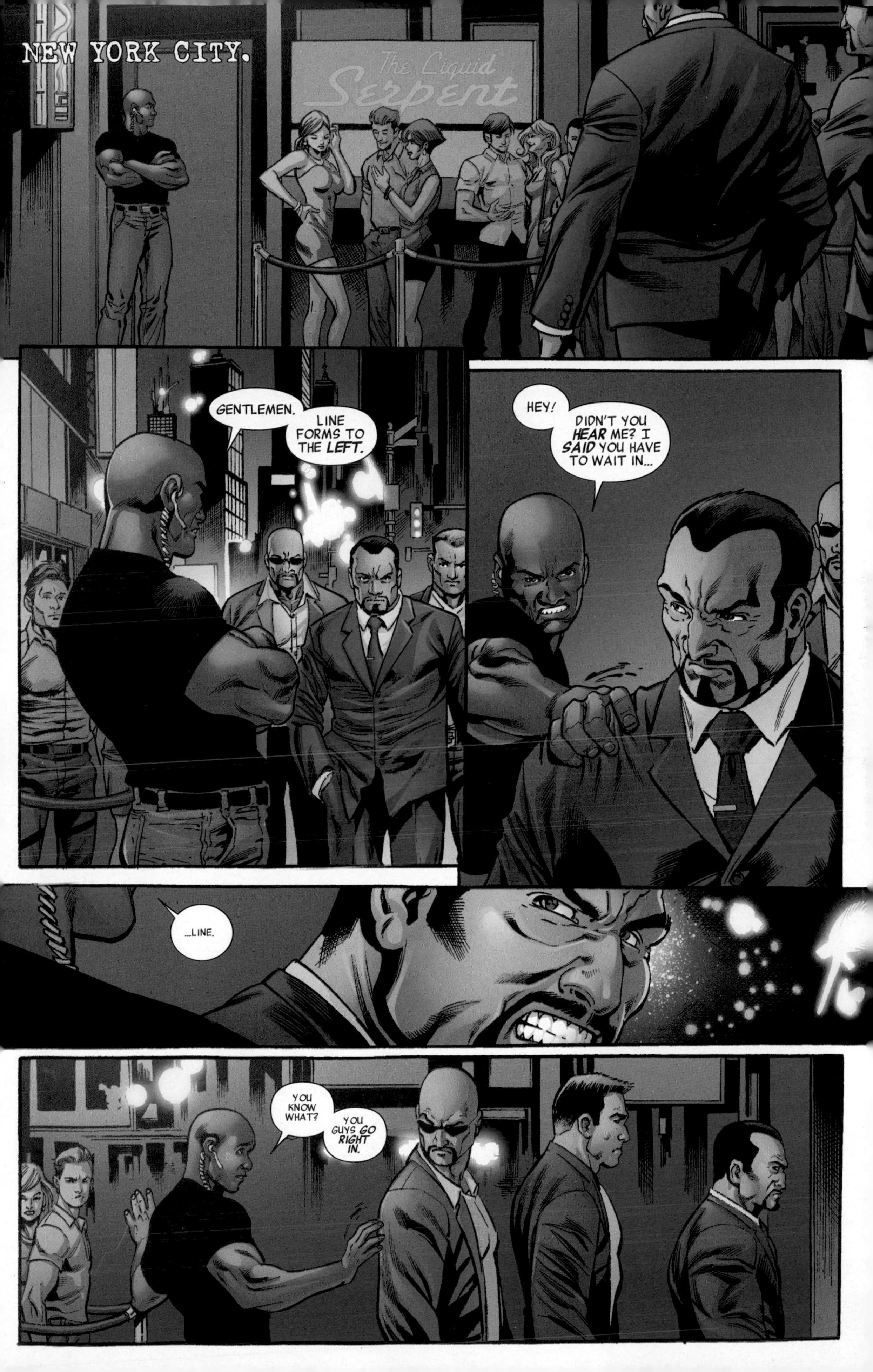
NEW YORK CITY.
The Liquid Serpent
GENTLEMEN.
LINE FORMS TO THE LEFT.
HEY!
DIDN'T YOU HEAR ME? I SAID YOU HAVE TO WAIT IN...
...LINE.
YOU KNOW WHAT?
YOU GUYS GO RIGHT IN.

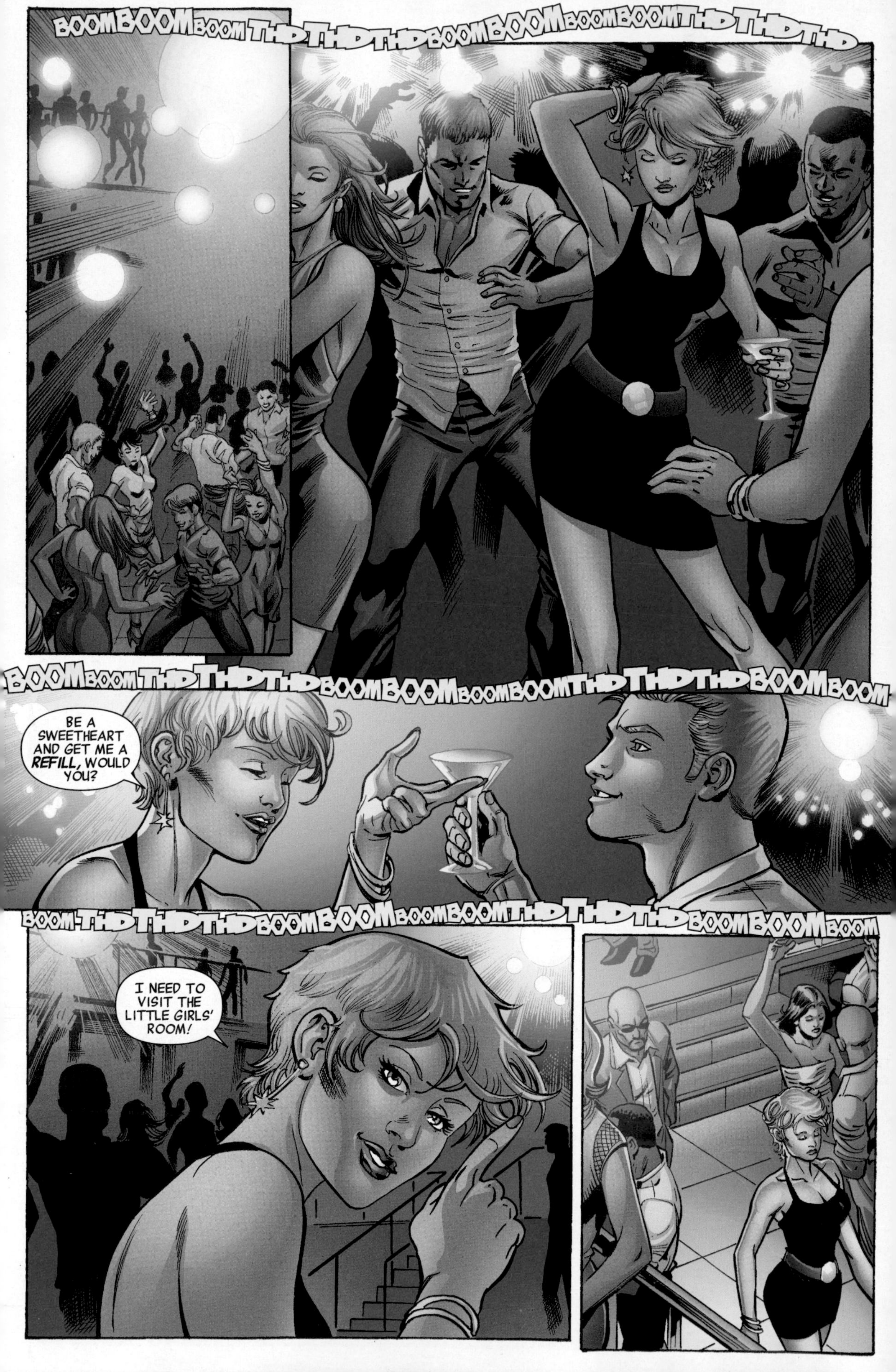
BOOMBOOMboomTHDTHDTHDBOOMBOOMboomBOOMTHDTHDTHD
BOOMboomTHDTHDTHDBOOMBOOMboomBOOMTHDTHDTHDBOOMboom
BE A SWEETHEART AND GET ME A **REFILL**, WOULD YOU?
BOOMTHDTHDTHDBOOMBOOMboomBOOMTHDTHDTHDBOOMBOOMboom
I NEED TO VISIT THE LITTLE GIRLS' ROOM!

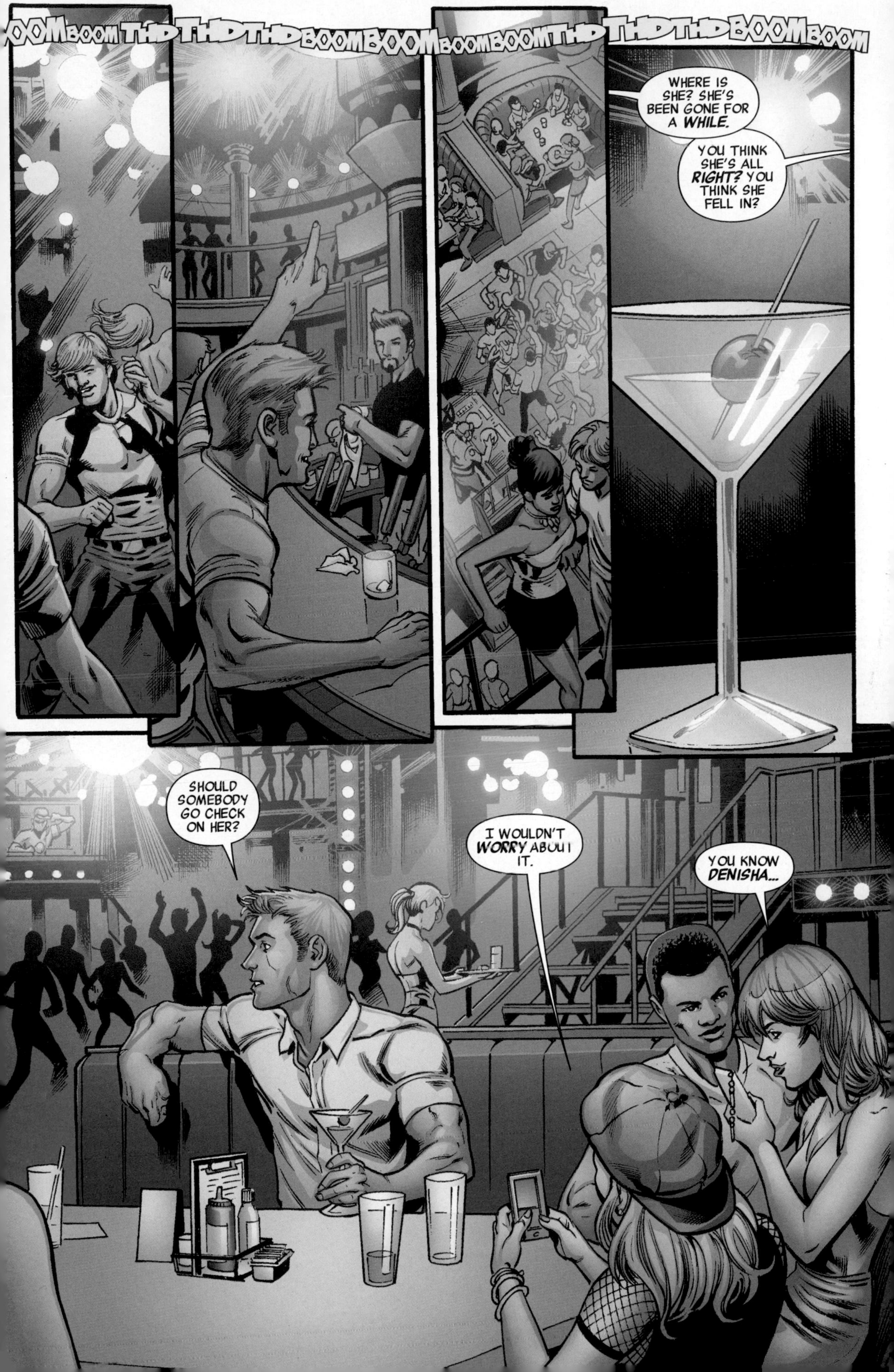

OOMboomTHDTHDTHDBOOMBOOMboomBOOMTHDTHDTHDBOOMboom
WHERE IS SHE? SHE'S BEEN GONE FOR A WHILE.
YOU THINK SHE'S ALL RIGHT? YOU THINK SHE FELL IN?
SHOULD SOMEBODY GO CHECK ON HER?
I WOULDN'T WORRY ABOUT IT.
YOU KNOW DENISHA...

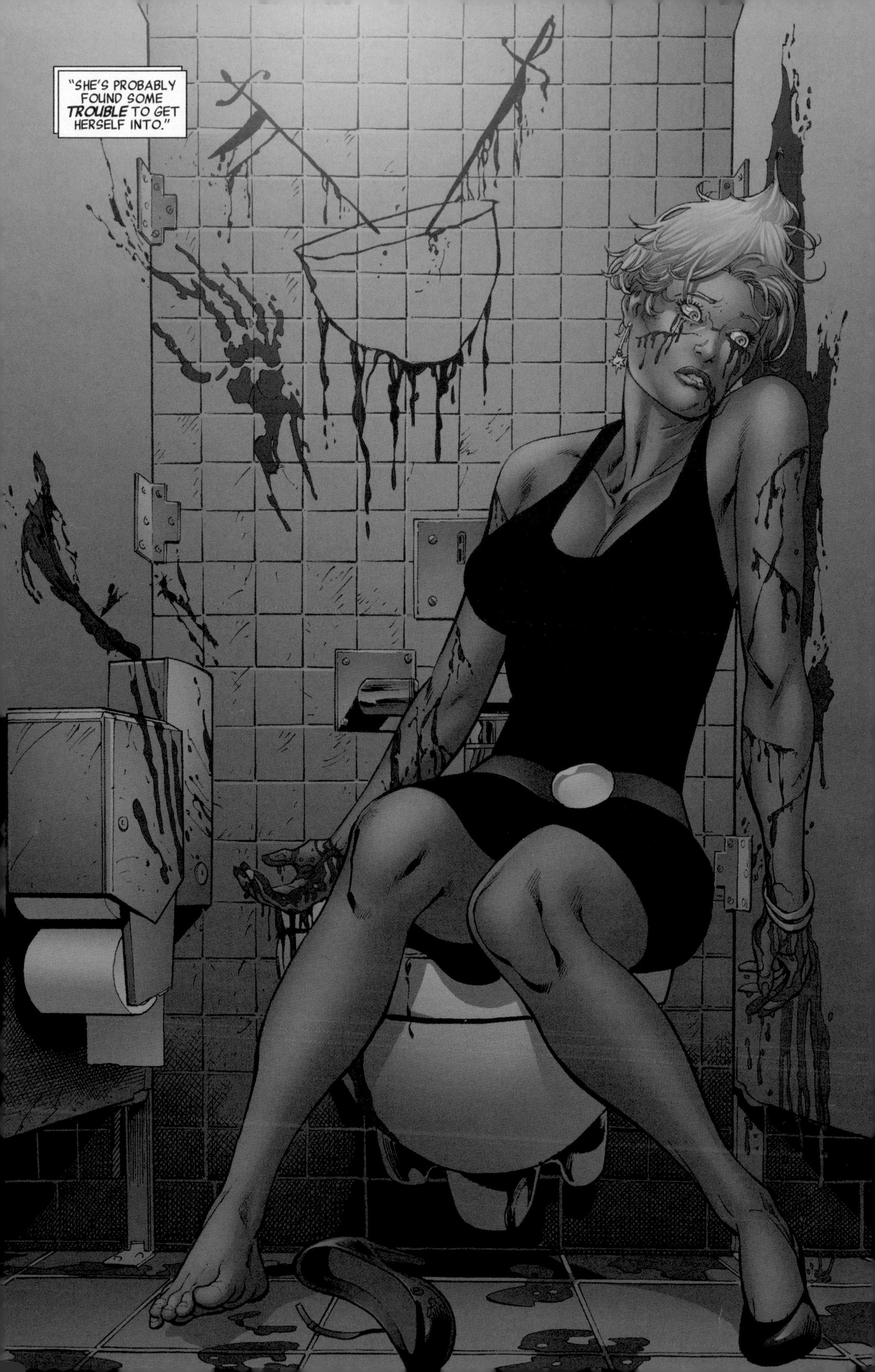
"SHE'S PROBABLY FOUND SOME TROUBLE TO GET HERSELF INTO."

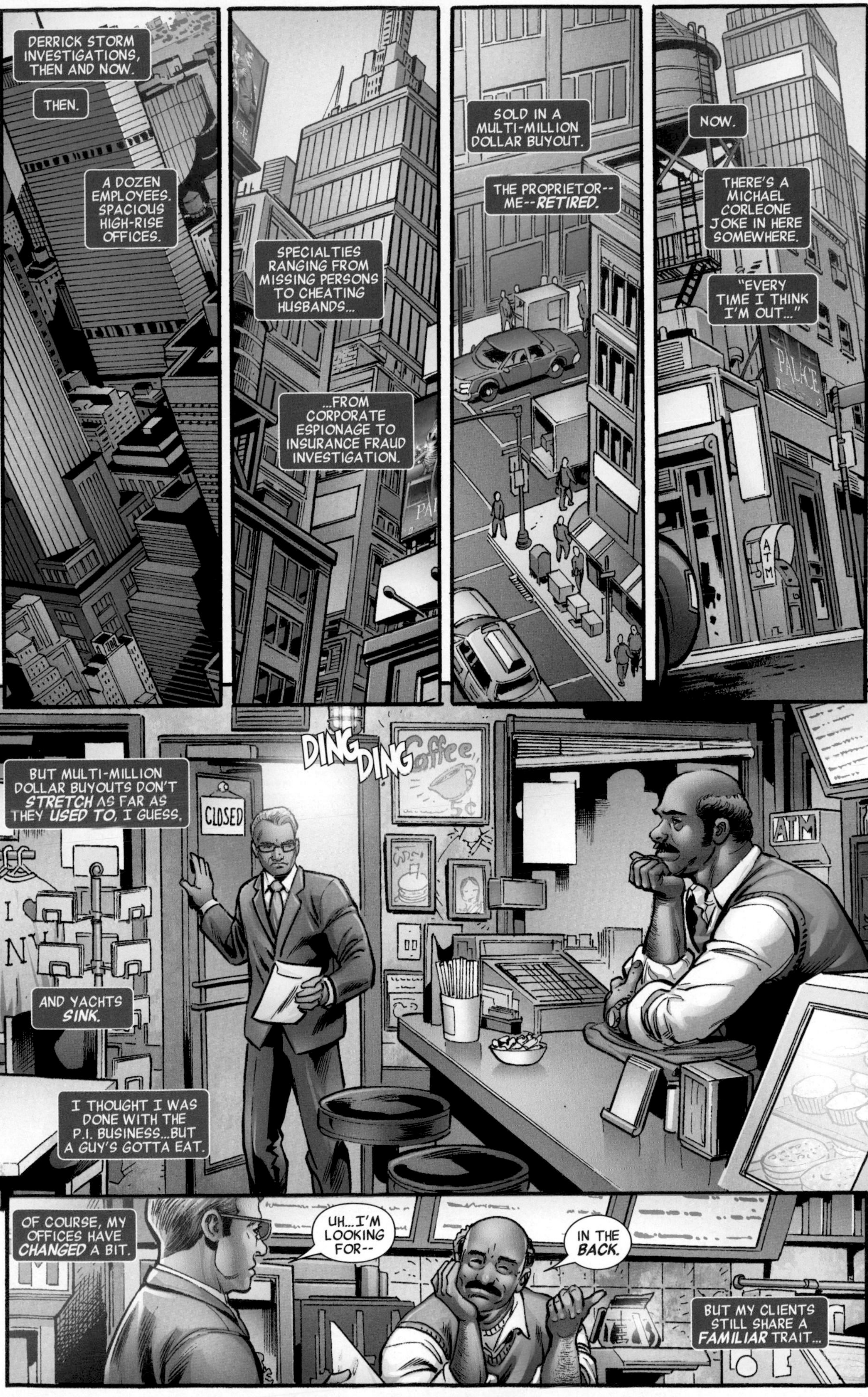
DERRICK STORM INVESTIGATIONS, THEN AND NOW.
THEN.
A DOZEN EMPLOYEES. SPACIOUS HIGH-RISE OFFICES.
SPECIALTIES RANGING FROM MISSING PERSONS TO CHEATING HUSBANDS...
...FROM CORPORATE ESPIONAGE TO INSURANCE FRAUD INVESTIGATION.
SOLD IN A MULTI-MILLION DOLLAR BUYOUT.
THE PROPRIETOR--ME--RETIRED.
NOW.
THERE'S A MICHAEL CORLEONE JOKE IN HERE SOMEWHERE.
"EVERY TIME I THINK I'M OUT..."
PALACE
ATM
BUT MULTI-MILLION DOLLAR BUYOUTS DON'T STRETCH AS FAR AS THEY USED TO, I GUESS.
DING DING
Coffee
5¢
CLOSED
ATM
AND YACHTS SINK.
I THOUGHT I WAS DONE WITH THE P.I. BUSINESS...BUT A GUY'S GOTTA EAT.
OF COURSE, MY OFFICES HAVE CHANGED A BIT.
UH...I'M LOOKING FOR--
IN THE BACK.
BUT MY CLIENTS STILL SHARE A FAMILIAR TRAIT...

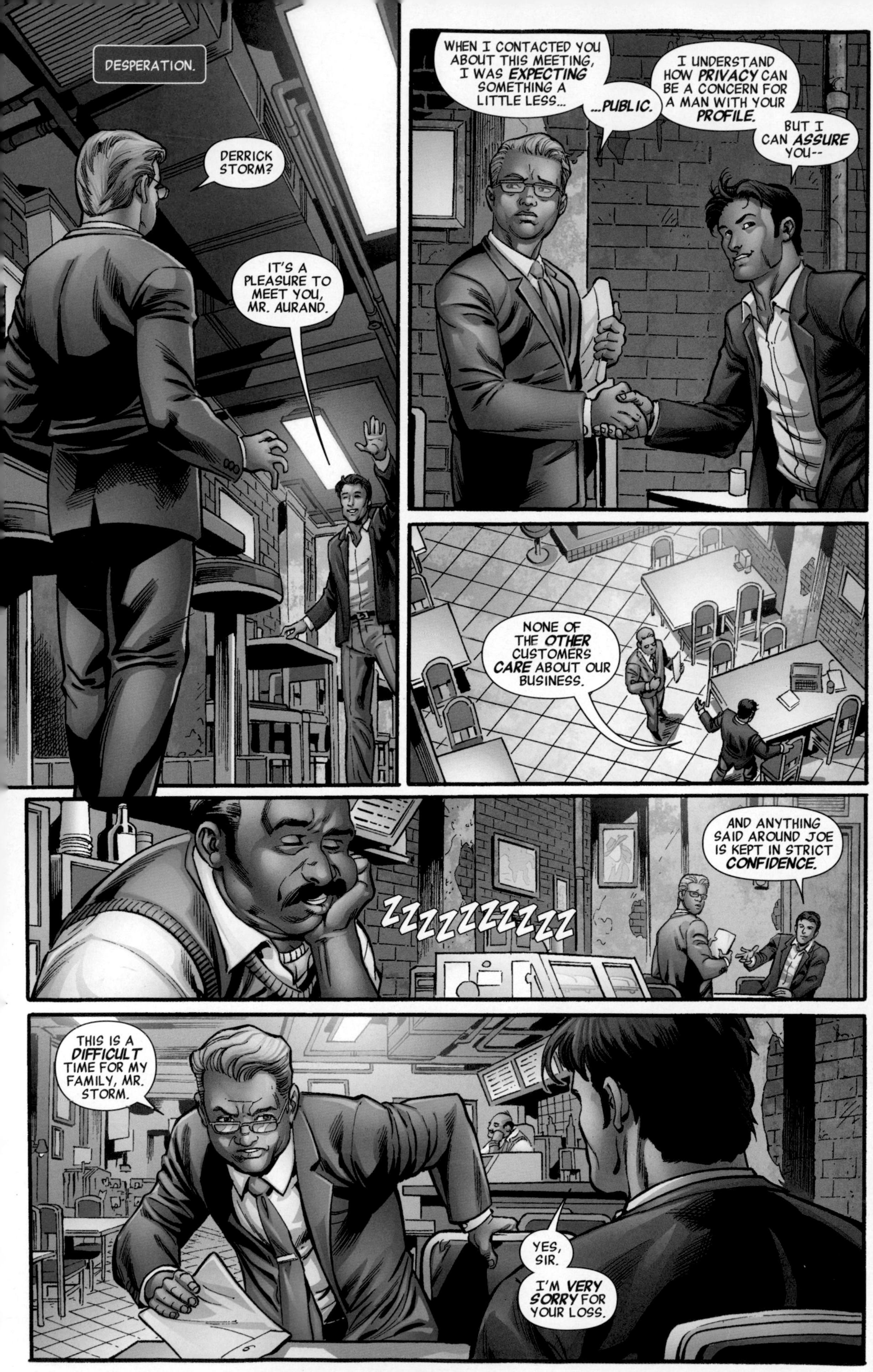
DESPERATION.
DERRICK STORM?
IT'S A PLEASURE TO MEET YOU, MR. AURAND.
WHEN I CONTACTED YOU ABOUT THIS MEETING, I WAS EXPECTING SOMETHING A LITTLE LESS...
...PUBLIC.
I UNDERSTAND HOW PRIVACY CAN BE A CONCERN FOR A MAN WITH YOUR PROFILE.
BUT I CAN ASSURE YOU--
NONE OF THE OTHER CUSTOMERS CARE ABOUT OUR BUSINESS.
ZZZZZZZZZZ
AND ANYTHING SAID AROUND JOE IS KEPT IN STRICT CONFIDENCE.
THIS IS A DIFFICULT TIME FOR MY FAMILY, MR. STORM.
YES, SIR.
I'M VERY SORRY FOR YOUR LOSS.

THUS FAR, LAW ENFORCEMENT HAS BEEN UNABLE TO FIND THE PERSON RESPONSIBLE.

IT'S BEEN *THREE* WEEKS.

AND I'VE ALWAYS HEARD THAT IF THE CRIME IS NOT SOLVED IN THE FIRST FEW DAYS, IT IS LIKELY A *LOST CAUSE.*

THAT'S A TRUE STATISTIC FOR *TRADITIONAL INVESTIGATION.*

A MAN WITH YOUR RESOURCES, THOUGH...I'M *SURPRISED* YOU HAVEN'T RETAINED A *PRIVATE CONTRACTOR* BEFORE NOW.

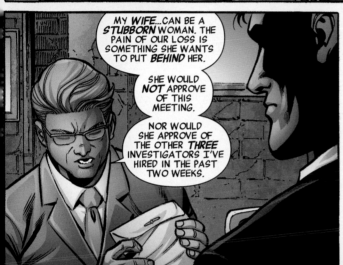

MY *WIFE*...CAN BE A *STUBBORN* WOMAN. THE PAIN OF OUR LOSS IS SOMETHING SHE WANTS TO PUT *BEHIND* HER.

SHE WOULD *NOT* APPROVE OF THIS MEETING.

NOR WOULD SHE APPROVE OF THE OTHER *THREE* INVESTIGATORS I'VE HIRED IN THE PAST TWO WEEKS.

AND THESE OTHER INVESTIGATORS...

WHAT DID YOU LEARN FROM THEM?

I LEARNED THAT IF I WANT TO FIND OUT WHO KILLED MY DAUGHTER, I NEED TO HIRE A MAN LIKE *YOU.*

UNLIKE MY WIFE, I WANT *JUSTICE,* NOT ACCEPTANCE.

AND I'M SURE THE FATHERS OF THESE OTHER GIRLS FEEL THE SAME.

OTHER GIRLS?

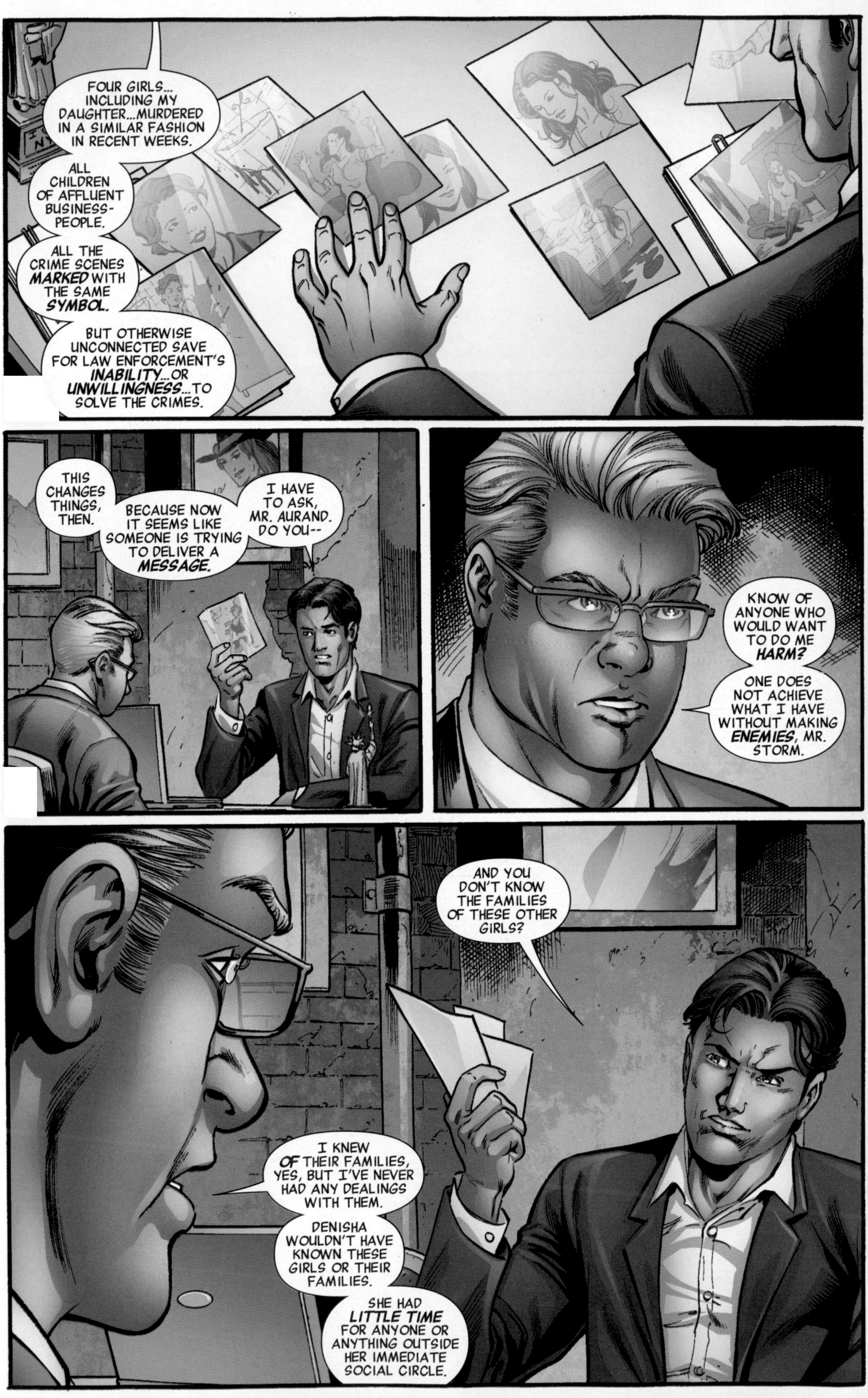
FOUR GIRLS... INCLUDING MY DAUGHTER...MURDERED IN A SIMILAR FASHION IN RECENT WEEKS.
ALL CHILDREN OF AFFLUENT BUSINESS-PEOPLE.
ALL THE CRIME SCENES MARKED WITH THE SAME SYMBOL.
BUT OTHERWISE UNCONNECTED SAVE FOR LAW ENFORCEMENT'S INABILITY...OR UNWILLINGNESS...TO SOLVE THE CRIMES.
THIS CHANGES THINGS, THEN.
BECAUSE NOW IT SEEMS LIKE SOMEONE IS TRYING TO DELIVER A MESSAGE.
I HAVE TO ASK, MR. AURAND. DO YOU--
KNOW OF ANYONE WHO WOULD WANT TO DO ME HARM?
ONE DOES NOT ACHIEVE WHAT I HAVE WITHOUT MAKING ENEMIES, MR. STORM.
AND YOU DON'T KNOW THE FAMILIES OF THESE OTHER GIRLS?
I KNEW OF THEIR FAMILIES, YES, BUT I'VE NEVER HAD ANY DEALINGS WITH THEM.
DENISHA WOULDN'T HAVE KNOWN THESE GIRLS OR THEIR FAMILIES.
SHE HAD LITTLE TIME FOR ANYONE OR ANYTHING OUTSIDE HER IMMEDIATE SOCIAL CIRCLE.

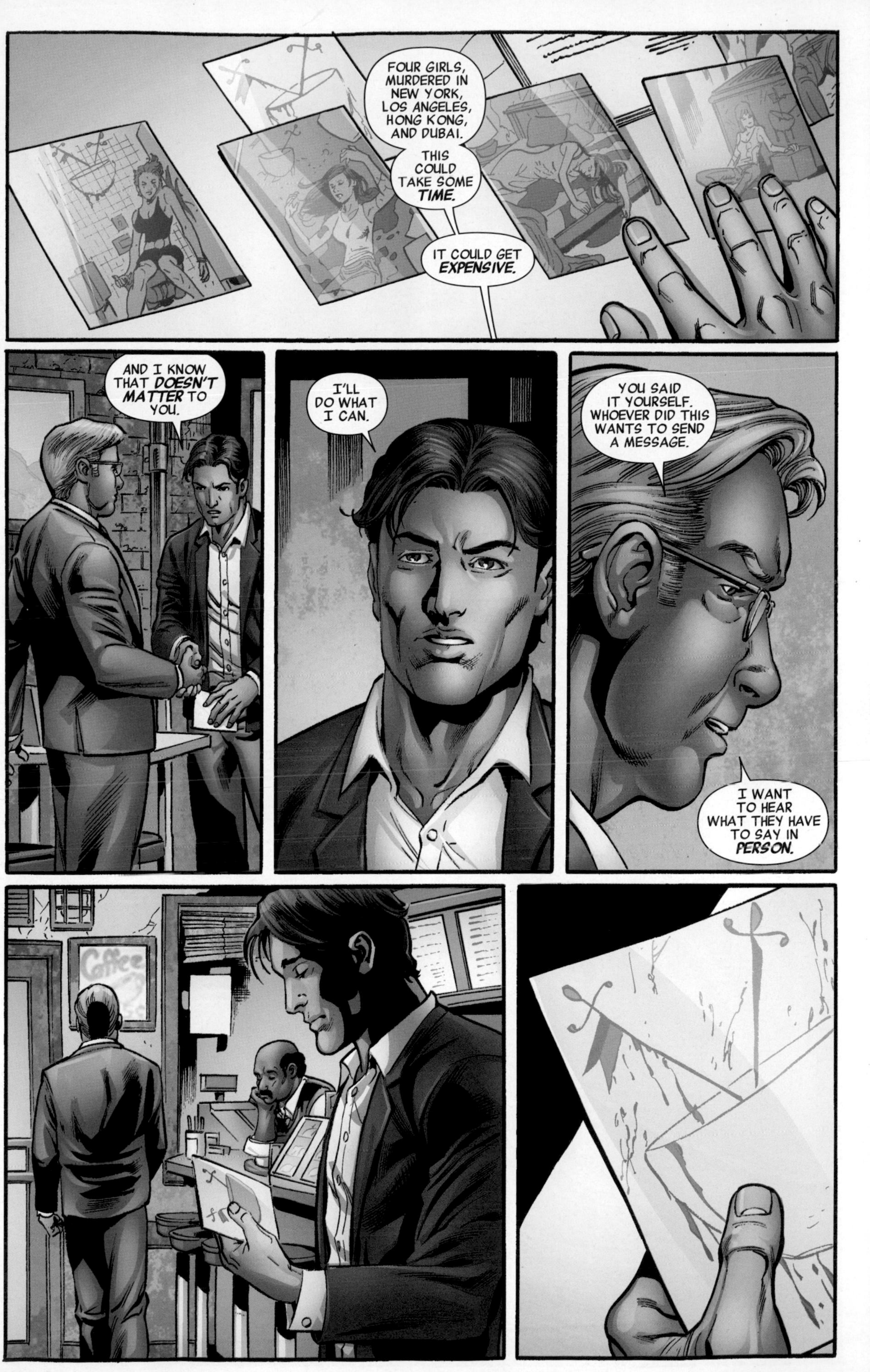
FOUR GIRLS, MURDERED IN NEW YORK, LOS ANGELES, HONG KONG, AND DUBAI.
THIS COULD TAKE SOME TIME.
IT COULD GET EXPENSIVE.
AND I KNOW THAT DOESN'T MATTER TO YOU.
I'LL DO WHAT I CAN.
YOU SAID IT YOURSELF. WHOEVER DID THIS WANTS TO SEND A MESSAGE.
I WANT TO HEAR WHAT THEY HAVE TO SAY IN PERSON.
Coffee

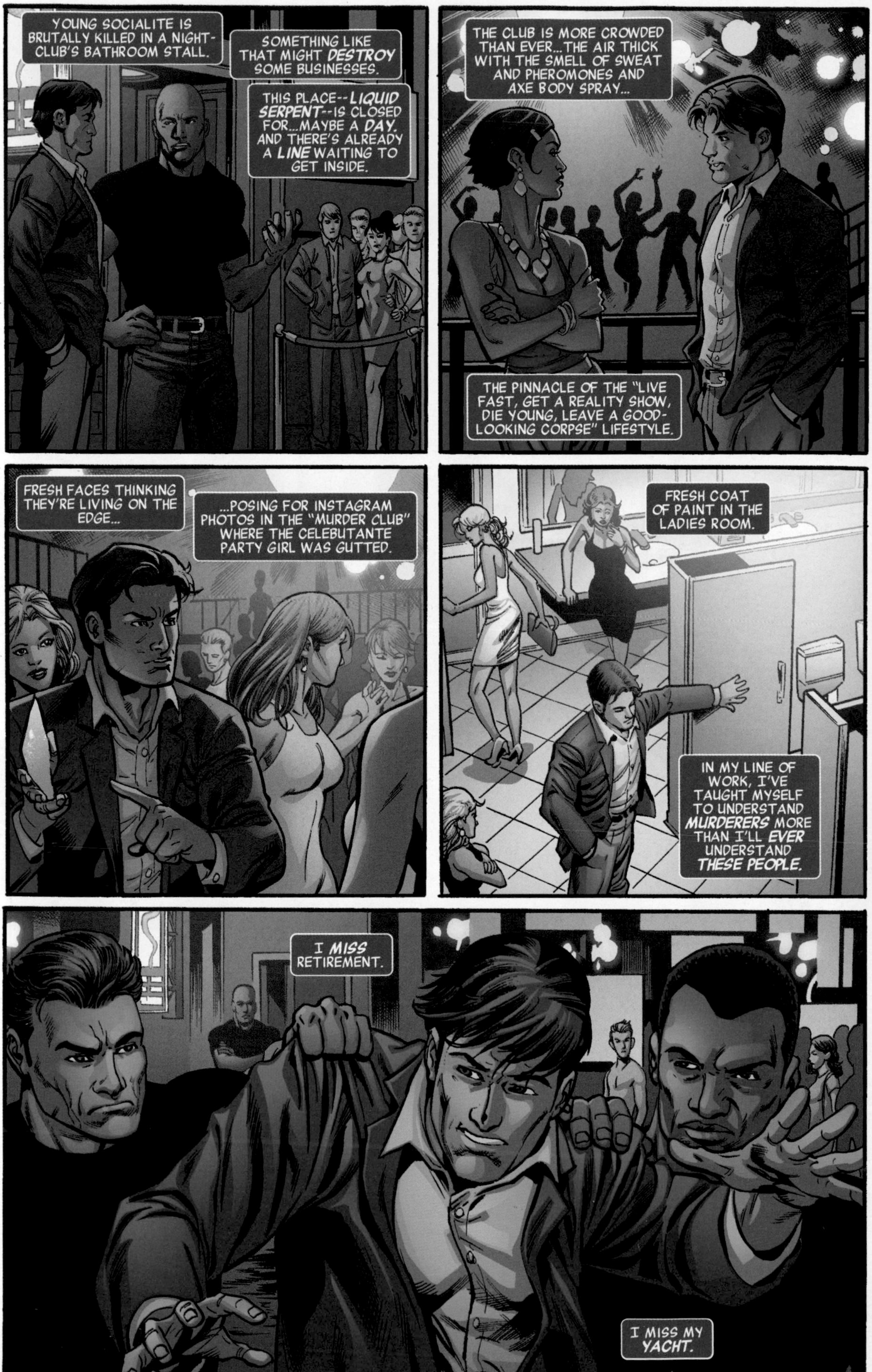
YOUNG SOCIALITE IS BRUTALLY KILLED IN A NIGHT-CLUB'S BATHROOM STALL.
SOMETHING LIKE THAT MIGHT DESTROY SOME BUSINESSES.
THIS PLACE--LIQUID SERPENT--IS CLOSED FOR...MAYBE A DAY. AND THERE'S ALREADY A LINE WAITING TO GET INSIDE.
THE CLUB IS MORE CROWDED THAN EVER...THE AIR THICK WITH THE SMELL OF SWEAT AND PHEROMONES AND AXE BODY SPRAY...
THE PINNACLE OF THE "LIVE FAST, GET A REALITY SHOW, DIE YOUNG, LEAVE A GOOD-LOOKING CORPSE" LIFESTYLE.
FRESH FACES THINKING THEY'RE LIVING ON THE EDGE...
...POSING FOR INSTAGRAM PHOTOS IN THE "MURDER CLUB" WHERE THE CELEBUTANTE PARTY GIRL WAS GUTTED.
FRESH COAT OF PAINT IN THE LADIES ROOM.
IN MY LINE OF WORK, I'VE TAUGHT MYSELF TO UNDERSTAND MURDERERS MORE THAN I'LL EVER UNDERSTAND THESE PEOPLE.
I MISS RETIREMENT.
I MISS MY YACHT.

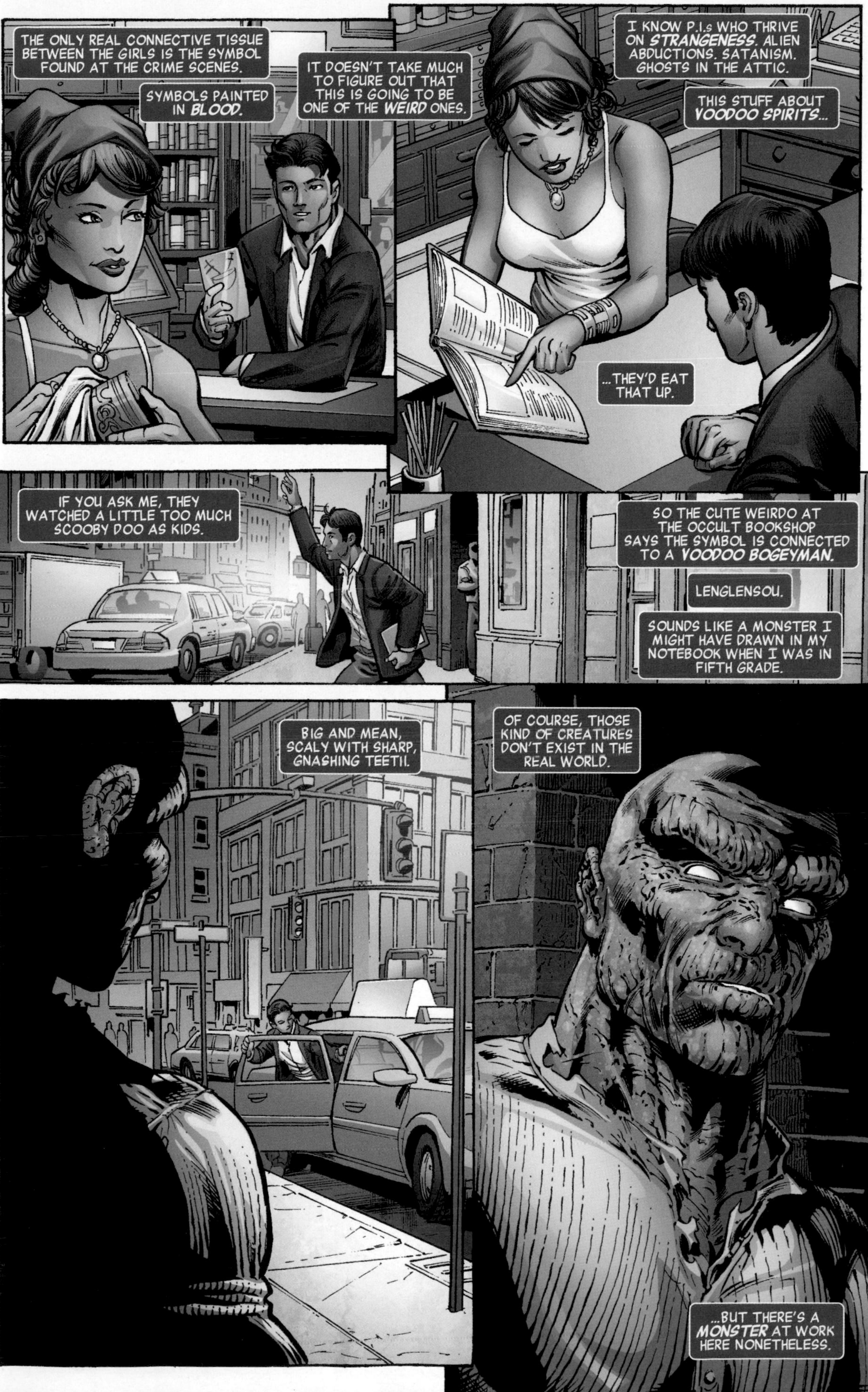
THE ONLY REAL CONNECTIVE TISSUE BETWEEN THE GIRLS IS THE SYMBOL FOUND AT THE CRIME SCENES.
SYMBOLS PAINTED IN BLOOD.
IT DOESN'T TAKE MUCH TO FIGURE OUT THAT THIS IS GOING TO BE ONE OF THE WEIRD ONES.
I KNOW P.I.s WHO THRIVE ON STRANGENESS. ALIEN ABDUCTIONS. SATANISM. GHOSTS IN THE ATTIC.
THIS STUFF ABOUT VOODOO SPIRITS...
...THEY'D EAT THAT UP.
IF YOU ASK ME, THEY WATCHED A LITTLE TOO MUCH SCOOBY DOO AS KIDS.
SO THE CUTE WEIRDO AT THE OCCULT BOOKSHOP SAYS THE SYMBOL IS CONNECTED TO A VOODOO BOGEYMAN.
LENGLENSOU.
SOUNDS LIKE A MONSTER I MIGHT HAVE DRAWN IN MY NOTEBOOK WHEN I WAS IN FIFTH GRADE.
BIG AND MEAN, SCALY WITH SHARP, GNASHING TEETH.
OF COURSE, THOSE KIND OF CREATURES DON'T EXIST IN THE REAL WORLD.
...BUT THERE'S A MONSTER AT WORK HERE NONETHELESS.

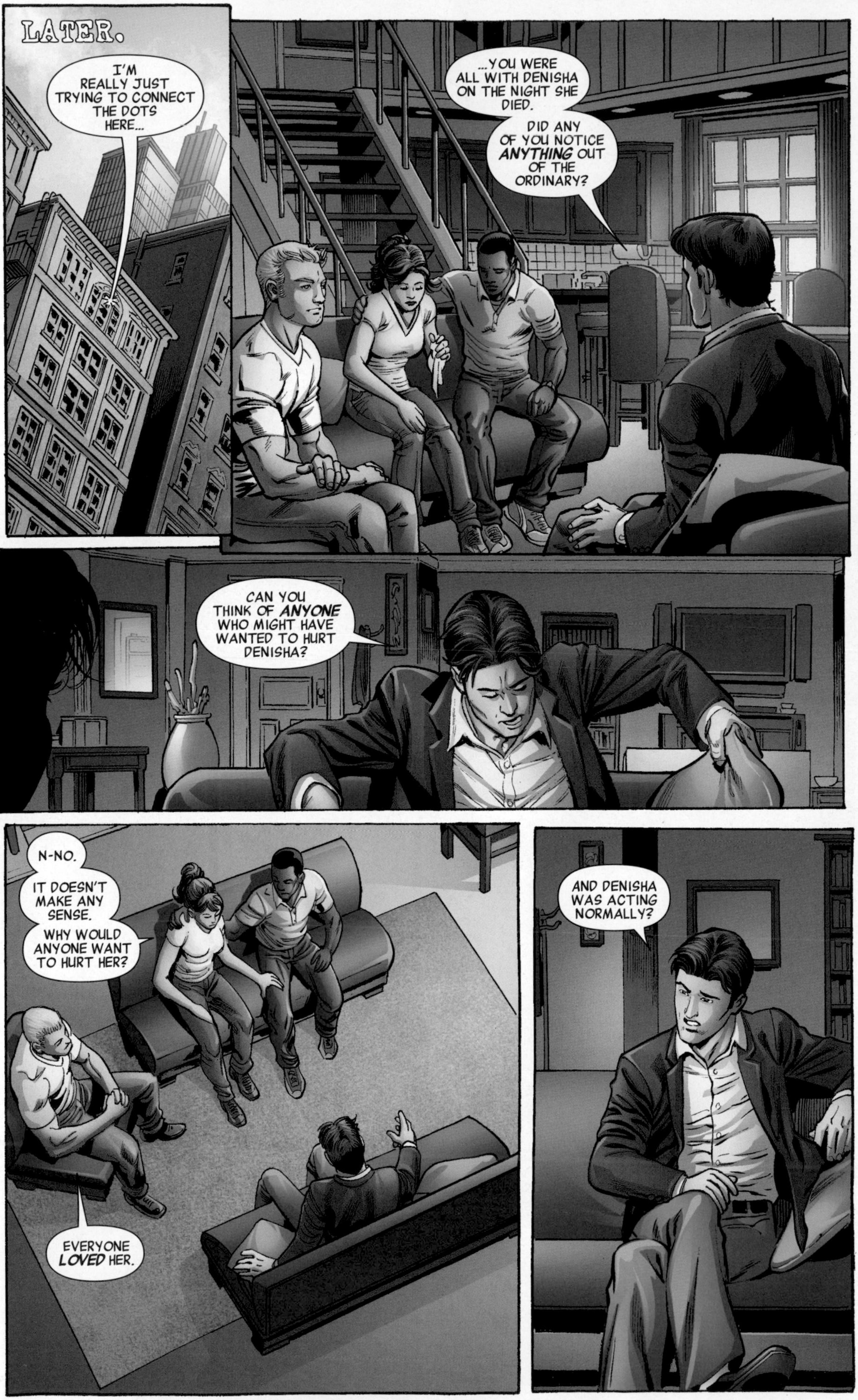
LATER.
I'M REALLY JUST TRYING TO CONNECT THE DOTS HERE...
...YOU WERE ALL WITH DENISHA ON THE NIGHT SHE DIED.
DID ANY OF YOU NOTICE ANYTHING OUT OF THE ORDINARY?
CAN YOU THINK OF ANYONE WHO MIGHT HAVE WANTED TO HURT DENISHA?
N-NO.
IT DOESN'T MAKE ANY SENSE.
WHY WOULD ANYONE WANT TO HURT HER?
EVERYONE LOVED HER.
AND DENISHA WAS ACTING NORMALLY?

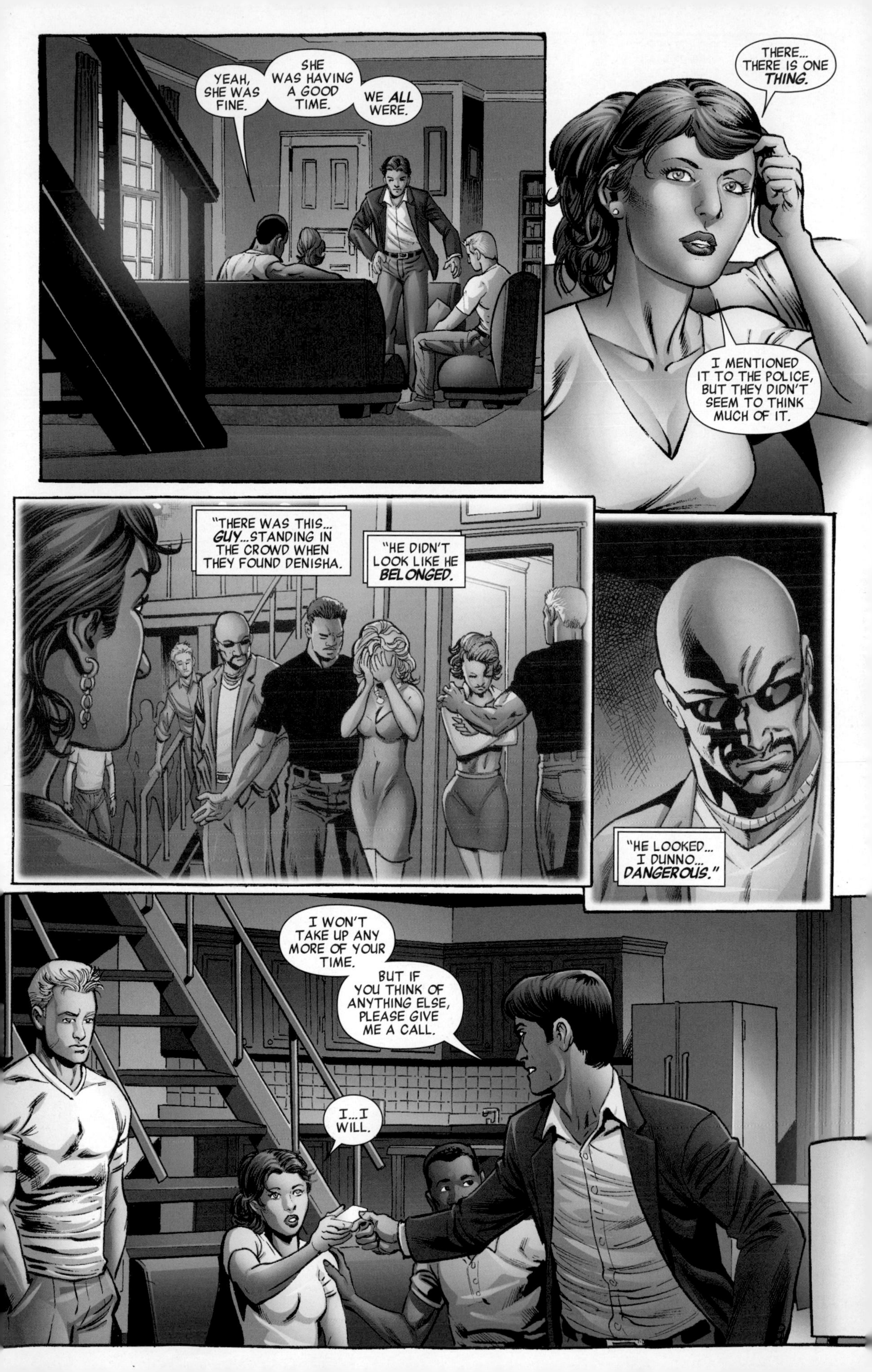
YEAH, SHE WAS FINE.
SHE WAS HAVING A GOOD TIME.
WE ALL WERE.
THERE... THERE IS ONE THING.
I MENTIONED IT TO THE POLICE, BUT THEY DIDN'T SEEM TO THINK MUCH OF IT.
"THERE WAS THIS... GUY...STANDING IN THE CROWD WHEN THEY FOUND DENISHA.
"HE DIDN'T LOOK LIKE HE BELONGED.
"HE LOOKED... I DUNNO... DANGEROUS."
I WON'T TAKE UP ANY MORE OF YOUR TIME.
BUT IF YOU THINK OF ANYTHING ELSE, PLEASE GIVE ME A CALL.
I...I WILL.

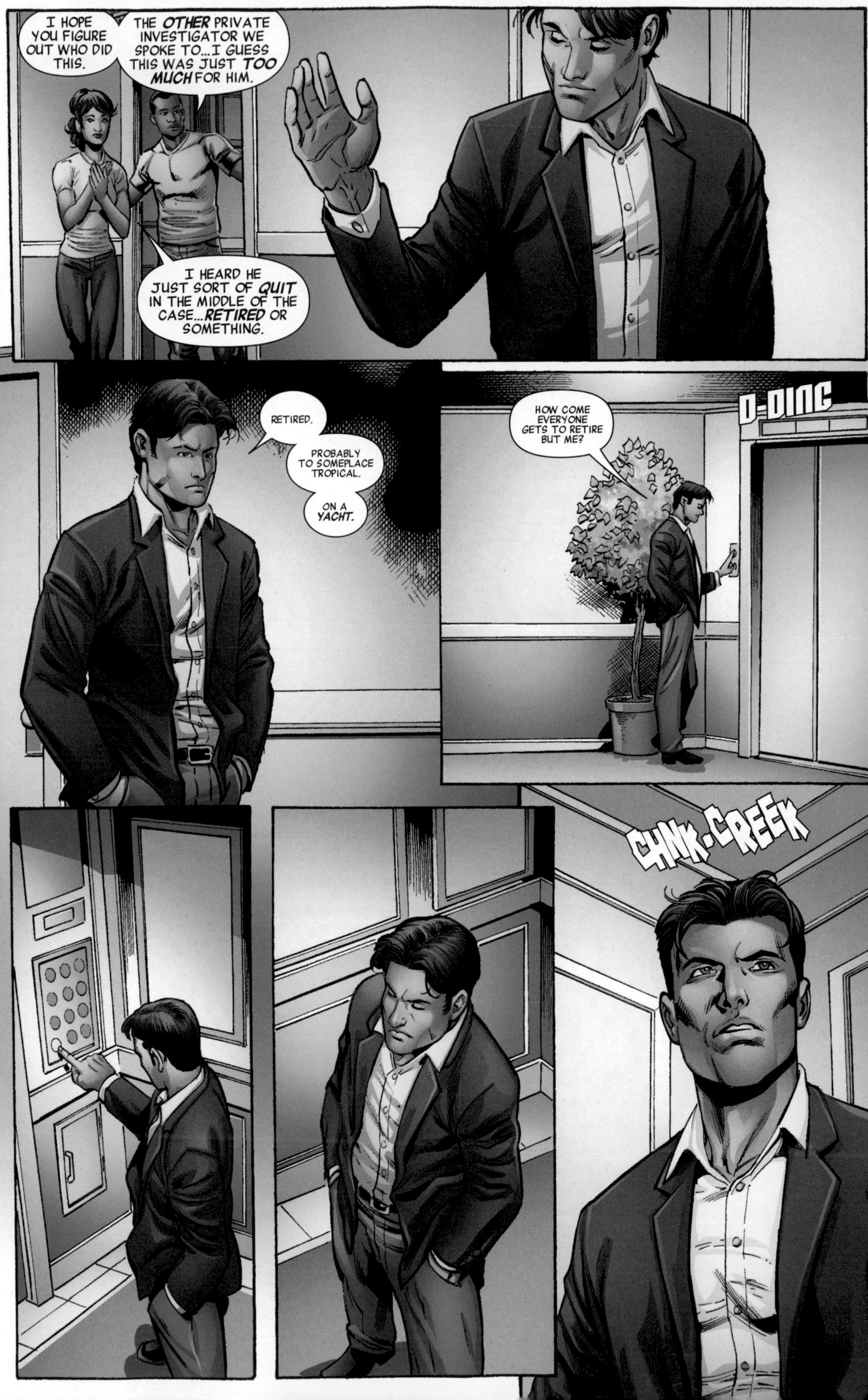
I HOPE YOU FIGURE OUT WHO DID THIS.
THE OTHER PRIVATE INVESTIGATOR WE SPOKE TO...I GUESS THIS WAS JUST TOO MUCH FOR HIM.
I HEARD HE JUST SORT OF QUIT IN THE MIDDLE OF THE CASE...RETIRED OR SOMETHING.
RETIRED.
PROBABLY TO SOMEPLACE TROPICAL.
ON A YACHT.
D-DING
HOW COME EVERYONE GETS TO RETIRE BUT ME?
CHNK-CREEK

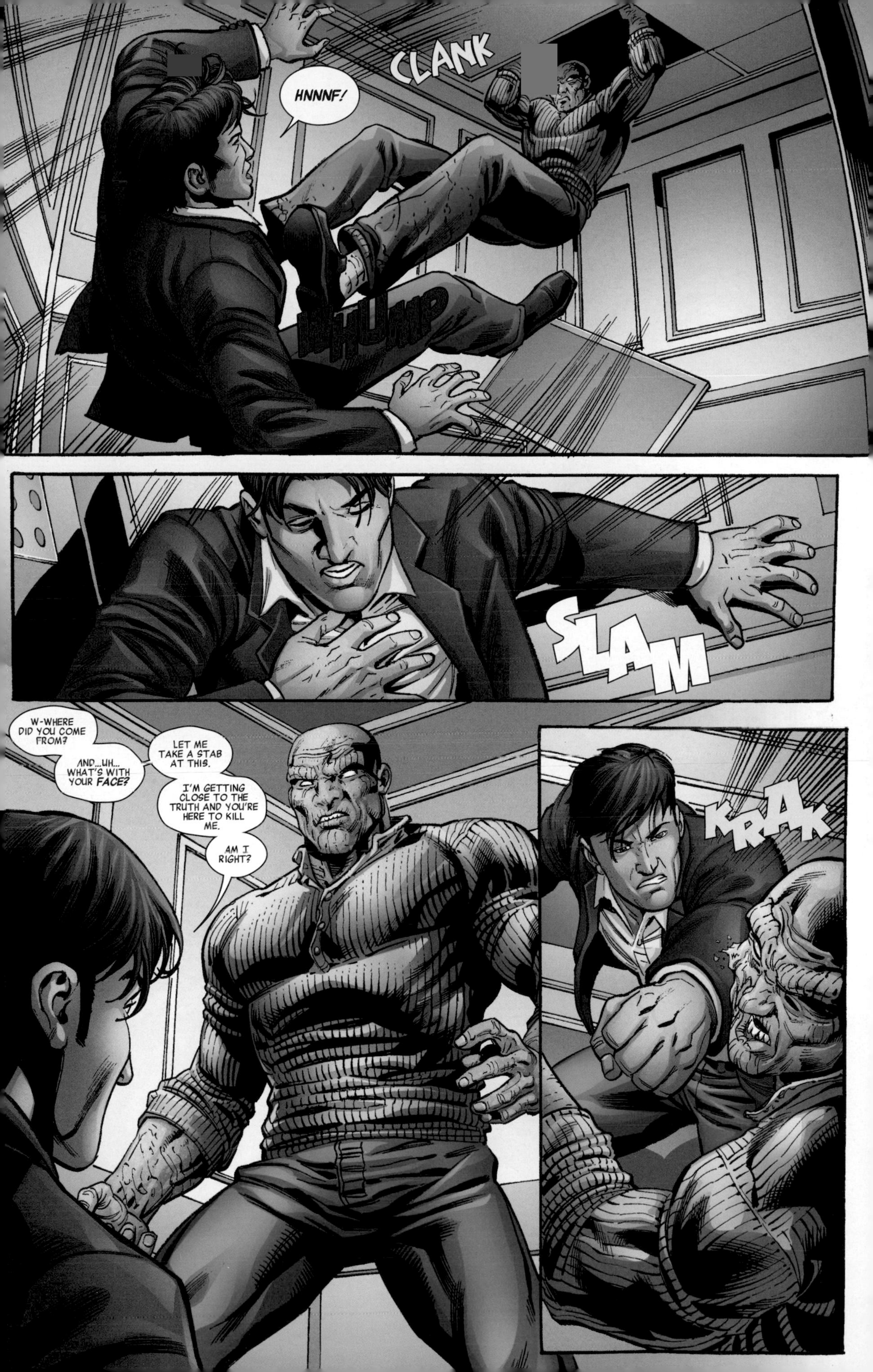
CLANK
HNNNF!
WHUMP
SLAM
W-WHERE DID YOU COME FROM?
AND...UH... WHAT'S WITH YOUR FACE?
LET ME TAKE A STAB AT THIS.
I'M GETTING CLOSE TO THE TRUTH AND YOU'RE HERE TO KILL ME.
AM I RIGHT?
KRAK

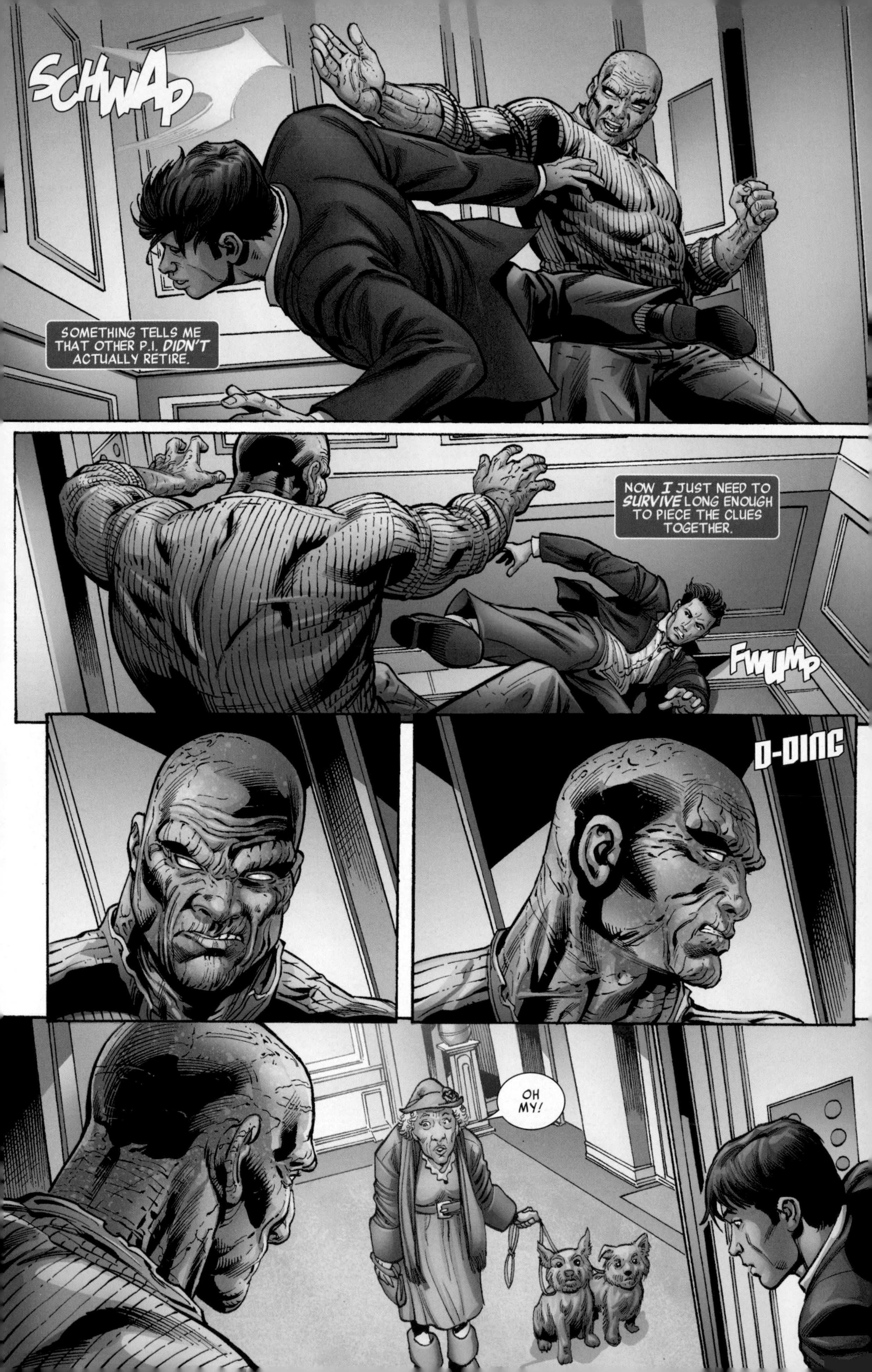
SCHWAP
SOMETHING TELLS ME THAT OTHER P.I. DIDN'T ACTUALLY RETIRE.
NOW I JUST NEED TO SURVIVE LONG ENOUGH TO PIECE THE CLUES TOGETHER.
FWUMP
D-DING
OH MY!

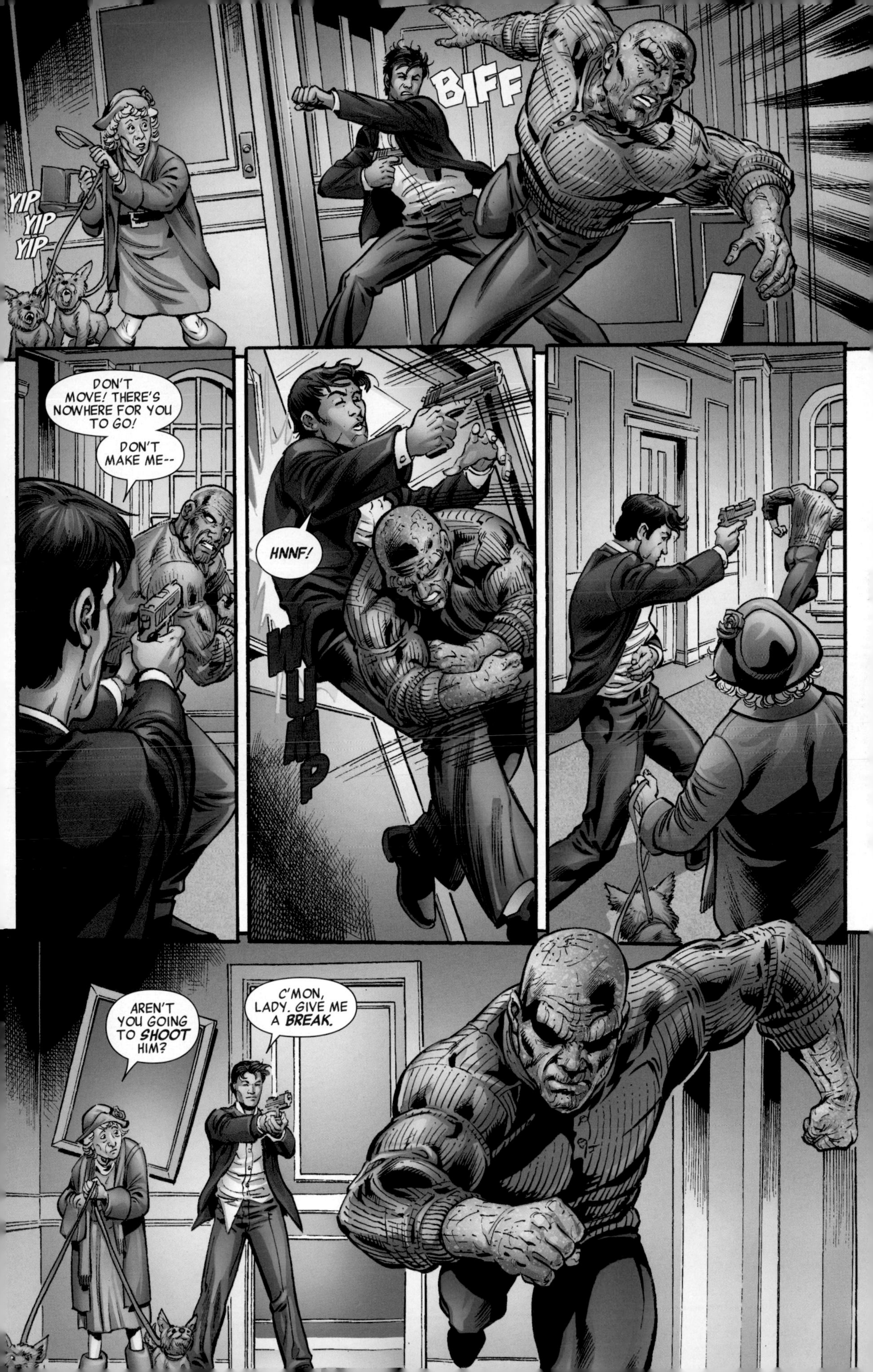
YIP
YIP
YIP
BIFF
DON'T MOVE! THERE'S NOWHERE FOR YOU TO GO!
DON'T MAKE ME--
HNNF!
WUMP
AREN'T YOU GOING TO SHOOT HIM?
C'MON, LADY. GIVE ME A BREAK.

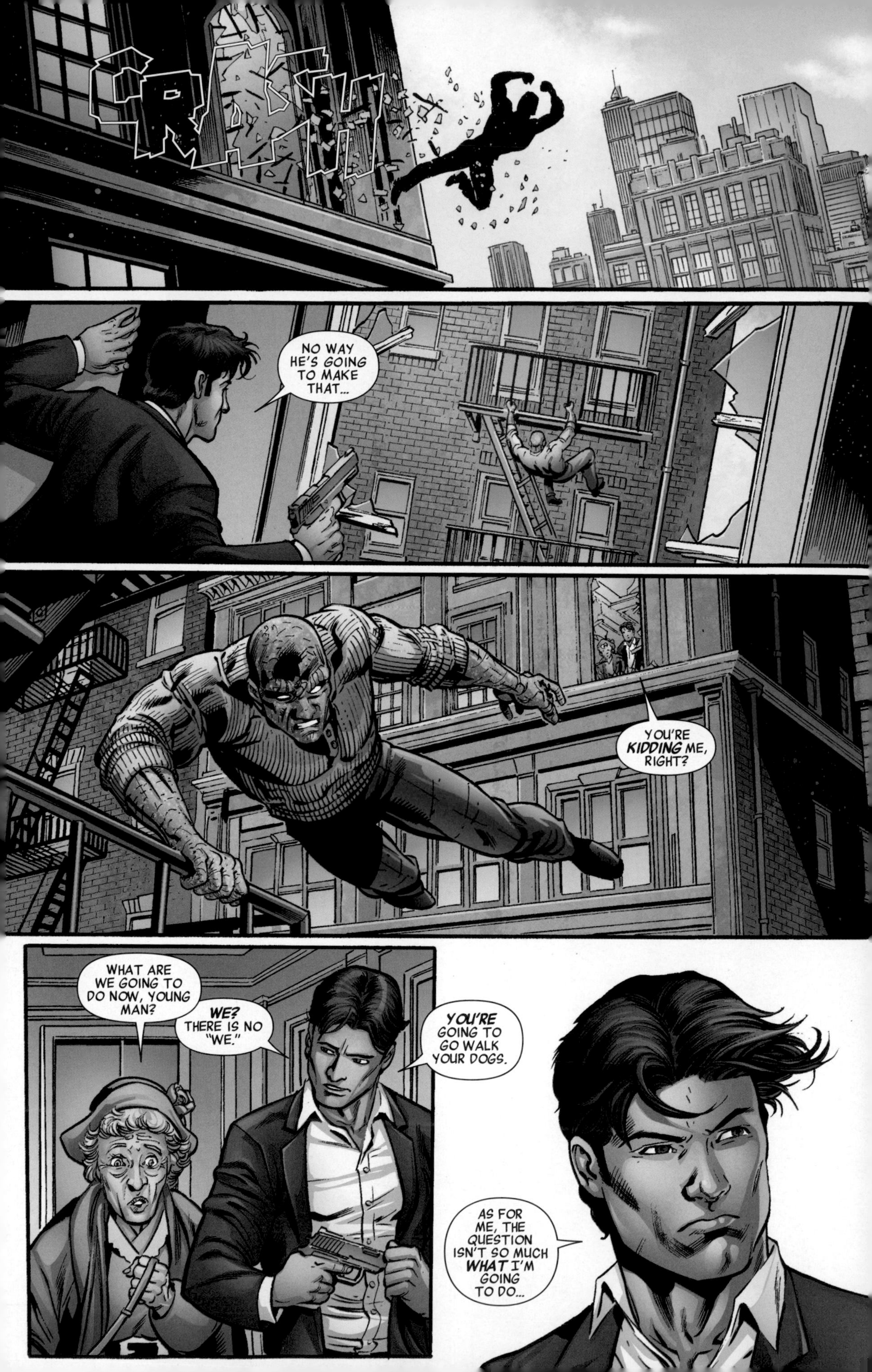
CRASH
NO WAY HE'S GOING TO MAKE THAT...
YOU'RE KIDDING ME, RIGHT?
WHAT ARE WE GOING TO DO NOW, YOUNG MAN?
WE? THERE IS NO "WE."
YOU'RE GOING TO GO WALK YOUR DOGS.
AS FOR ME, THE QUESTION ISN'T SO MUCH WHAT I'M GOING TO DO...

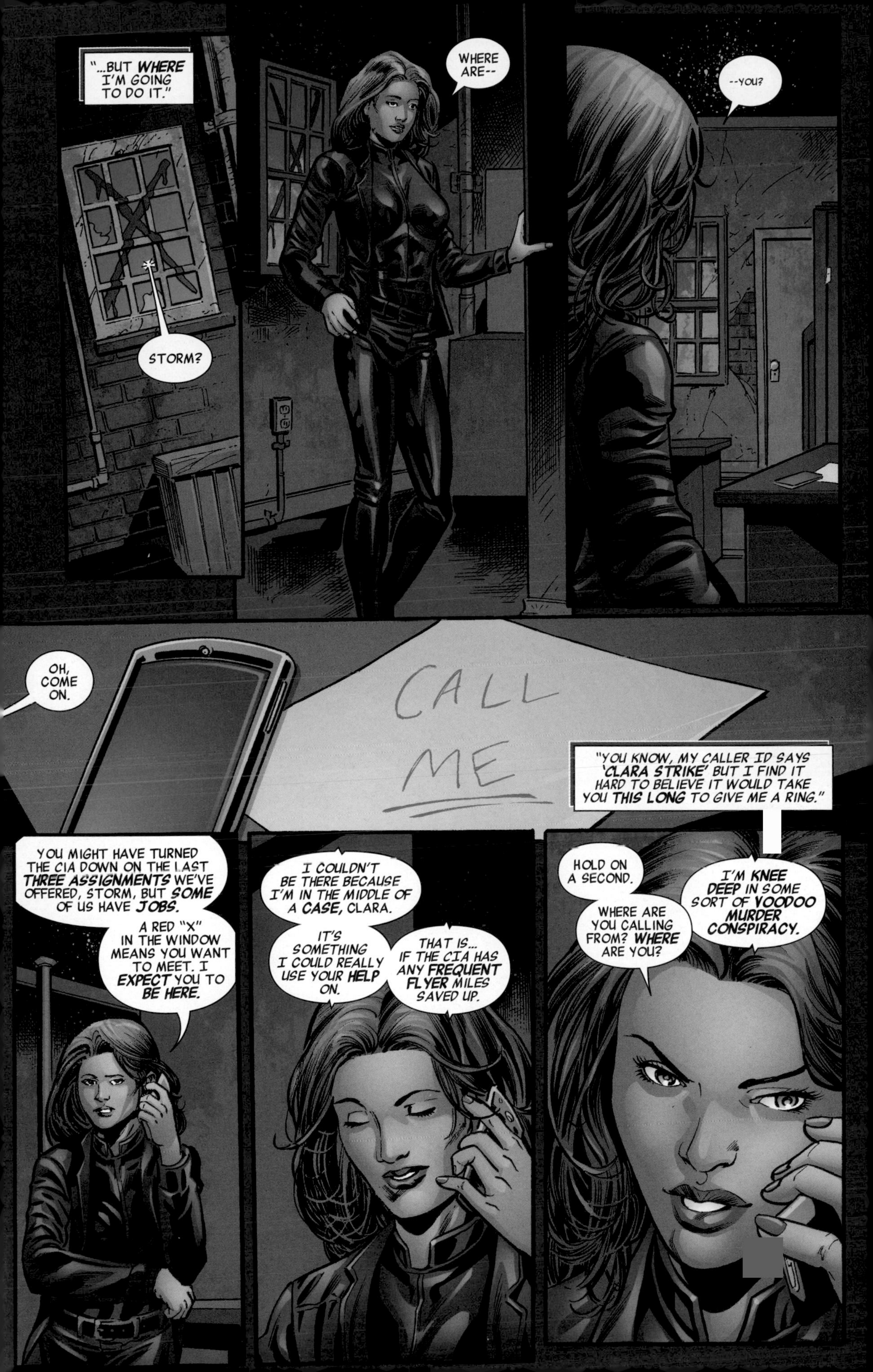
"...BUT WHERE I'M GOING TO DO IT."
STORM?
WHERE ARE--
--YOU?
OH, COME ON.
CALL ME
"YOU KNOW, MY CALLER ID SAYS 'CLARA STRIKE' BUT I FIND IT HARD TO BELIEVE IT WOULD TAKE YOU THIS LONG TO GIVE ME A RING."
YOU MIGHT HAVE TURNED THE CIA DOWN ON THE LAST THREE ASSIGNMENTS WE'VE OFFERED, STORM, BUT SOME OF US HAVE JOBS.
A RED "X" IN THE WINDOW MEANS YOU WANT TO MEET. I EXPECT YOU TO BE HERE.
I COULDN'T BE THERE BECAUSE I'M IN THE MIDDLE OF A CASE, CLARA.
IT'S SOMETHING I COULD REALLY USE YOUR HELP ON.
THAT IS... IF THE CIA HAS ANY FREQUENT FLYER MILES SAVED UP.
HOLD ON A SECOND.
WHERE ARE YOU CALLING FROM? WHERE ARE YOU?
I'M KNEE DEEP IN SOME SORT OF VOODOO MURDER CONSPIRACY.

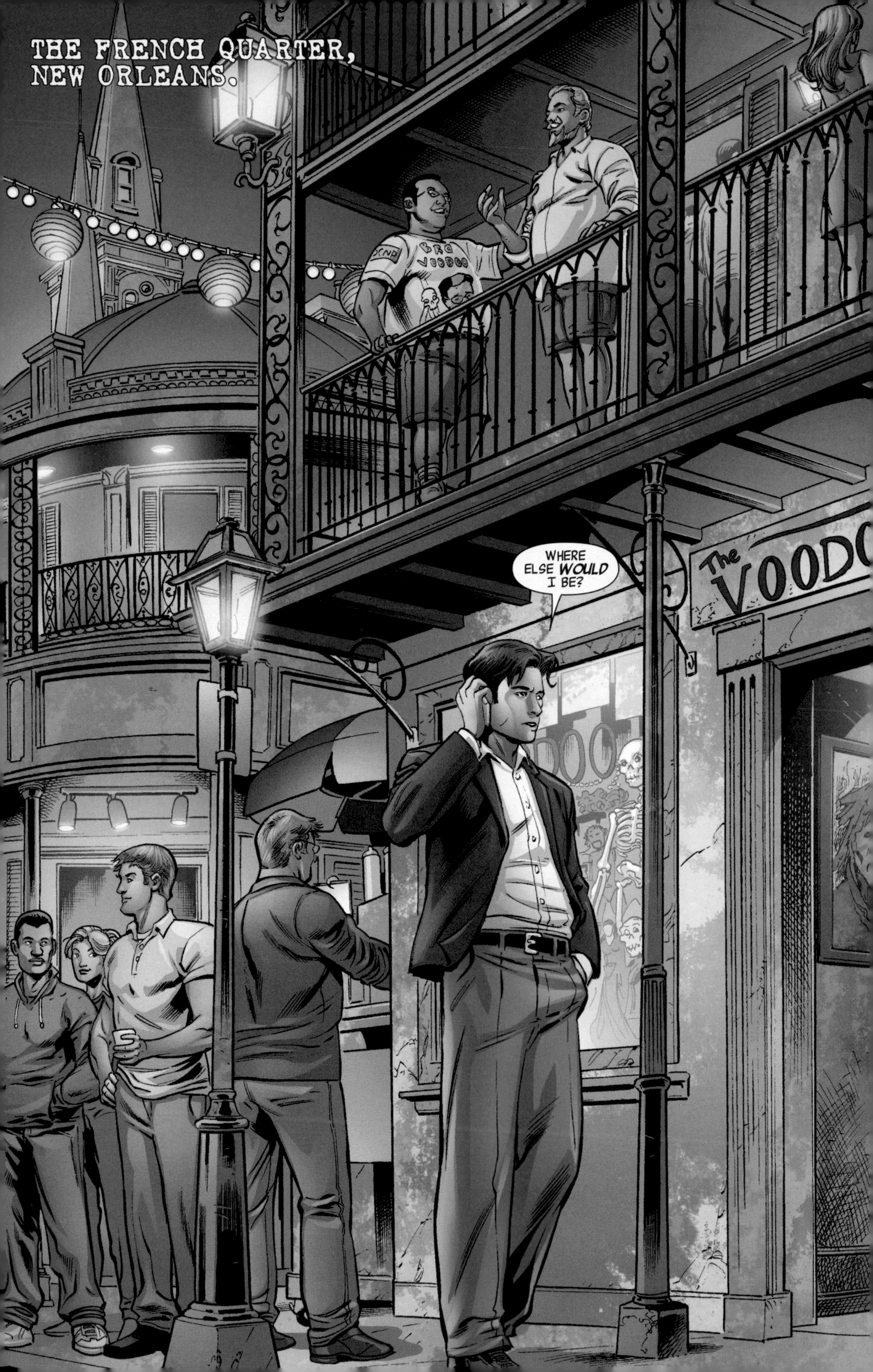
THE FRENCH QUARTER, NEW ORLEANS.
WHERE ELSE WOULD I BE?
The VOODO

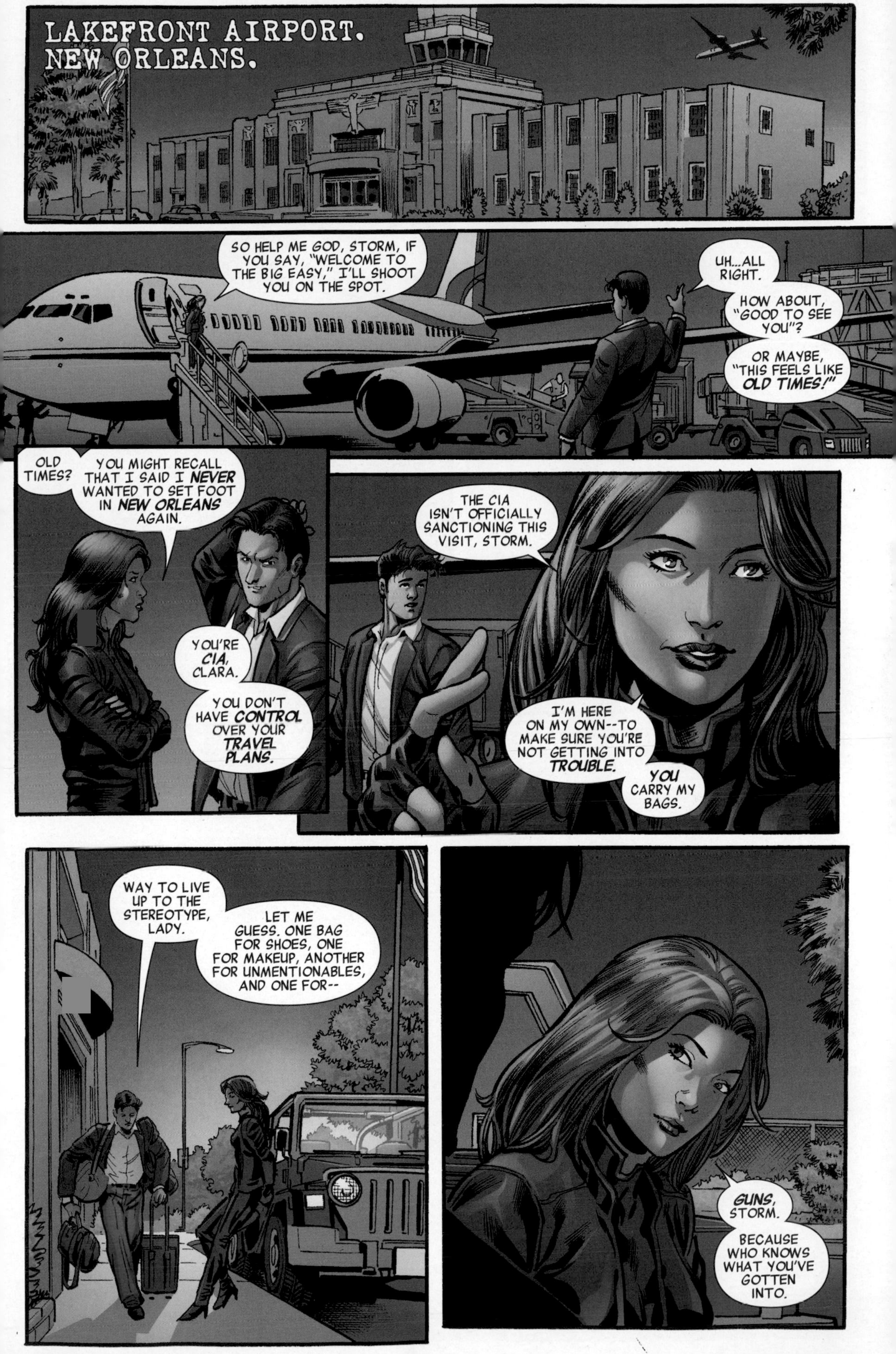
LAKEFRONT AIRPORT. NEW ORLEANS.
SO HELP ME GOD, STORM, IF YOU SAY, "WELCOME TO THE BIG EASY," I'LL SHOOT YOU ON THE SPOT.
UH...ALL RIGHT.
HOW ABOUT, "GOOD TO SEE YOU"?
OR MAYBE, "THIS FEELS LIKE OLD TIMES!"
OLD TIMES?
YOU MIGHT RECALL THAT I SAID I NEVER WANTED TO SET FOOT IN NEW ORLEANS AGAIN.
YOU'RE CIA, CLARA.
YOU DON'T HAVE CONTROL OVER YOUR TRAVEL PLANS.
THE CIA ISN'T OFFICIALLY SANCTIONING THIS VISIT, STORM.
I'M HERE ON MY OWN--TO MAKE SURE YOU'RE NOT GETTING INTO TROUBLE.
YOU CARRY MY BAGS.
WAY TO LIVE UP TO THE STEREOTYPE, LADY.
LET ME GUESS. ONE BAG FOR SHOES, ONE FOR MAKEUP, ANOTHER FOR UNMENTIONABLES, AND ONE FOR--
GUNS, STORM.
BECAUSE WHO KNOWS WHAT YOU'VE GOTTEN INTO.

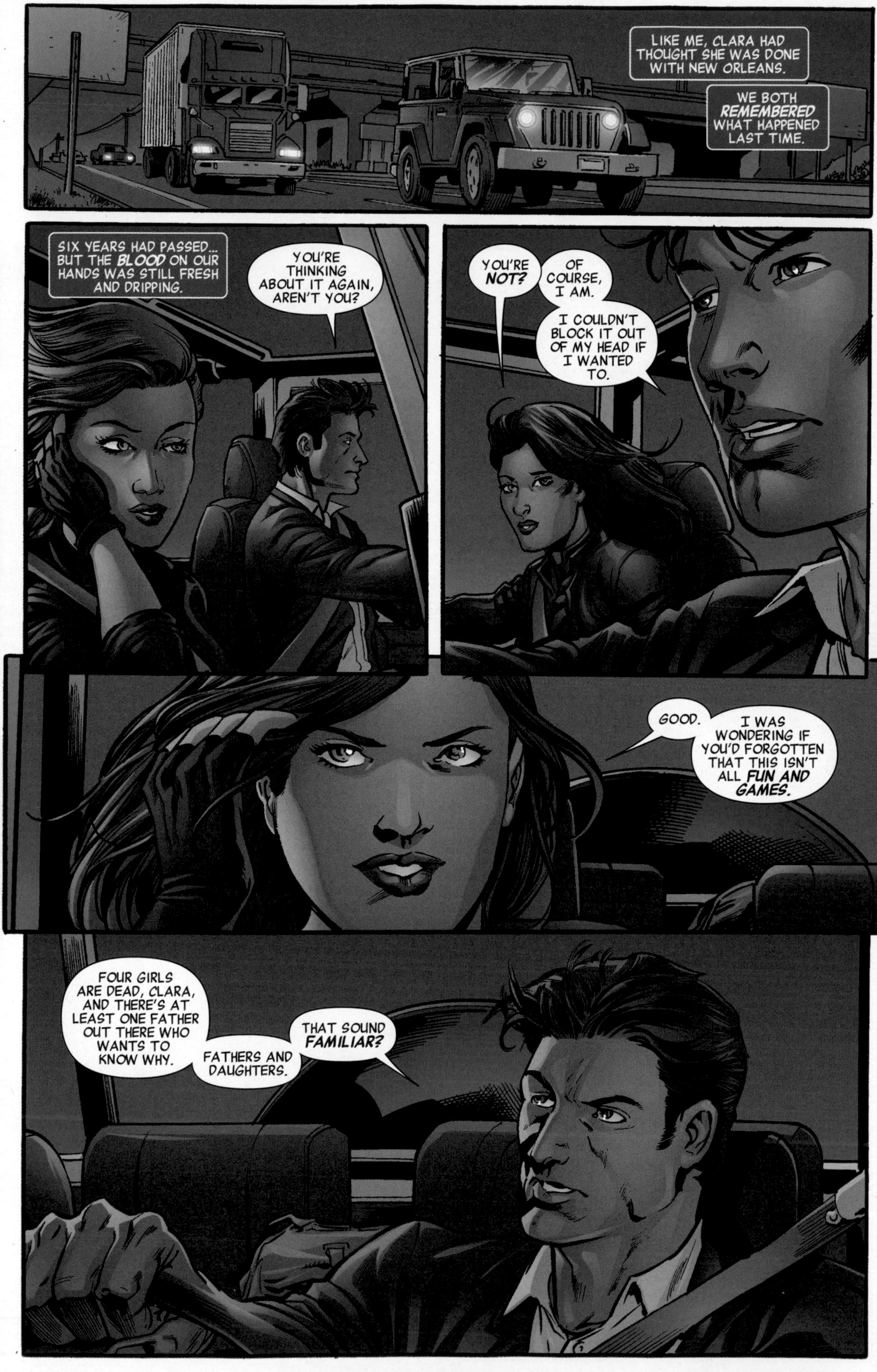

LIKE ME, CLARA HAD THOUGHT SHE WAS DONE WITH NEW ORLEANS.
WE BOTH REMEMBERED WHAT HAPPENED LAST TIME.
SIX YEARS HAD PASSED... BUT THE BLOOD ON OUR HANDS WAS STILL FRESH AND DRIPPING.
YOU'RE THINKING ABOUT IT AGAIN, AREN'T YOU?
YOU'RE NOT?
OF COURSE, I AM.
I COULDN'T BLOCK IT OUT OF MY HEAD IF I WANTED TO.
GOOD.
I WAS WONDERING IF YOU'D FORGOTTEN THAT THIS ISN'T ALL FUN AND GAMES.
FOUR GIRLS ARE DEAD, CLARA, AND THERE'S AT LEAST ONE FATHER OUT THERE WHO WANTS TO KNOW WHY.
FATHERS AND DAUGHTERS.
THAT SOUND FAMILIAR?

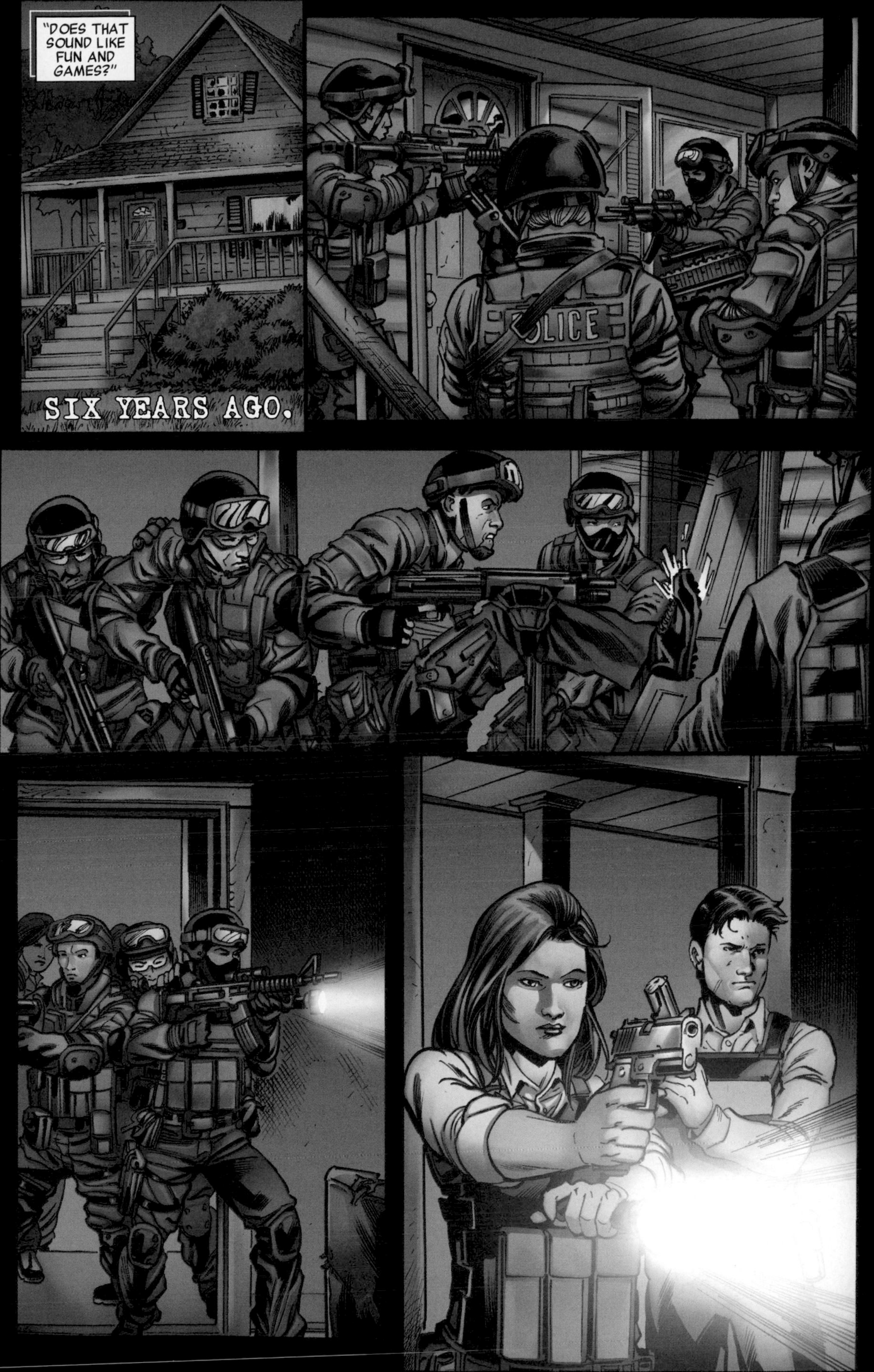
"DOES THAT SOUND LIKE FUN AND GAMES?"
SIX YEARS AGO.
POLICE

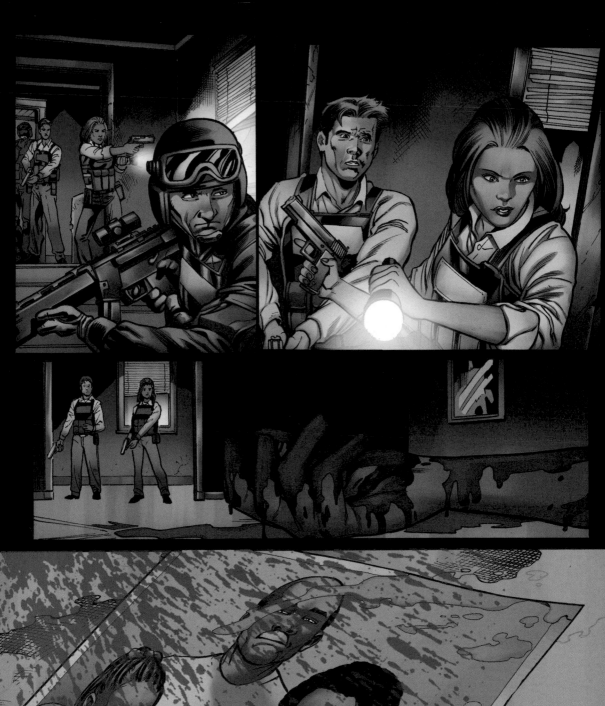

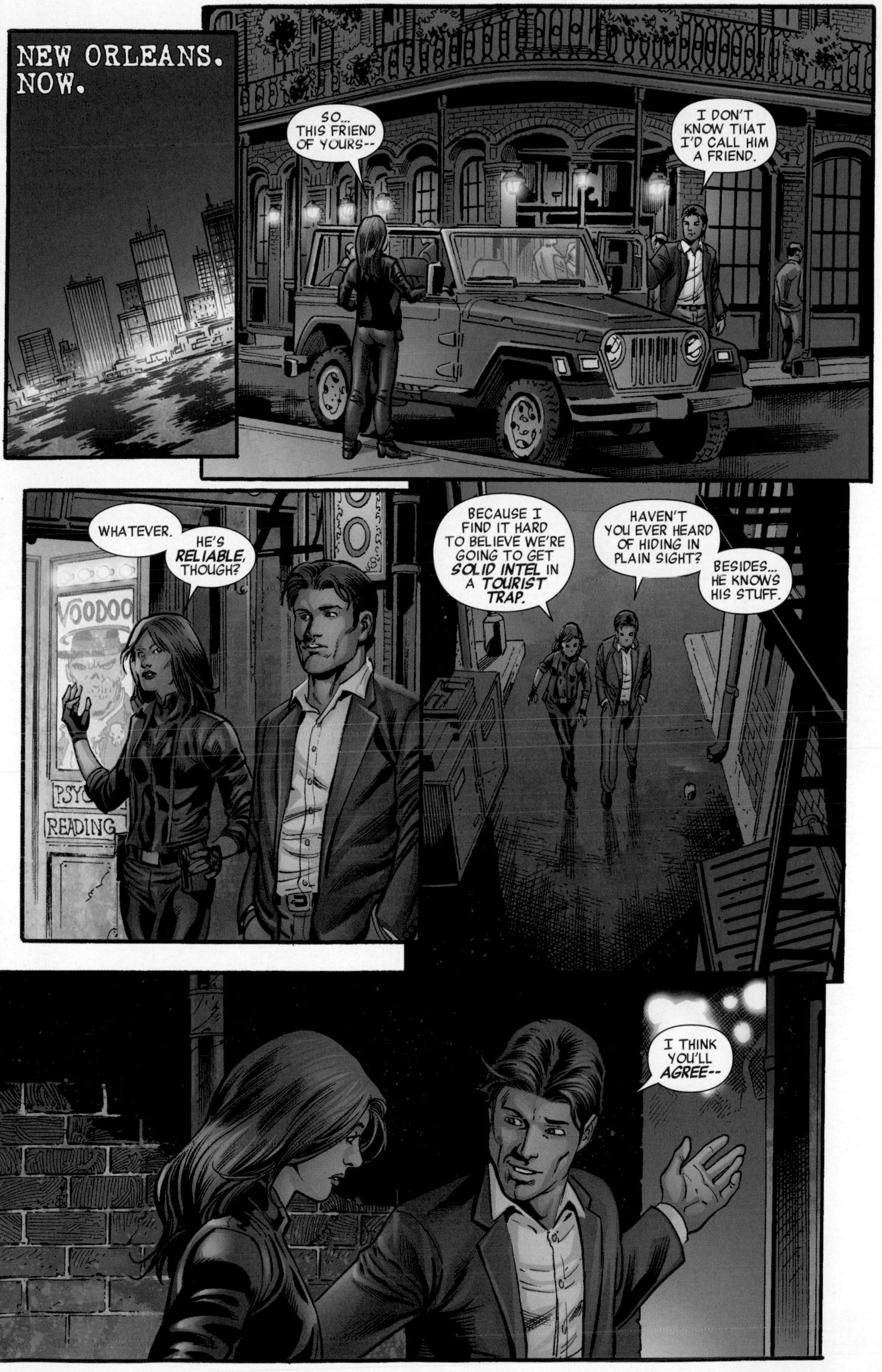
NEW ORLEANS.
NOW.
SO... THIS FRIEND OF YOURS--
I DON'T KNOW THAT I'D CALL HIM A FRIEND.
WHATEVER.
HE'S RELIABLE, THOUGH?
BECAUSE I FIND IT HARD TO BELIEVE WE'RE GOING TO GET SOLID INTEL IN A TOURIST TRAP.
HAVEN'T YOU EVER HEARD OF HIDING IN PLAIN SIGHT?
BESIDES... HE KNOWS HIS STUFF.
VOODOO
PSYC
READING
I THINK YOU'LL AGREE--

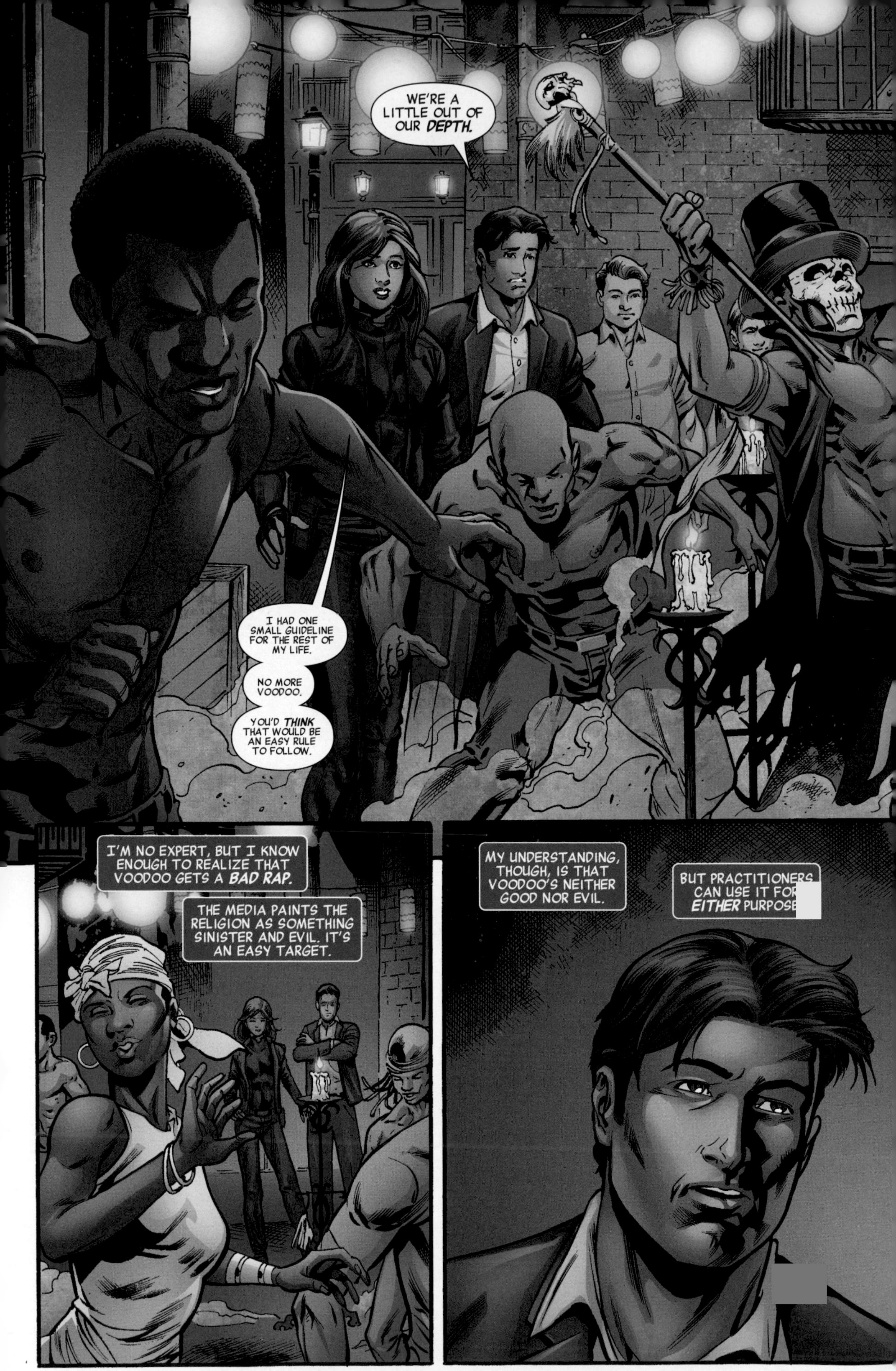
WE'RE A LITTLE OUT OF OUR DEPTH.
I HAD ONE SMALL GUIDELINE FOR THE REST OF MY LIFE.
NO MORE VOODOO.
YOU'D THINK THAT WOULD BE AN EASY RULE TO FOLLOW.
I'M NO EXPERT, BUT I KNOW ENOUGH TO REALIZE THAT VOODOO GETS A BAD RAP.
THE MEDIA PAINTS THE RELIGION AS SOMETHING SINISTER AND EVIL. IT'S AN EASY TARGET.
MY UNDERSTANDING, THOUGH, IS THAT VOODOO'S NEITHER GOOD NOR EVIL.
BUT PRACTITIONERS CAN USE IT FOR EITHER PURPOSE

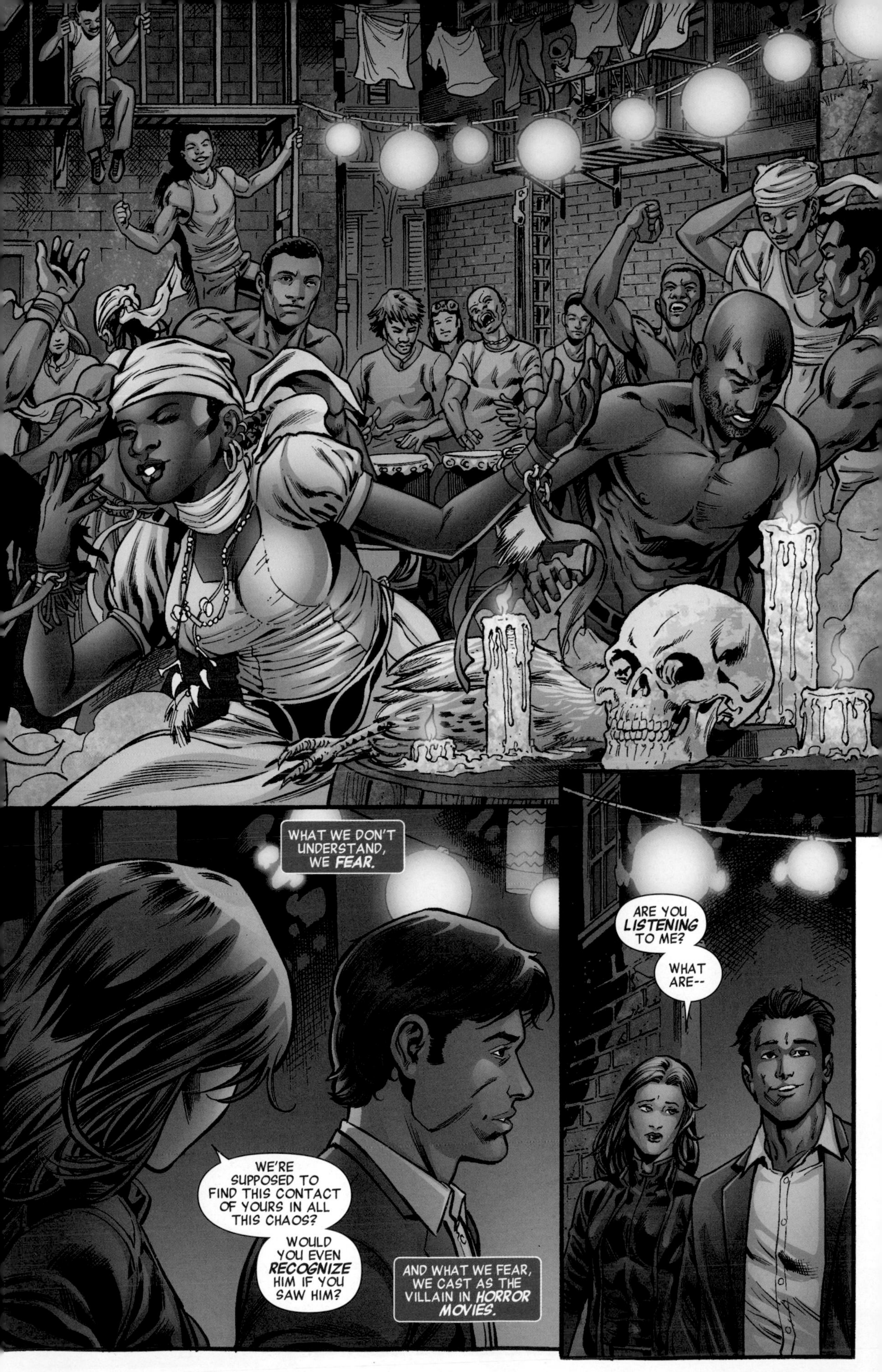

WHAT WE DON'T UNDERSTAND, WE FEAR.
WE'RE SUPPOSED TO FIND THIS CONTACT OF YOURS IN ALL THIS CHAOS?
WOULD YOU EVEN RECOGNIZE HIM IF YOU SAW HIM?
AND WHAT WE FEAR, WE CAST AS THE VILLAIN IN HORROR MOVIES.
ARE YOU LISTENING TO ME?
WHAT ARE--

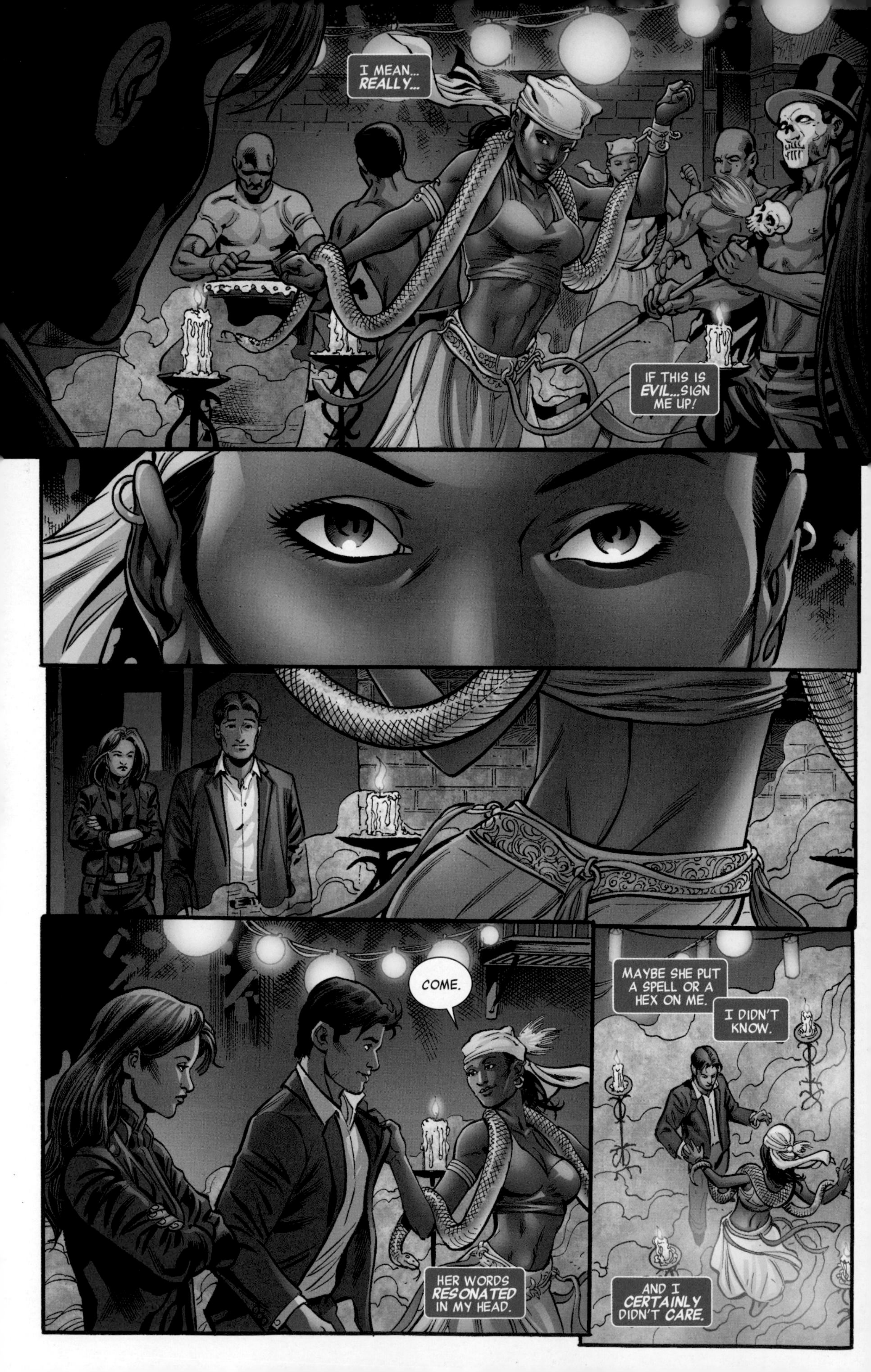

I MEAN... REALLY...
IF THIS IS EVIL...SIGN ME UP!
COME.
HER WORDS RESONATED IN MY HEAD.
MAYBE SHE PUT A SPELL OR A HEX ON ME.
I DIDN'T KNOW.
AND I CERTAINLY DIDN'T CARE.

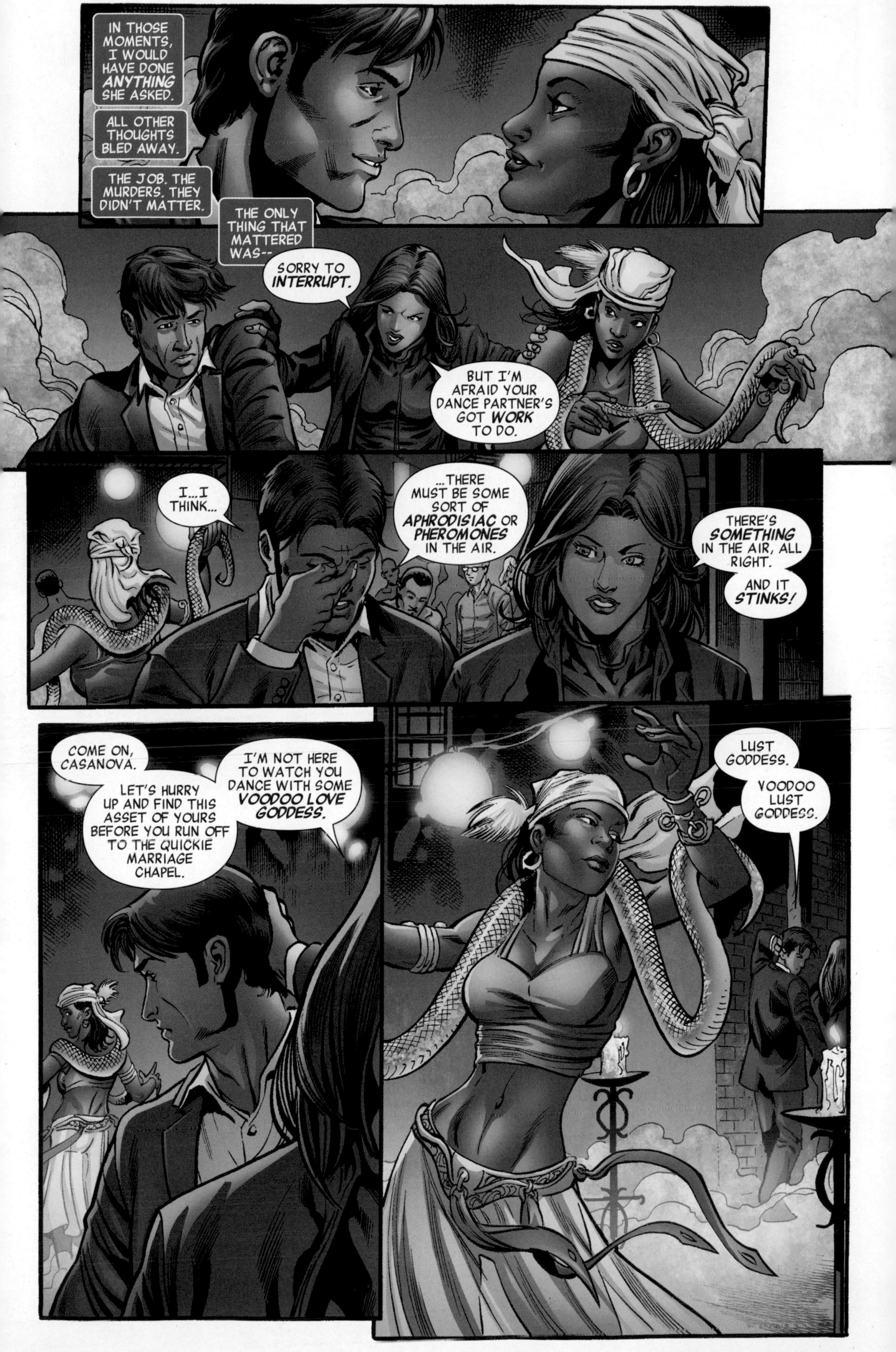
IN THOSE MOMENTS, I WOULD HAVE DONE ANYTHING SHE ASKED.
ALL OTHER THOUGHTS BLED AWAY.
THE JOB. THE MURDERS. THEY DIDN'T MATTER.
THE ONLY THING THAT MATTERED WAS--
SORRY TO INTERRUPT.
BUT I'M AFRAID YOUR DANCE PARTNER'S GOT WORK TO DO.
I...I THINK...
...THERE MUST BE SOME SORT OF APHRODISIAC OR PHEROMONES IN THE AIR.
THERE'S SOMETHING IN THE AIR, ALL RIGHT.
AND IT STINKS!
COME ON, CASANOVA.
LET'S HURRY UP AND FIND THIS ASSET OF YOURS BEFORE YOU RUN OFF TO THE QUICKIE MARRIAGE CHAPEL.
I'M NOT HERE TO WATCH YOU DANCE WITH SOME VOODOO LOVE GODDESS.
LUST GODDESS.
VOODOO LUST GODDESS.

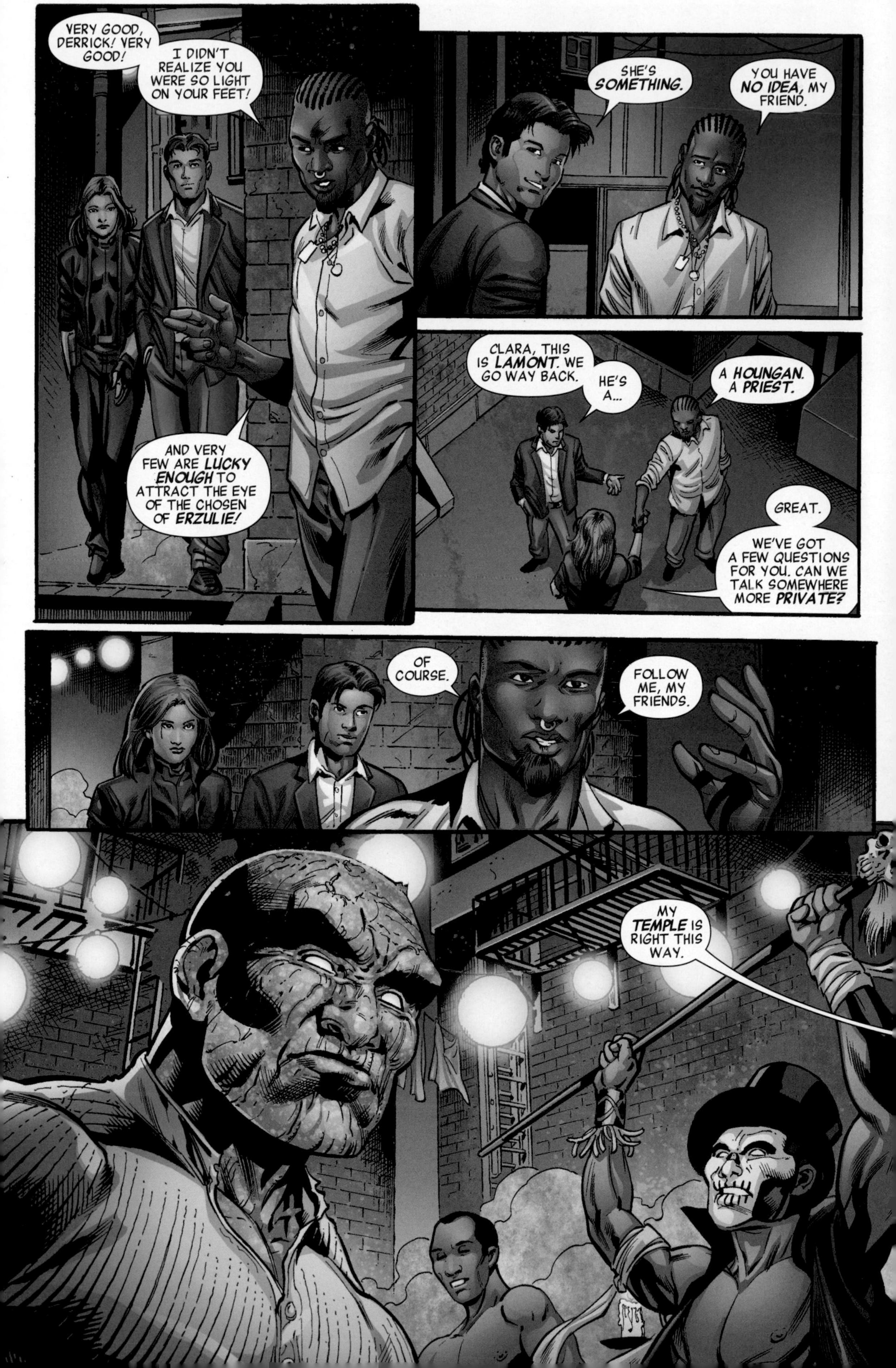
VERY GOOD, DERRICK! VERY GOOD!
I DIDN'T REALIZE YOU WERE SO LIGHT ON YOUR FEET!
AND VERY FEW ARE LUCKY ENOUGH TO ATTRACT THE EYE OF THE CHOSEN OF ERZULIE!
SHE'S SOMETHING.
YOU HAVE NO IDEA, MY FRIEND.
CLARA, THIS IS LAMONT. WE GO WAY BACK.
HE'S A...
A HOUNGAN. A PRIEST.
GREAT.
WE'VE GOT A FEW QUESTIONS FOR YOU. CAN WE TALK SOMEWHERE MORE PRIVATE?
OF COURSE.
FOLLOW ME, MY FRIENDS.
MY TEMPLE IS RIGHT THIS WAY.

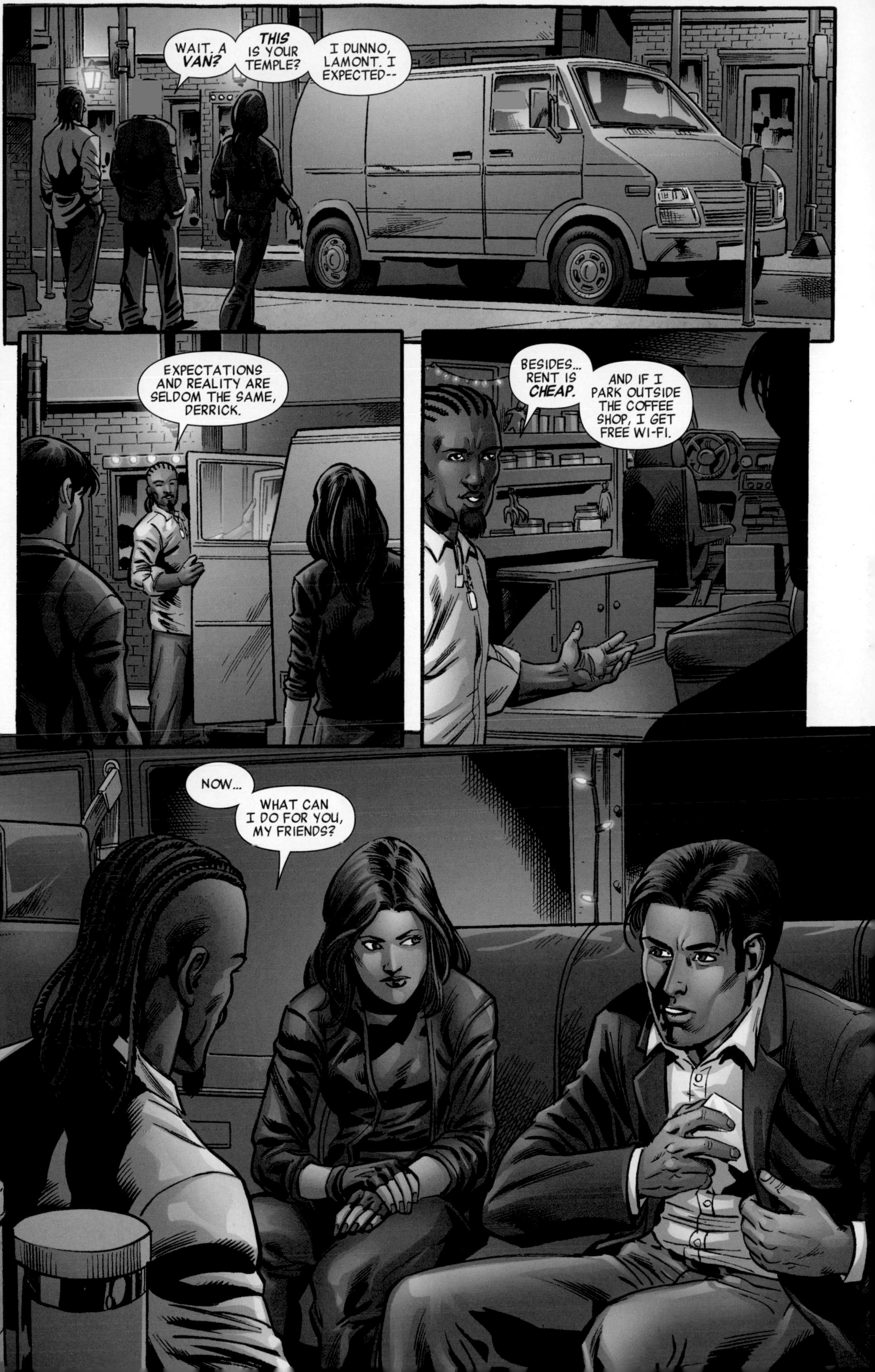
WAIT. A VAN?
THIS IS YOUR TEMPLE?
I DUNNO, LAMONT. I EXPECTED--
EXPECTATIONS AND REALITY ARE SELDOM THE SAME, DERRICK.
BESIDES... RENT IS CHEAP.
AND IF I PARK OUTSIDE THE COFFEE SHOP, I GET FREE WI-FI.
NOW...
WHAT CAN I DO FOR YOU, MY FRIENDS?

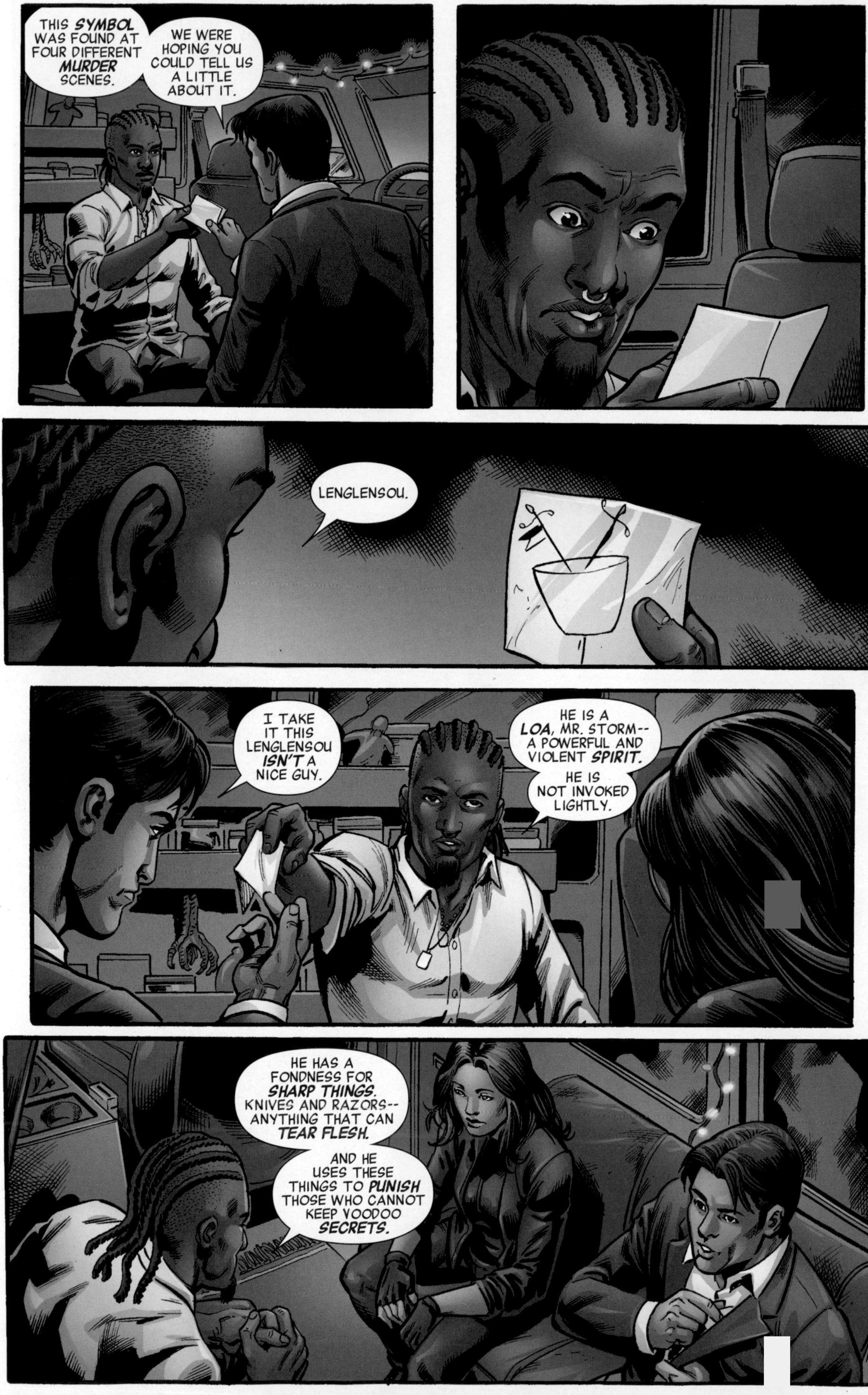
THIS SYMBOL WAS FOUND AT FOUR DIFFERENT MURDER SCENES.
WE WERE HOPING YOU COULD TELL US A LITTLE ABOUT IT.
LENGLENSOU.
I TAKE IT THIS LENGLENSOU ISN'T A NICE GUY.
HE IS A LOA, MR. STORM-- A POWERFUL AND VIOLENT SPIRIT.
HE IS NOT INVOKED LIGHTLY.
HE HAS A FONDNESS FOR SHARP THINGS. KNIVES AND RAZORS-- ANYTHING THAT CAN TEAR FLESH.
AND HE USES THESE THINGS TO PUNISH THOSE WHO CANNOT KEEP VOODOO SECRETS.

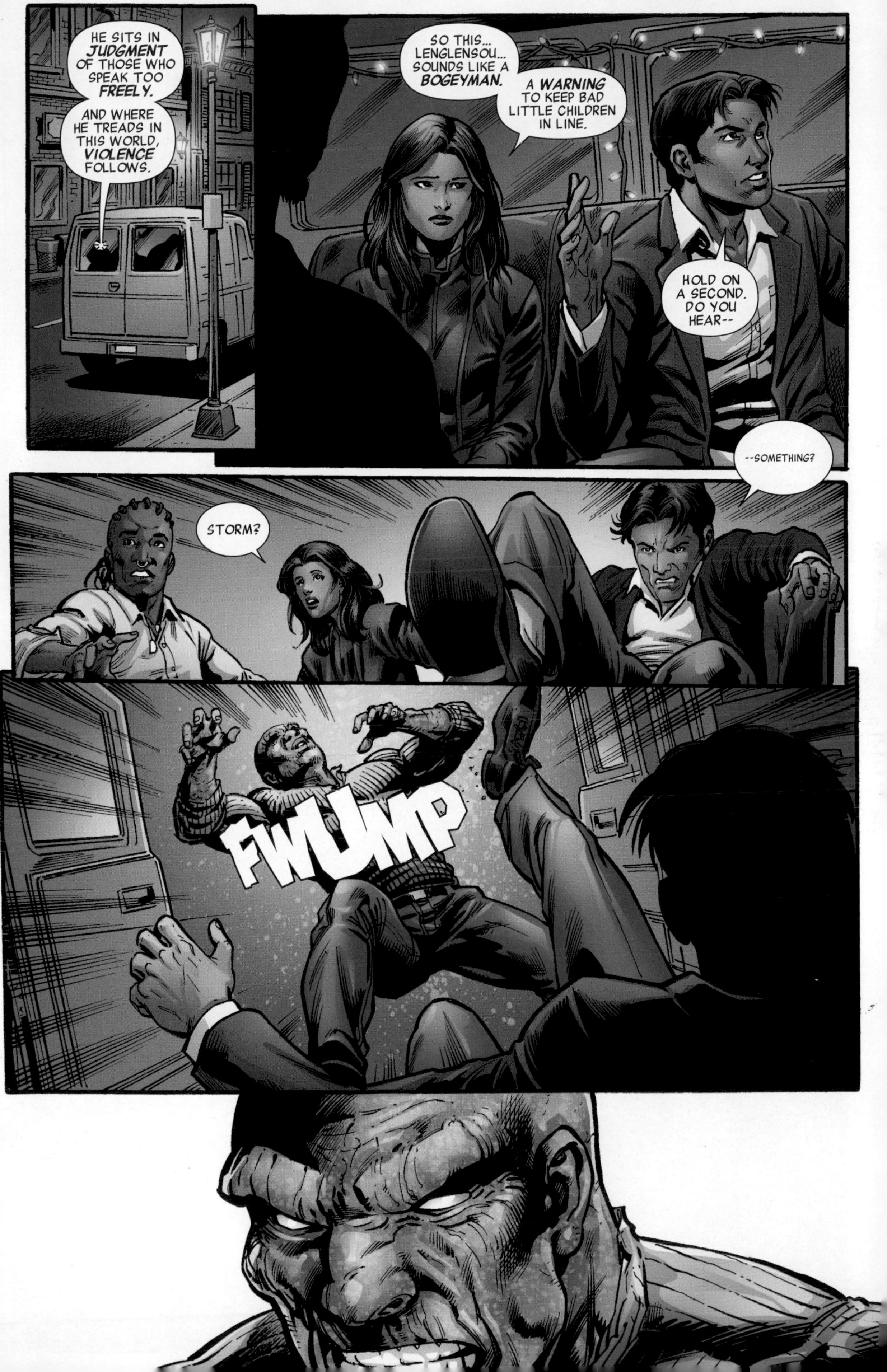

HE SITS IN JUDGMENT OF THOSE WHO SPEAK TOO FREELY.
AND WHERE HE TREADS IN THIS WORLD, VIOLENCE FOLLOWS.
SO THIS... LENGLENSOU... SOUNDS LIKE A BOGEYMAN.
A WARNING TO KEEP BAD LITTLE CHILDREN IN LINE.
HOLD ON A SECOND. DO YOU HEAR--
--SOMETHING?
STORM?
FWUMP

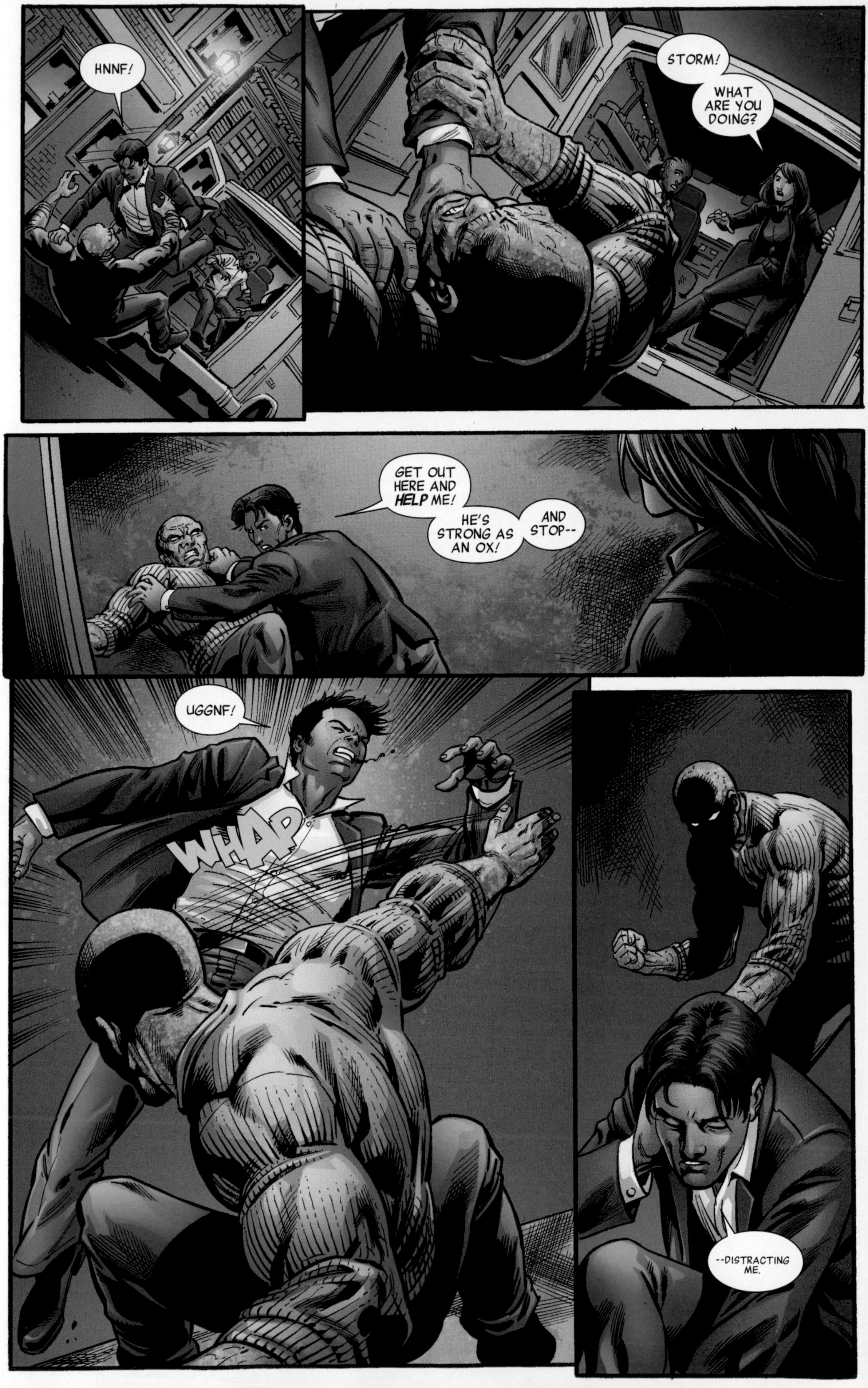
HNNF!
STORM!
WHAT ARE YOU DOING?
GET OUT HERE AND HELP ME!
HE'S STRONG AS AN OX!
AND STOP--
UGGNF!
WHAP
--DISTRACTING ME.

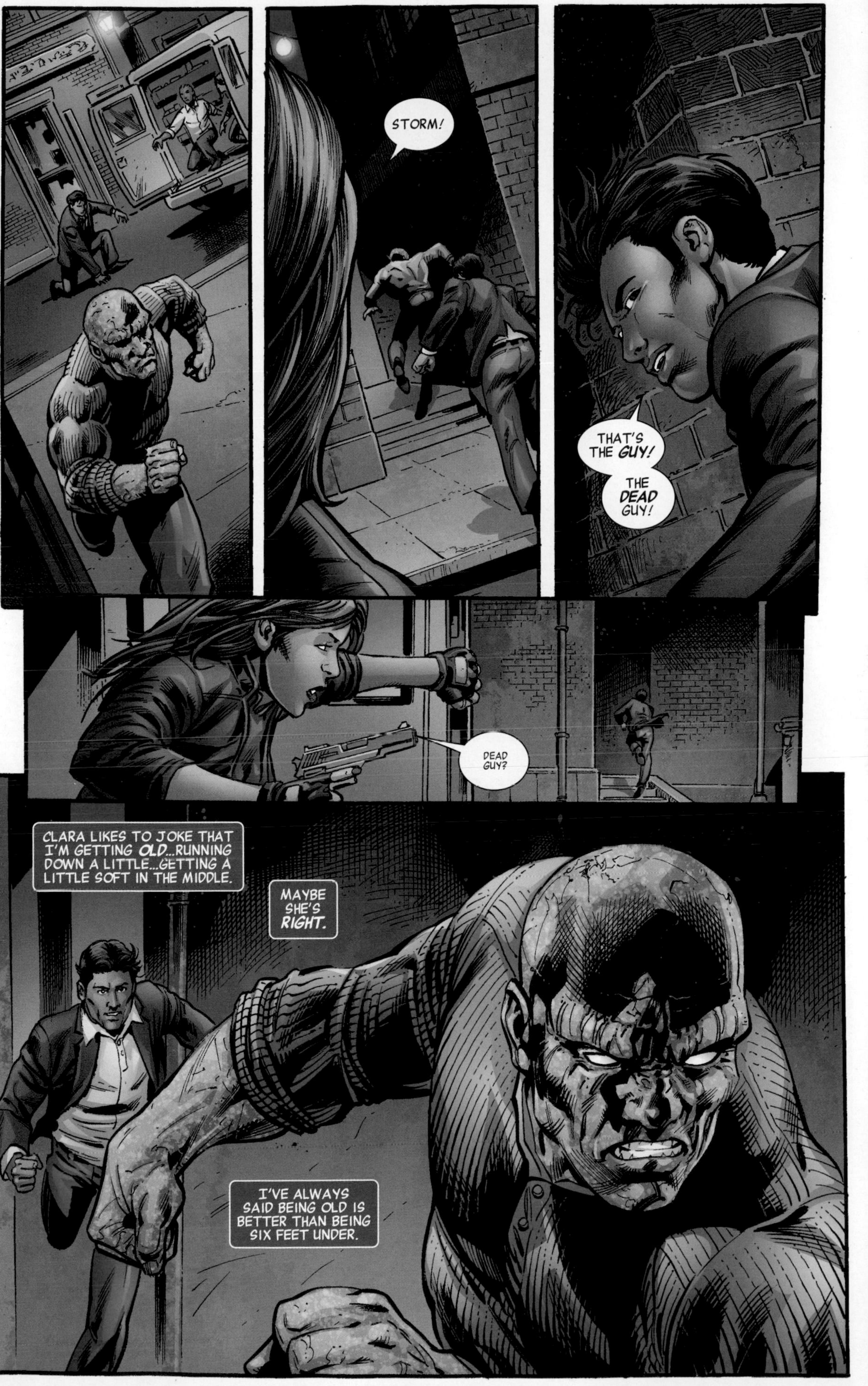
STORM!
THAT'S THE GUY!
THE DEAD GUY!
DEAD GUY?
CLARA LIKES TO JOKE THAT I'M GETTING OLD...RUNNING DOWN A LITTLE...GETTING A LITTLE SOFT IN THE MIDDLE.
MAYBE SHE'S RIGHT.
I'VE ALWAYS SAID BEING OLD IS BETTER THAN BEING SIX FEET UNDER.

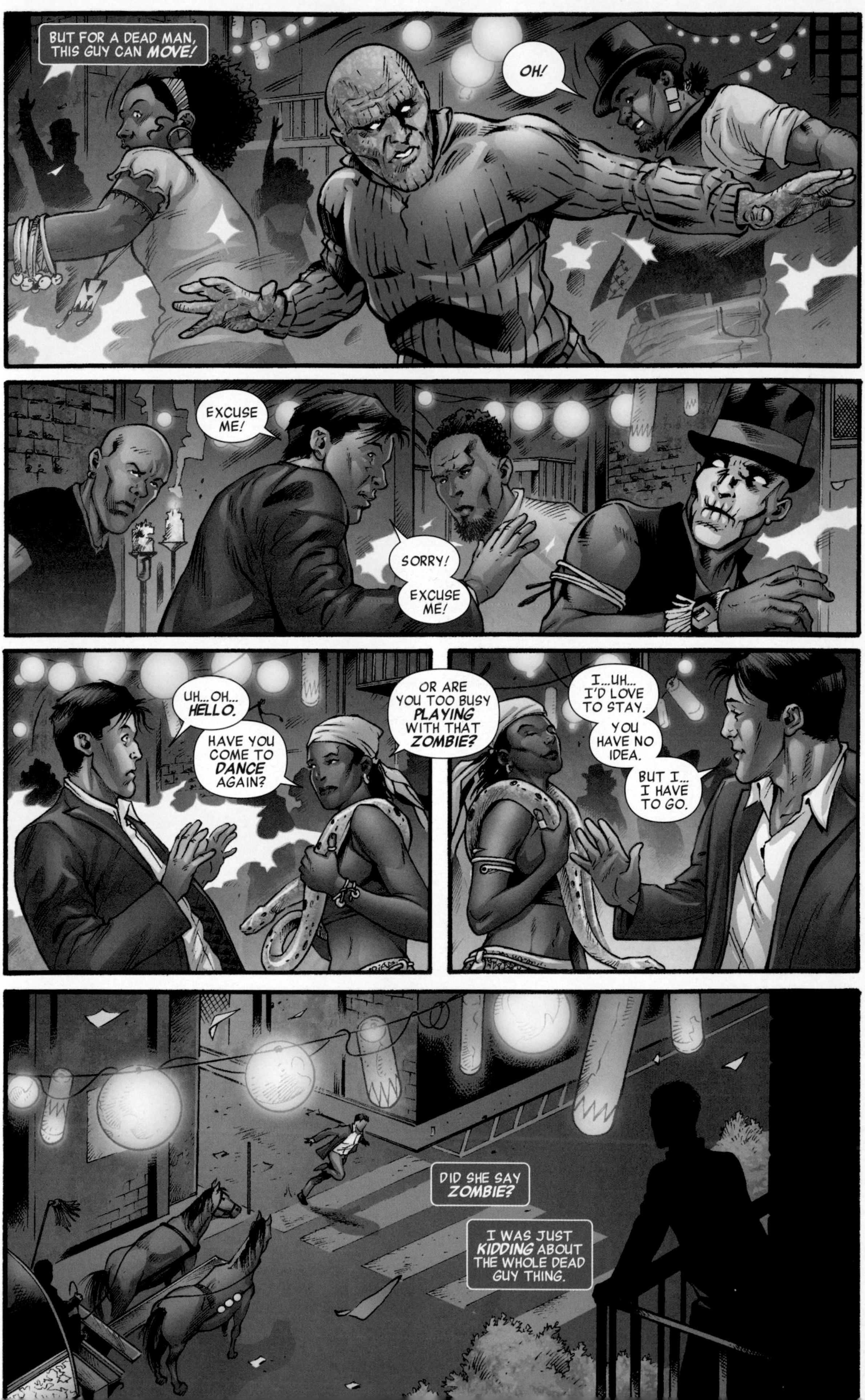
BUT FOR A DEAD MAN, THIS GUY CAN MOVE!
OH!
EXCUSE ME!
SORRY!
EXCUSE ME!
UH...OH... HELLO.
HAVE YOU COME TO DANCE AGAIN?
OR ARE YOU TOO BUSY PLAYING WITH THAT ZOMBIE?
I...UH... I'D LOVE TO STAY.
YOU HAVE NO IDEA.
BUT I... I HAVE TO GO.
DID SHE SAY ZOMBIE?
I WAS JUST KIDDING ABOUT THE WHOLE DEAD GUY THING.

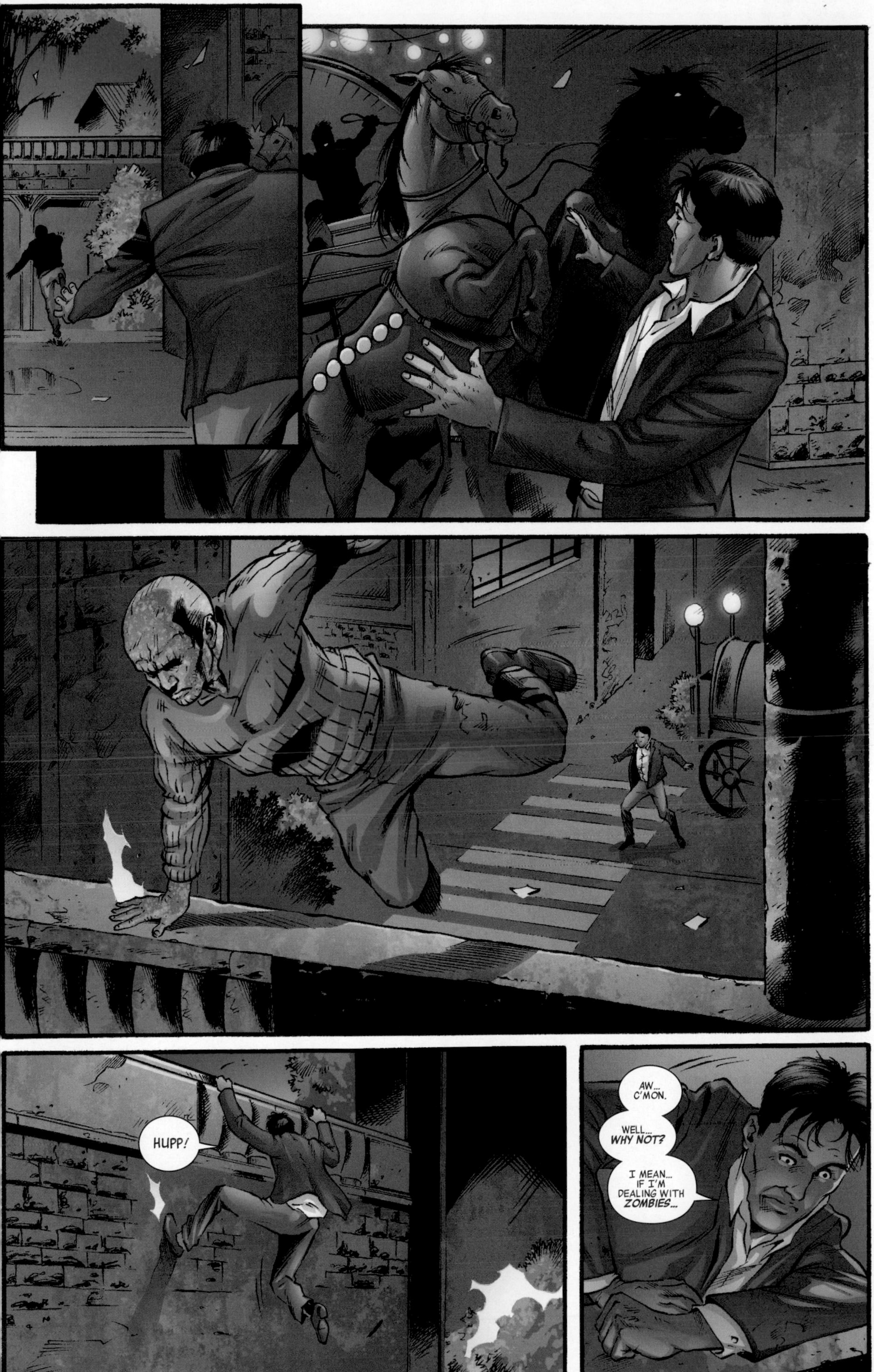
HUPP!
AW... C'MON.
WELL... WHY NOT?
I MEAN... IF I'M DEALING WITH ZOMBIES...

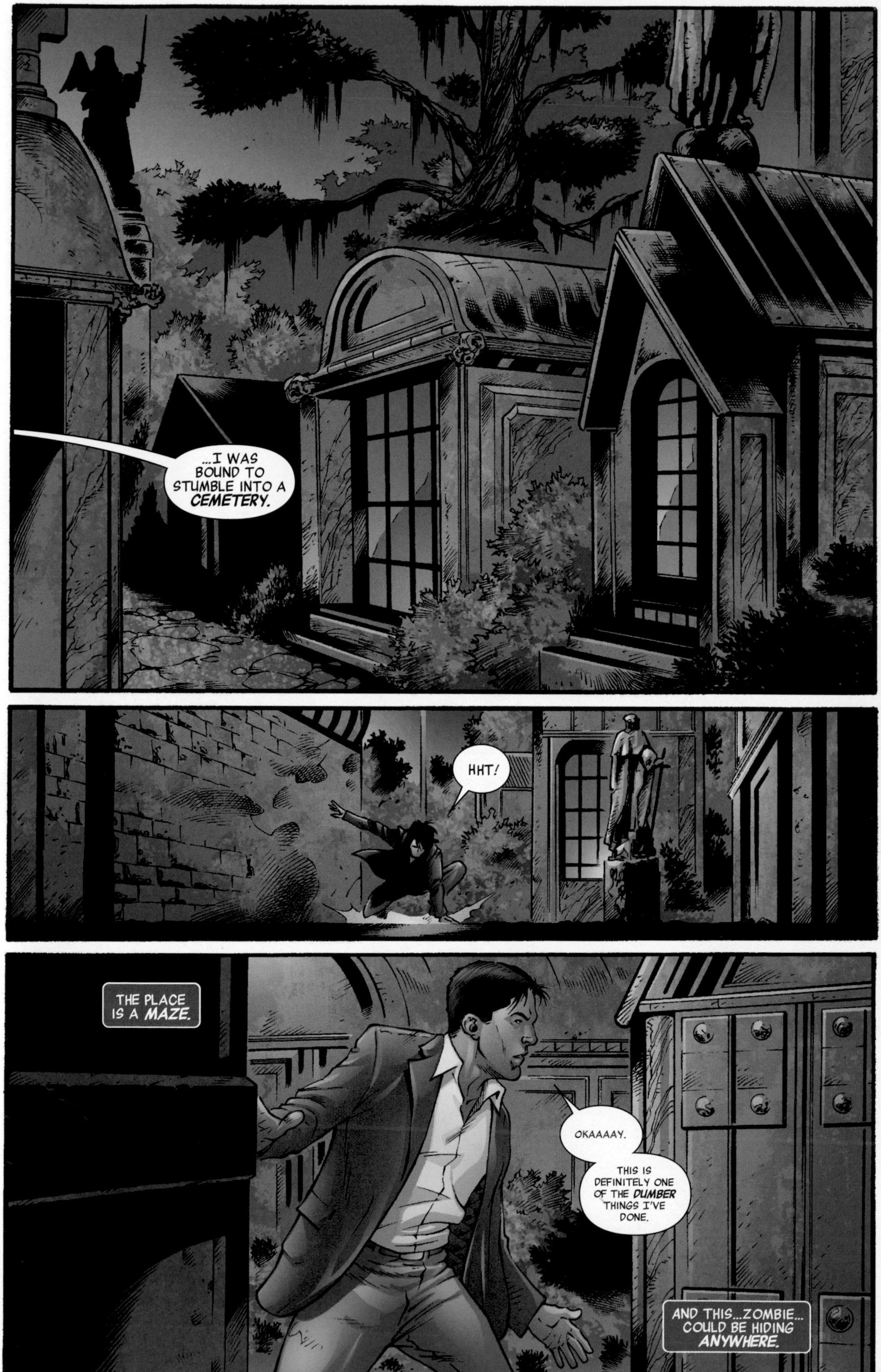
...I WAS BOUND TO STUMBLE INTO A CEMETERY.
HHT!
THE PLACE IS A MAZE.
OKAAAAY.
THIS IS DEFINITELY ONE OF THE DUMBER THINGS I'VE DONE.
AND THIS...ZOMBIE... COULD BE HIDING ANYWHERE.

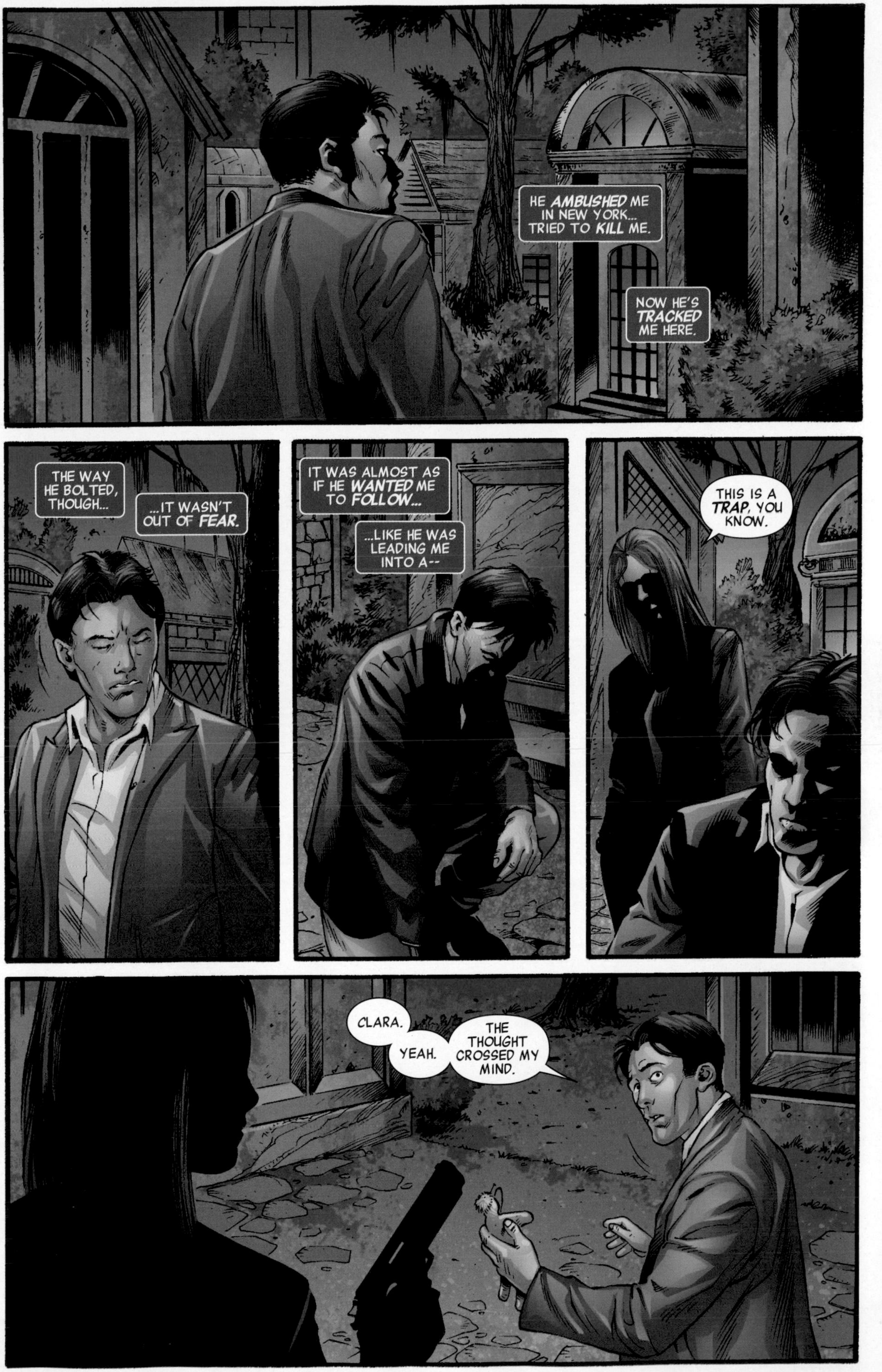
HE AMBUSHED ME IN NEW YORK... TRIED TO KILL ME.
NOW HE'S TRACKED ME HERE.
THE WAY HE BOLTED, THOUGH...
...IT WASN'T OUT OF FEAR.
IT WAS ALMOST AS IF HE WANTED ME TO FOLLOW...
...LIKE HE WAS LEADING ME INTO A--
THIS IS A TRAP, YOU KNOW.
CLARA.
YEAH.
THE THOUGHT CROSSED MY MIND.

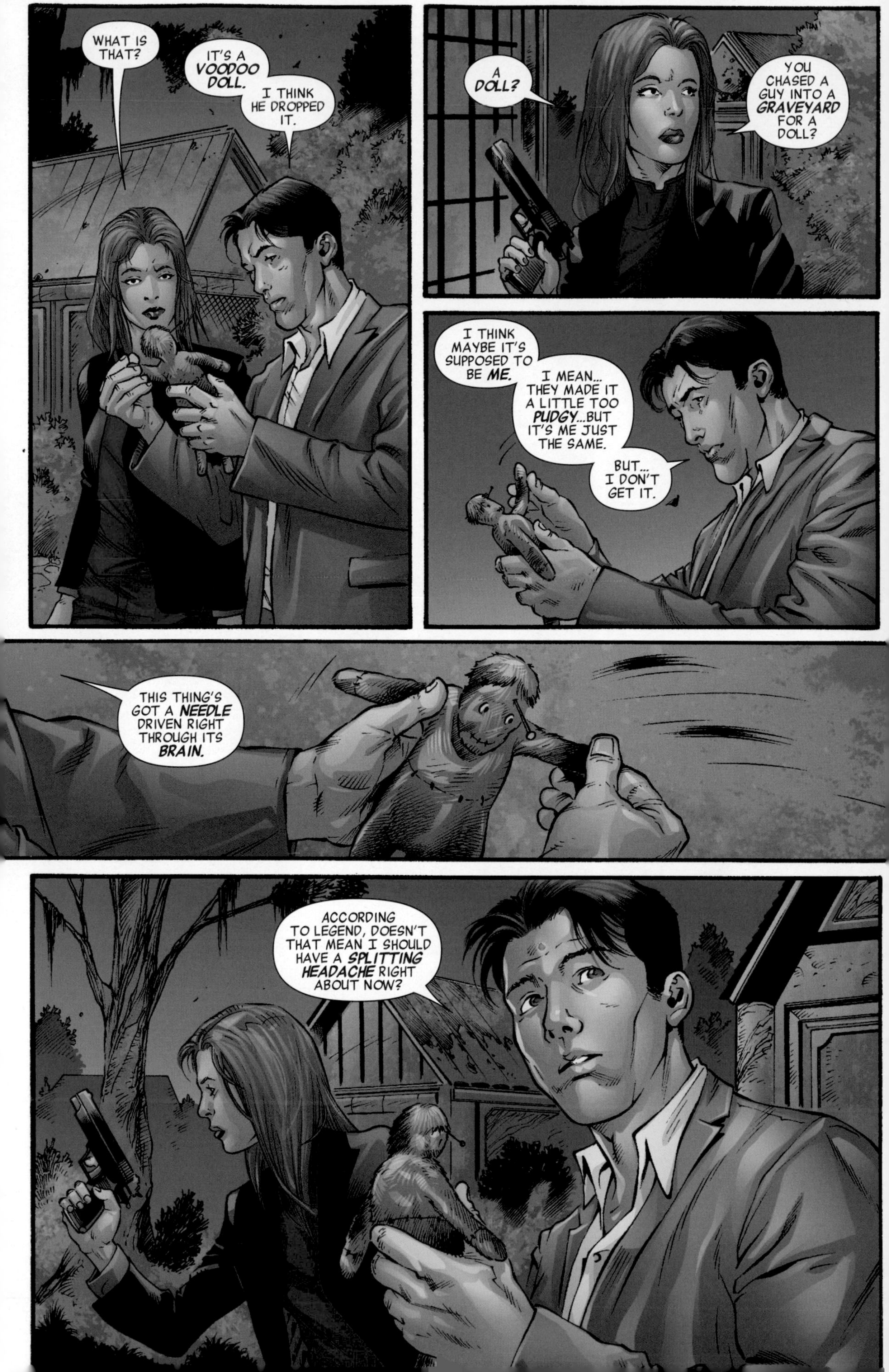
WHAT IS THAT?
IT'S A VOODOO DOLL.
I THINK HE DROPPED IT.
A DOLL?
YOU CHASED A GUY INTO A GRAVEYARD FOR A DOLL?
I THINK MAYBE IT'S SUPPOSED TO BE ME.
I MEAN... THEY MADE IT A LITTLE TOO PUDGY...BUT IT'S ME JUST THE SAME.
BUT... I DON'T GET IT.
THIS THING'S GOT A NEEDLE DRIVEN RIGHT THROUGH ITS BRAIN.
ACCORDING TO LEGEND, DOESN'T THAT MEAN I SHOULD HAVE A SPLITTING HEADACHE RIGHT ABOUT NOW?

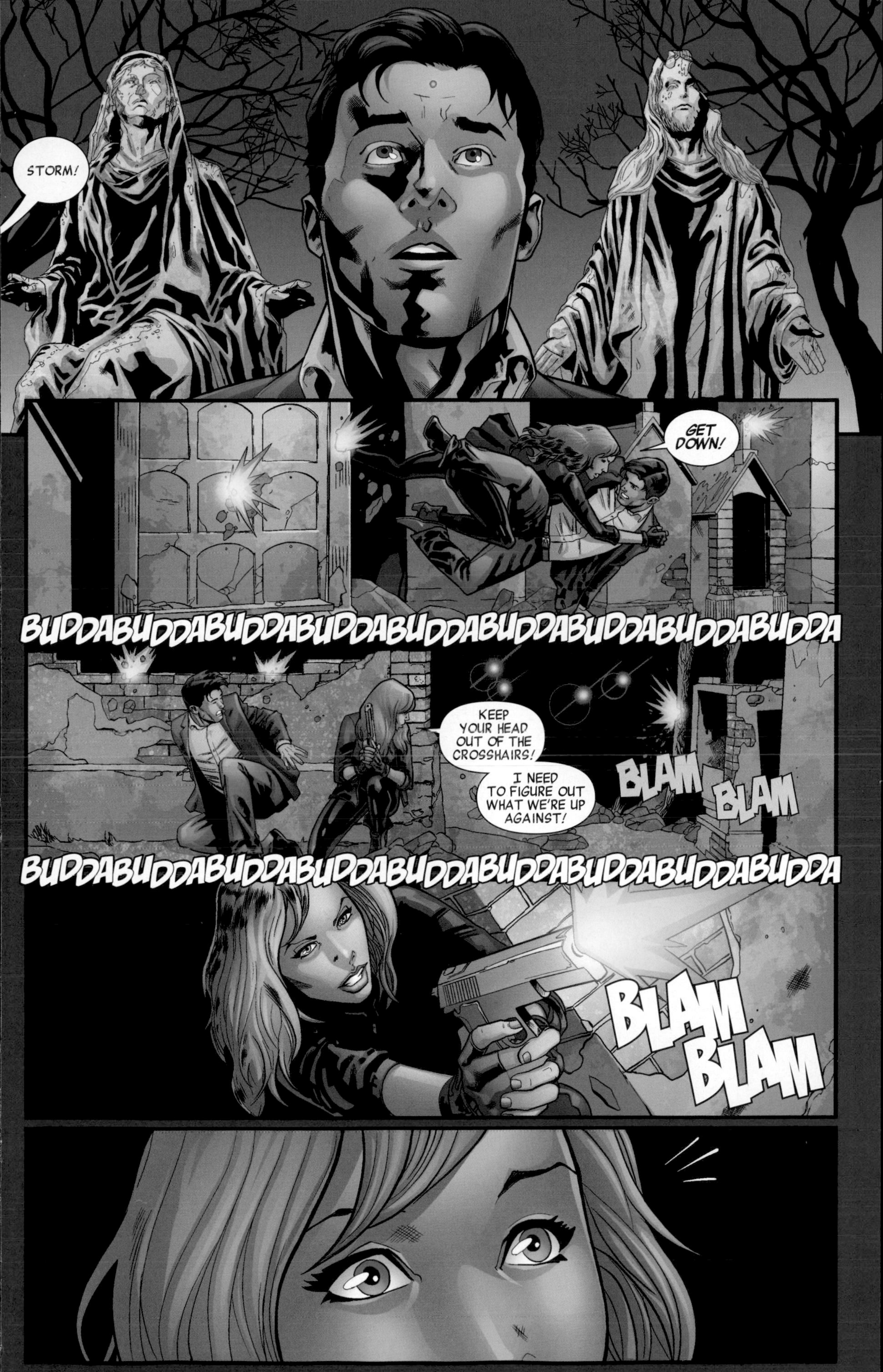
STORM!
GET DOWN!
BUDDABUDDABUDDABUDDABUDDABUDDABUDDABUDDABUDDABUDDA
KEEP YOUR HEAD OUT OF THE CROSSHAIRS!
I NEED TO FIGURE OUT WHAT WE'RE UP AGAINST!
BLAM BLAM
BUDDABUDDABUDDABUDDABUDDABUDDABUDDABUDDABUDDABUDDA
BLAM BLAM

THEY'RE **FANNING OUT**, TRYING TO **BOX** US IN.

SOUNDS LIKE WE **SHOULDN'T** LET THEM DO THAT.

BUDDABUDDABUDDABUDDABUDDABUDDABUDDABUDDABUDDA

WE NEED TO **MOVE!**

YOU KNOW, **NOW** MIGHT BE A GOOD TIME TO GIVE ME ONE OF THOSE **GUNS** YOU BROUGHT ALONG.

NOW MIGHT HAVE BEEN A GOOD TIME FOR YOU TO BRING YOUR OWN GUN.

WASN'T REALLY **EXPECTING** CEMETERY DEATH SQUADS.

THAT'S THE **DIFFERENCE** BETWEEN YOU AND ME, STORM...

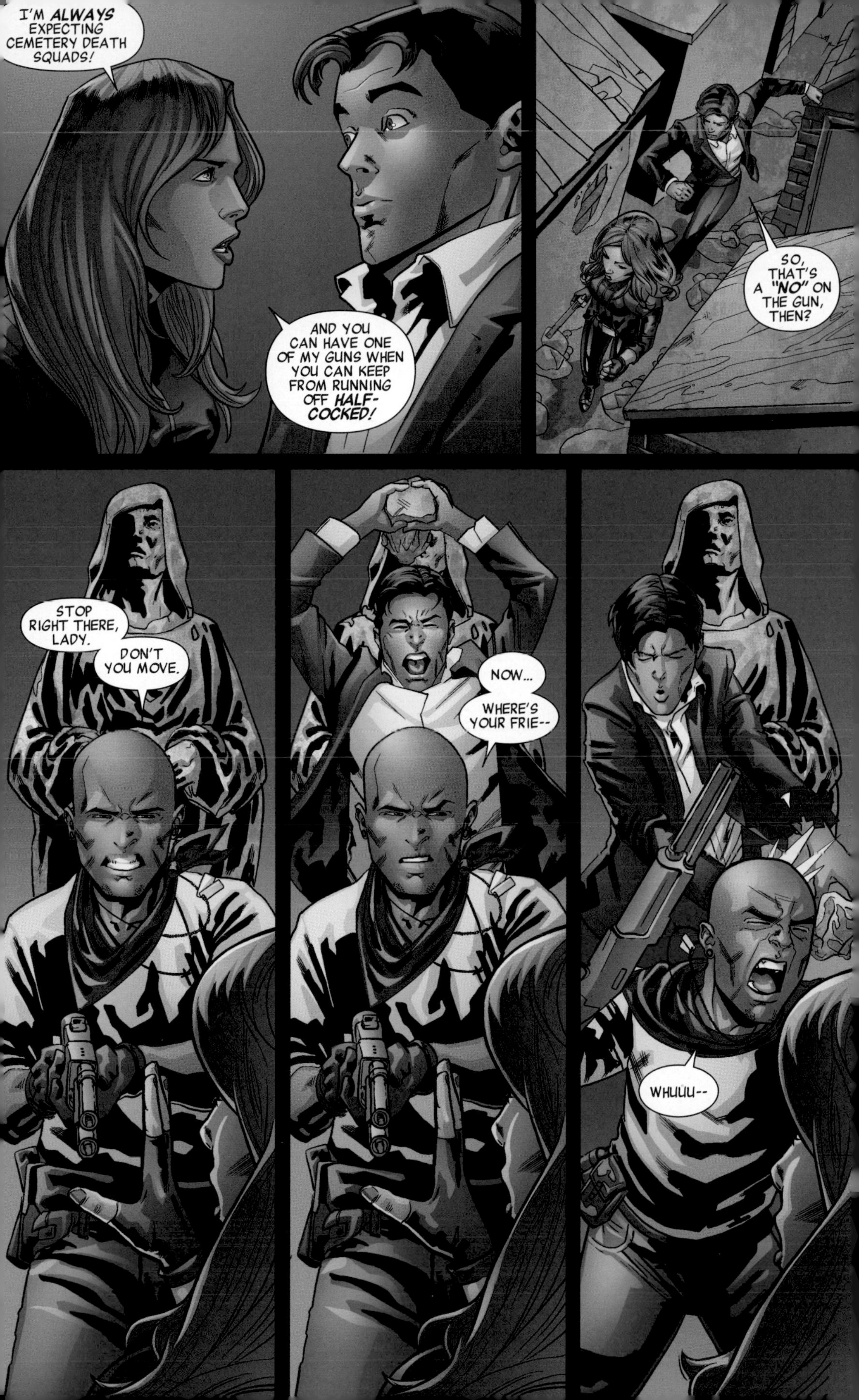
I'M ALWAYS EXPECTING CEMETERY DEATH SQUADS!
AND YOU CAN HAVE ONE OF MY GUNS WHEN YOU CAN KEEP FROM RUNNING OFF HALF-COCKED!
SO, THAT'S A "NO" ON THE GUN, THEN?
STOP RIGHT THERE, LADY.
DON'T YOU MOVE.
NOW...
WHERE'S YOUR FRIE--
WHUUU--

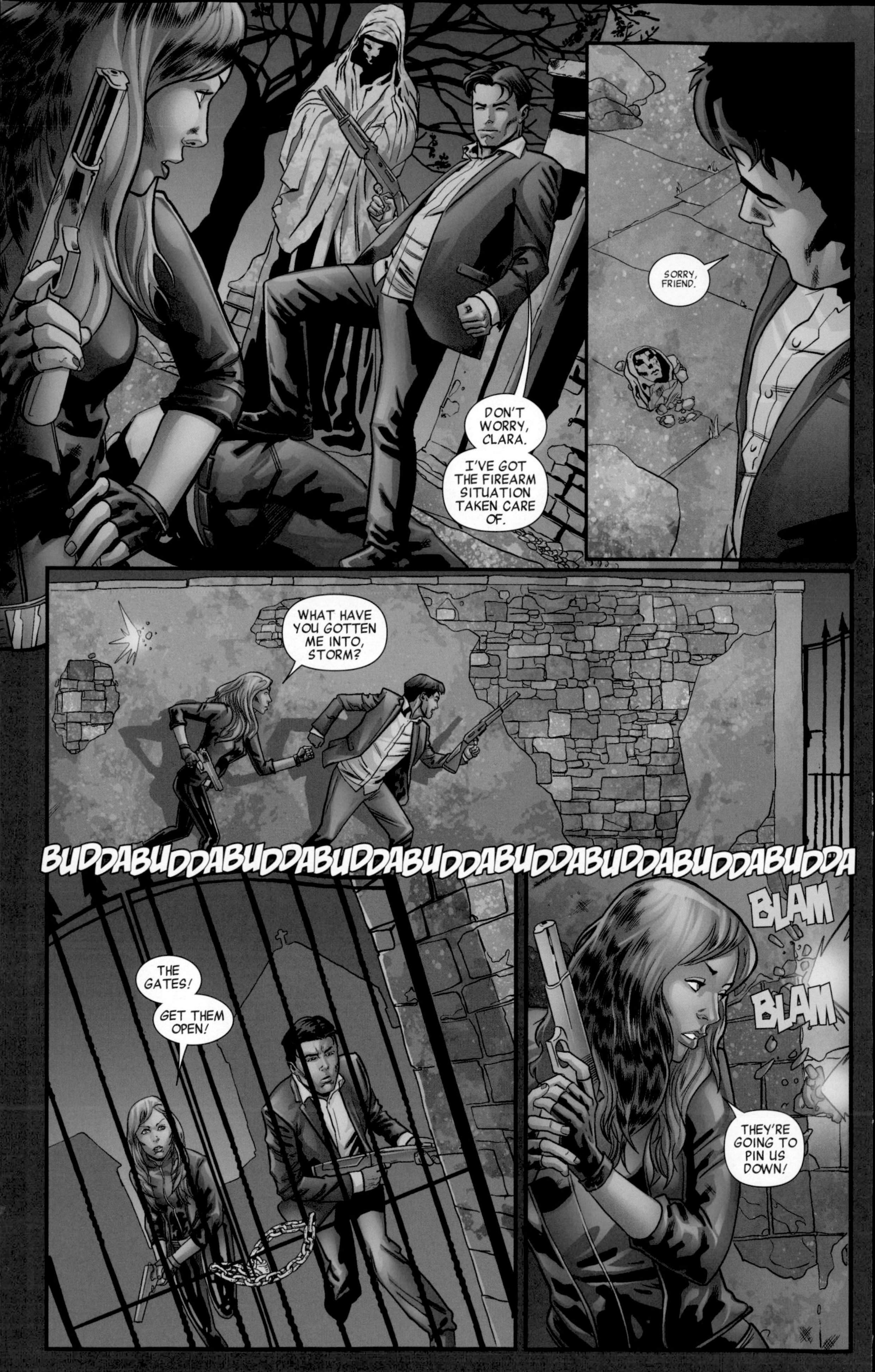
DON'T WORRY, CLARA.
I'VE GOT THE FIREARM SITUATION TAKEN CARE OF.
SORRY, FRIEND.
WHAT HAVE YOU GOTTEN ME INTO, STORM?
BUDDABUDDABUDDABUDDABUDDABUDDABUDDABUDDABUDDA
THE GATES!
GET THEM OPEN!
BLAM
BLAM
THEY'RE GOING TO PIN US DOWN!

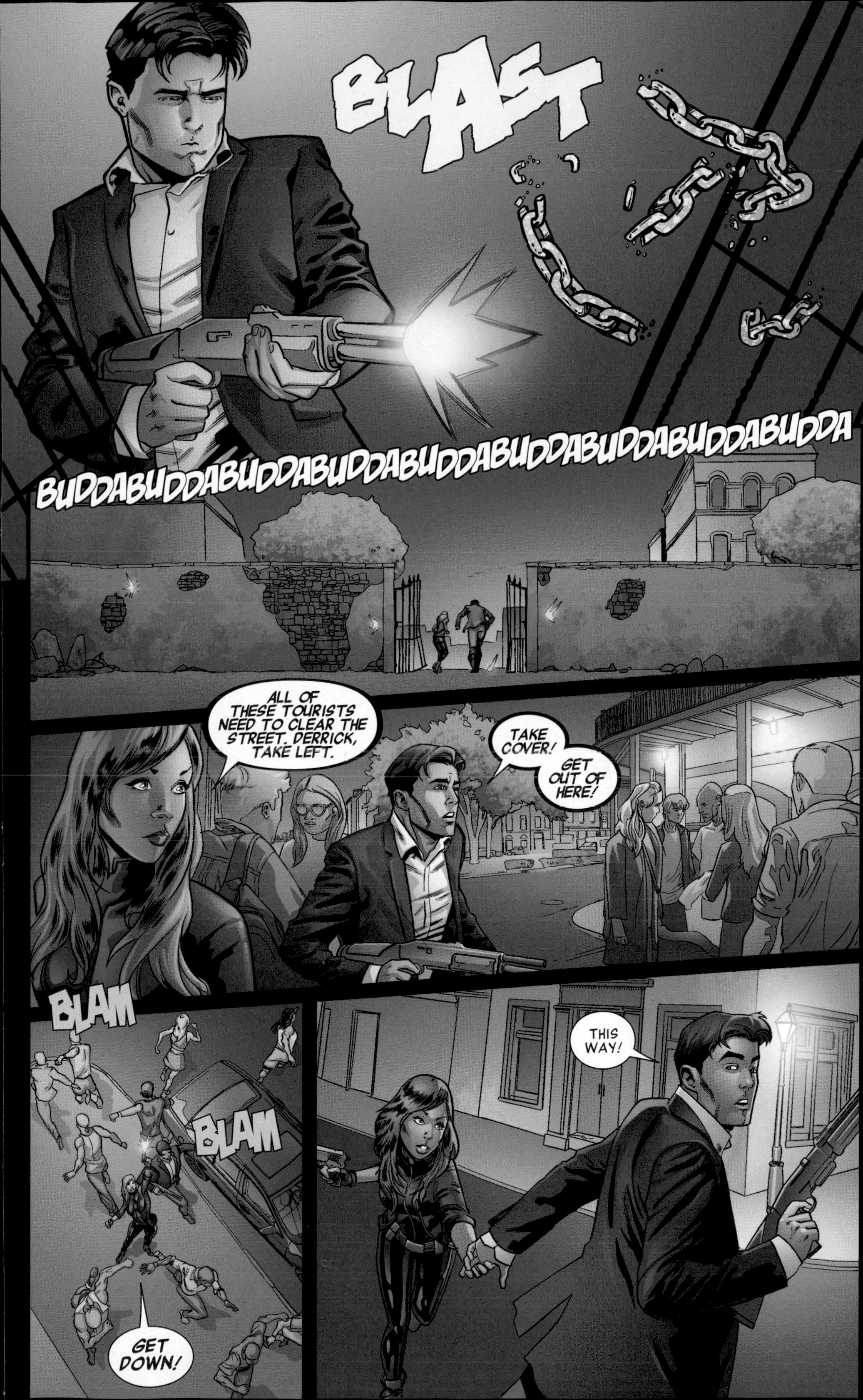
BLAST
BUDDABUDDABUDDABUDDABUDDABUDDABUDDABUDDABUDDA
ALL OF THESE TOURISTS NEED TO CLEAR THE STREET. DERRICK, TAKE LEFT.
TAKE COVER!
GET OUT OF HERE!
BLAM
BLAM
GET DOWN!
THIS WAY!

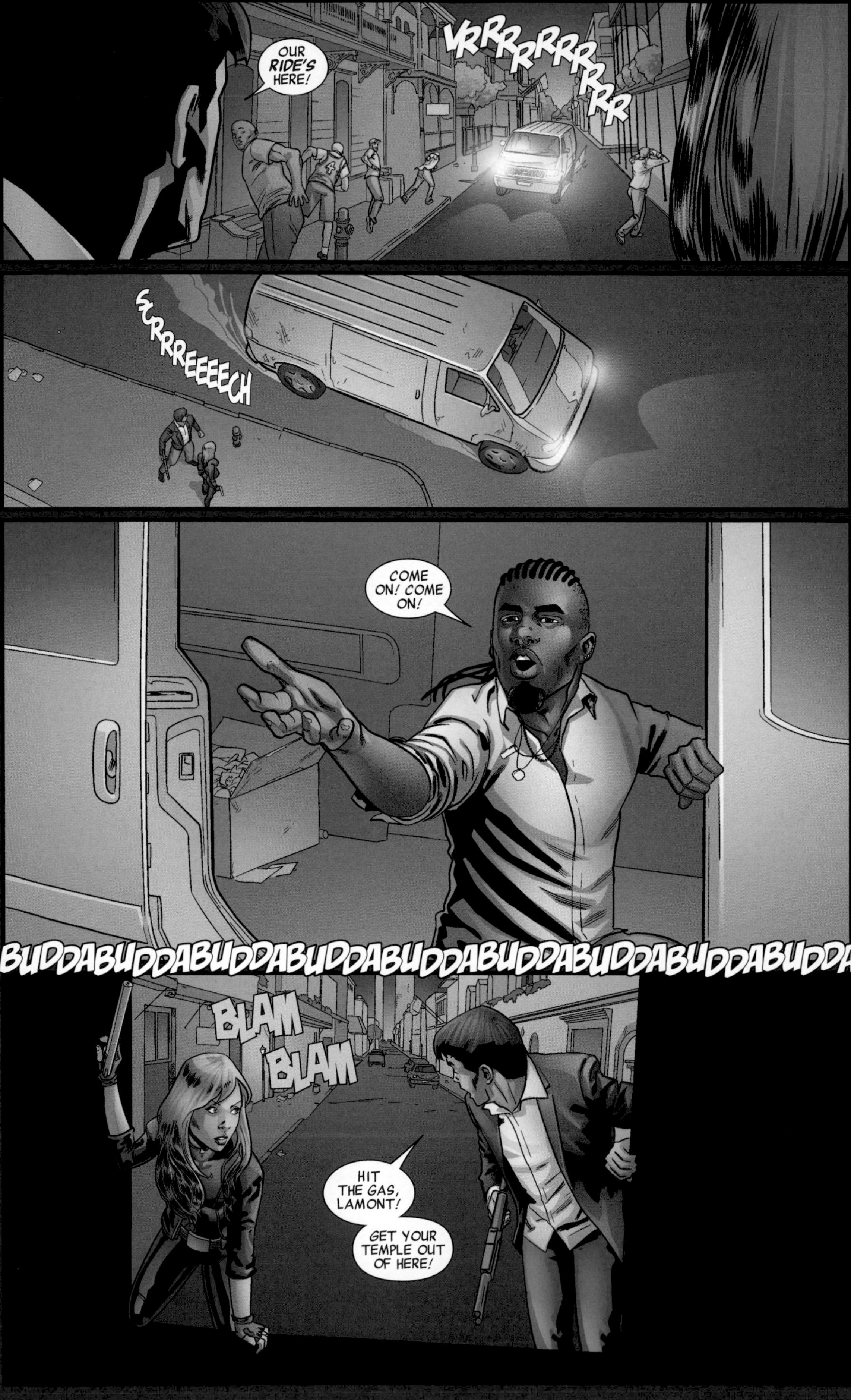
OUR RIDE'S HERE!
VRRRRRRRRRRRR
SCRRREEEEECH
COME ON! COME ON!
BUDDABUDDABUDDABUDDABUDDABUDDABUDDABUDDABUDDA
BLAM
BLAM
HIT THE GAS, LAMONT!
GET YOUR TEMPLE OUT OF HERE!

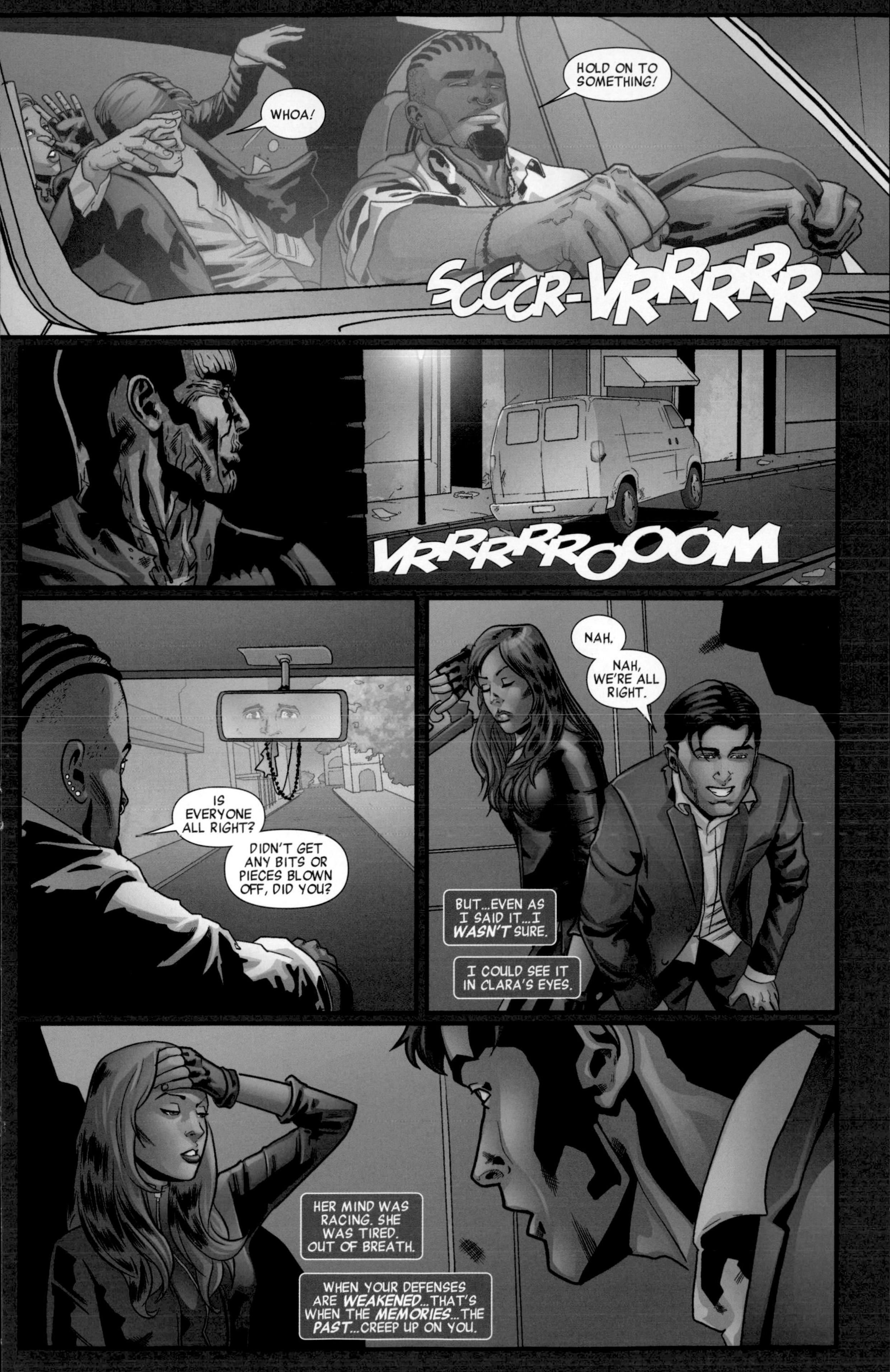
HOLD ON TO SOMETHING!
WHOA!
SCCCR-VRRRRRR
VRRRRROOOOM
IS EVERYONE ALL RIGHT?
DIDN'T GET ANY BITS OR PIECES BLOWN OFF, DID YOU?
NAH.
NAH, WE'RE ALL RIGHT.
BUT...EVEN AS I SAID IT...I WASN'T SURE.
I COULD SEE IT IN CLARA'S EYES.
HER MIND WAS RACING. SHE WAS TIRED. OUT OF BREATH.
WHEN YOUR DEFENSES ARE WEAKENED...THAT'S WHEN THE MEMORIES...THE PAST...CREEP UP ON YOU.

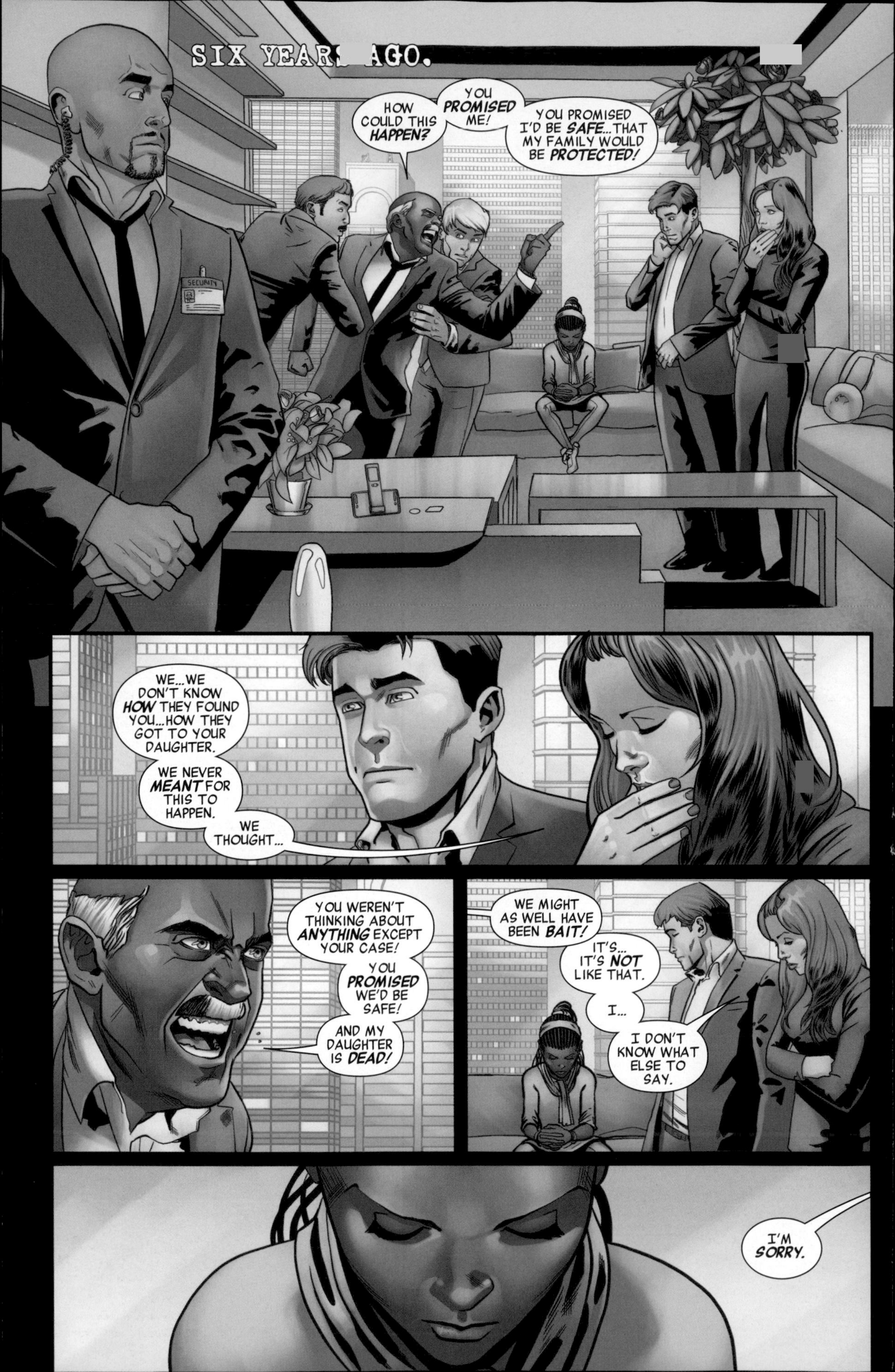
SIX YEARS AGO.
HOW COULD THIS HAPPEN?
YOU PROMISED ME!
YOU PROMISED I'D BE SAFE...THAT MY FAMILY WOULD BE PROTECTED!
WE...WE DON'T KNOW HOW THEY FOUND YOU...HOW THEY GOT TO YOUR DAUGHTER.
WE NEVER MEANT FOR THIS TO HAPPEN.
WE THOUGHT...
YOU WEREN'T THINKING ABOUT ANYTHING EXCEPT YOUR CASE!
YOU PROMISED WE'D BE SAFE!
AND MY DAUGHTER IS DEAD!
WE MIGHT AS WELL HAVE BEEN BAIT!
IT'S... IT'S NOT LIKE THAT.
I...
I DON'T KNOW WHAT ELSE TO SAY.
I'M SORRY.

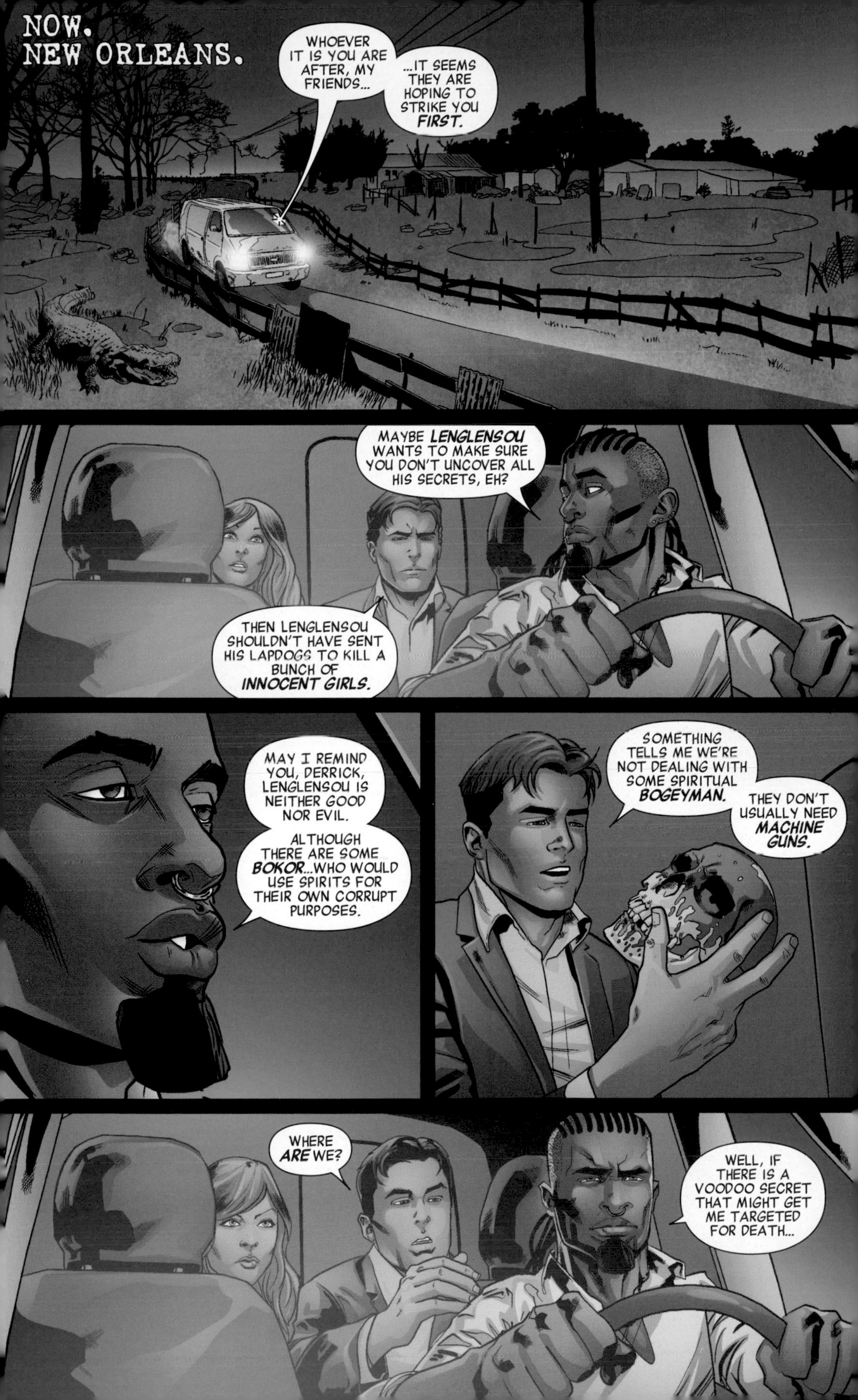
NOW. NEW ORLEANS.
WHOEVER IT IS YOU ARE AFTER, MY FRIENDS...
...IT SEEMS THEY ARE HOPING TO STRIKE YOU FIRST.
MAYBE LENGLENSOU WANTS TO MAKE SURE YOU DON'T UNCOVER ALL HIS SECRETS, EH?
THEN LENGLENSOU SHOULDN'T HAVE SENT HIS LAPDOGS TO KILL A BUNCH OF INNOCENT GIRLS.
MAY I REMIND YOU, DERRICK, LENGLENSOU IS NEITHER GOOD NOR EVIL.
ALTHOUGH THERE ARE SOME BOKOR...WHO WOULD USE SPIRITS FOR THEIR OWN CORRUPT PURPOSES.
SOMETHING TELLS ME WE'RE NOT DEALING WITH SOME SPIRITUAL BOGEYMAN.
THEY DON'T USUALLY NEED MACHINE GUNS.
WHERE ARE WE?
WELL, IF THERE IS A VOODOO SECRET THAT MIGHT GET ME TARGETED FOR DEATH...

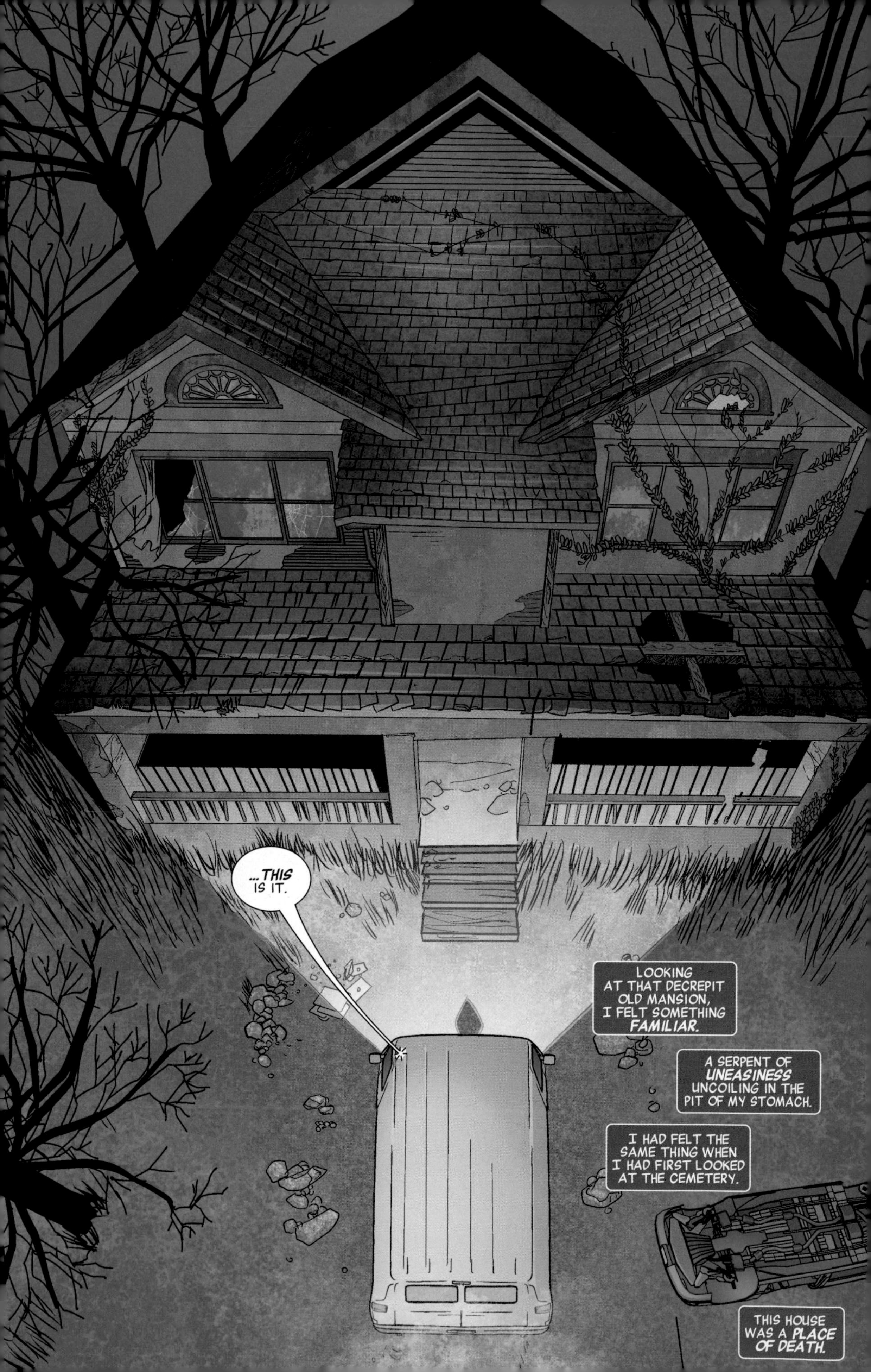
...THIS IS IT.
LOOKING AT THAT DECREPIT OLD MANSION, I FELT SOMETHING FAMILIAR.
A SERPENT OF UNEASINESS UNCOILING IN THE PIT OF MY STOMACH.
I HAD FELT THE SAME THING WHEN I HAD FIRST LOOKED AT THE CEMETERY.
THIS HOUSE WAS A PLACE OF DEATH.

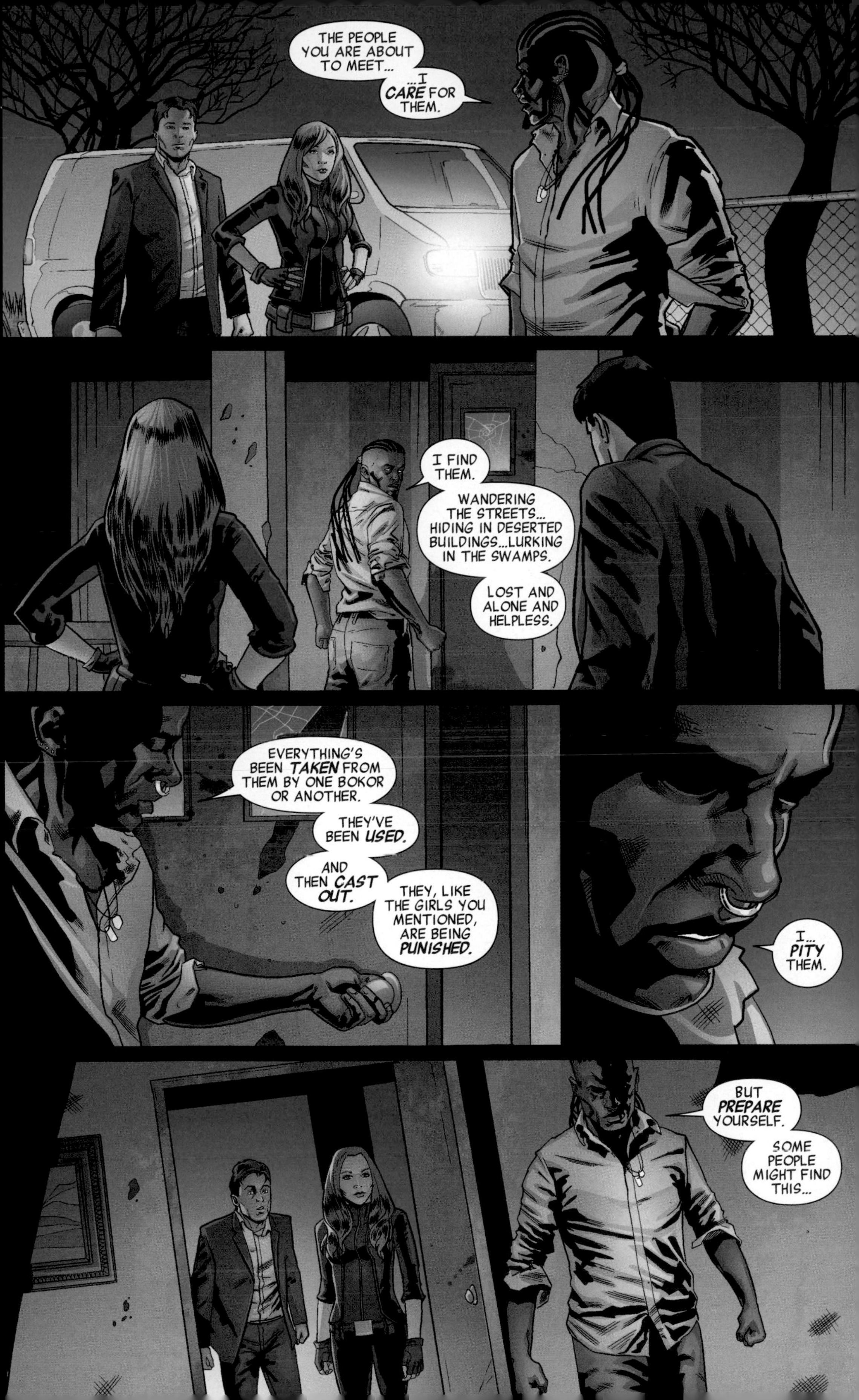
THE PEOPLE YOU ARE ABOUT TO MEET...
...I CARE FOR THEM.
I FIND THEM.
WANDERING THE STREETS... HIDING IN DESERTED BUILDINGS...LURKING IN THE SWAMPS.
LOST AND ALONE AND HELPLESS.
EVERYTHING'S BEEN TAKEN FROM THEM BY ONE BOKOR OR ANOTHER.
THEY'VE BEEN USED.
AND THEN CAST OUT.
THEY, LIKE THE GIRLS YOU MENTIONED, ARE BEING PUNISHED.
I... PITY THEM.
BUT PREPARE YOURSELF.
SOME PEOPLE MIGHT FIND THIS...

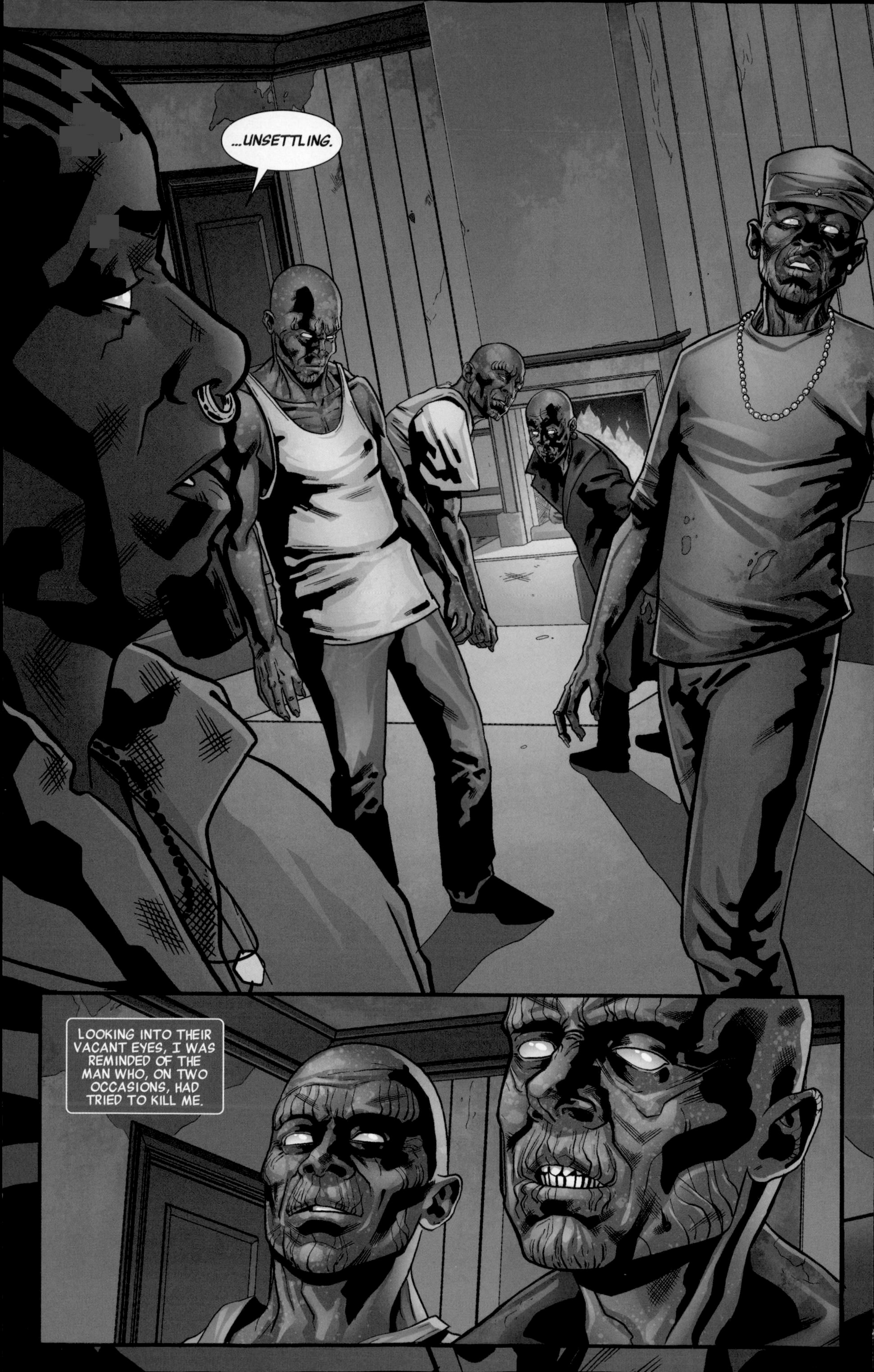
...UNSETTLING.
LOOKING INTO THEIR VACANT EYES, I WAS REMINDED OF THE MAN WHO, ON TWO OCCASIONS, HAD TRIED TO KILL ME.

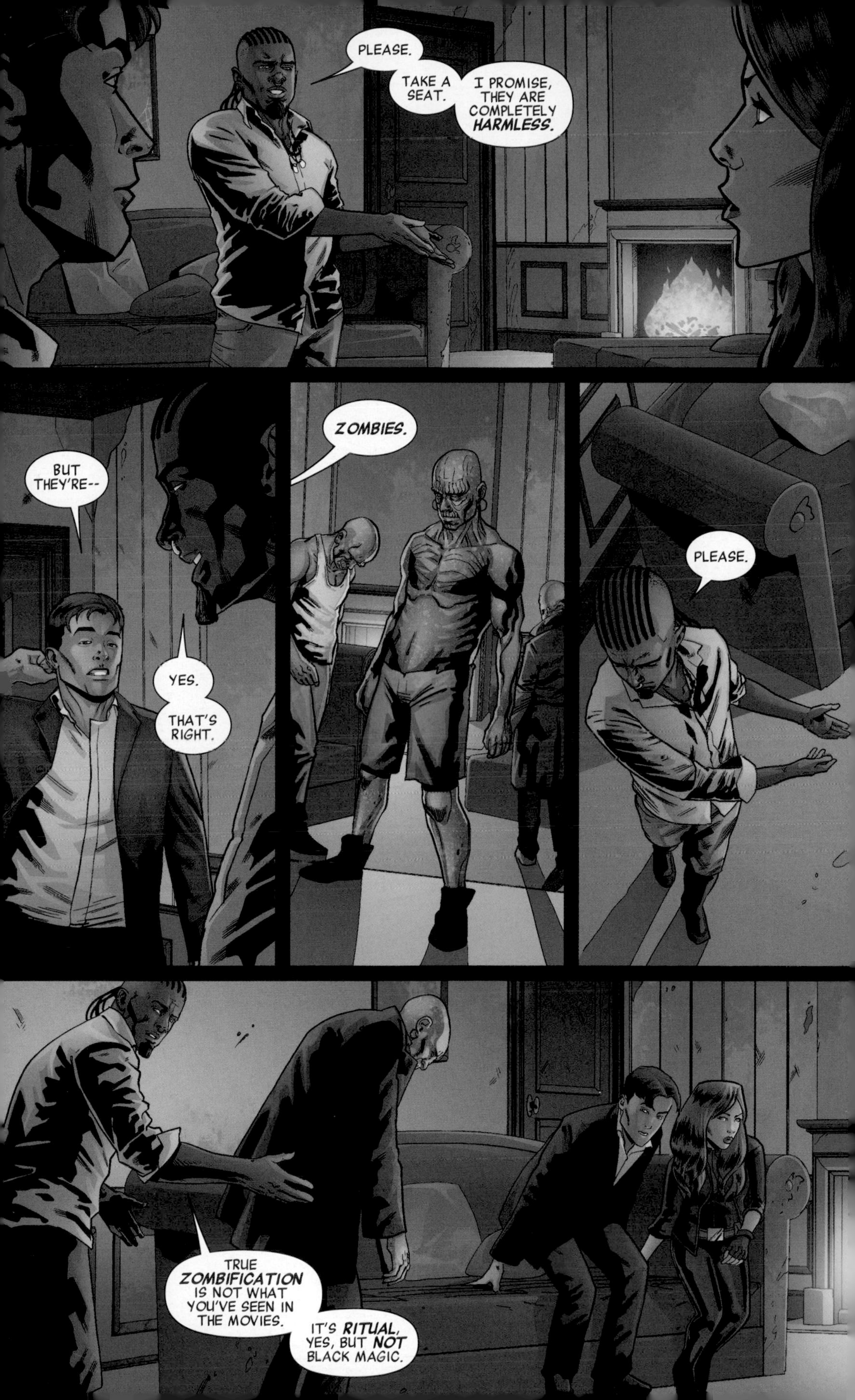
PLEASE.
TAKE A SEAT.
I PROMISE, THEY ARE COMPLETELY HARMLESS.
BUT THEY'RE--
YES.
THAT'S RIGHT.
ZOMBIES.
PLEASE.
TRUE ZOMBIFICATION IS NOT WHAT YOU'VE SEEN IN THE MOVIES.
IT'S RITUAL, YES, BUT NOT BLACK MAGIC.

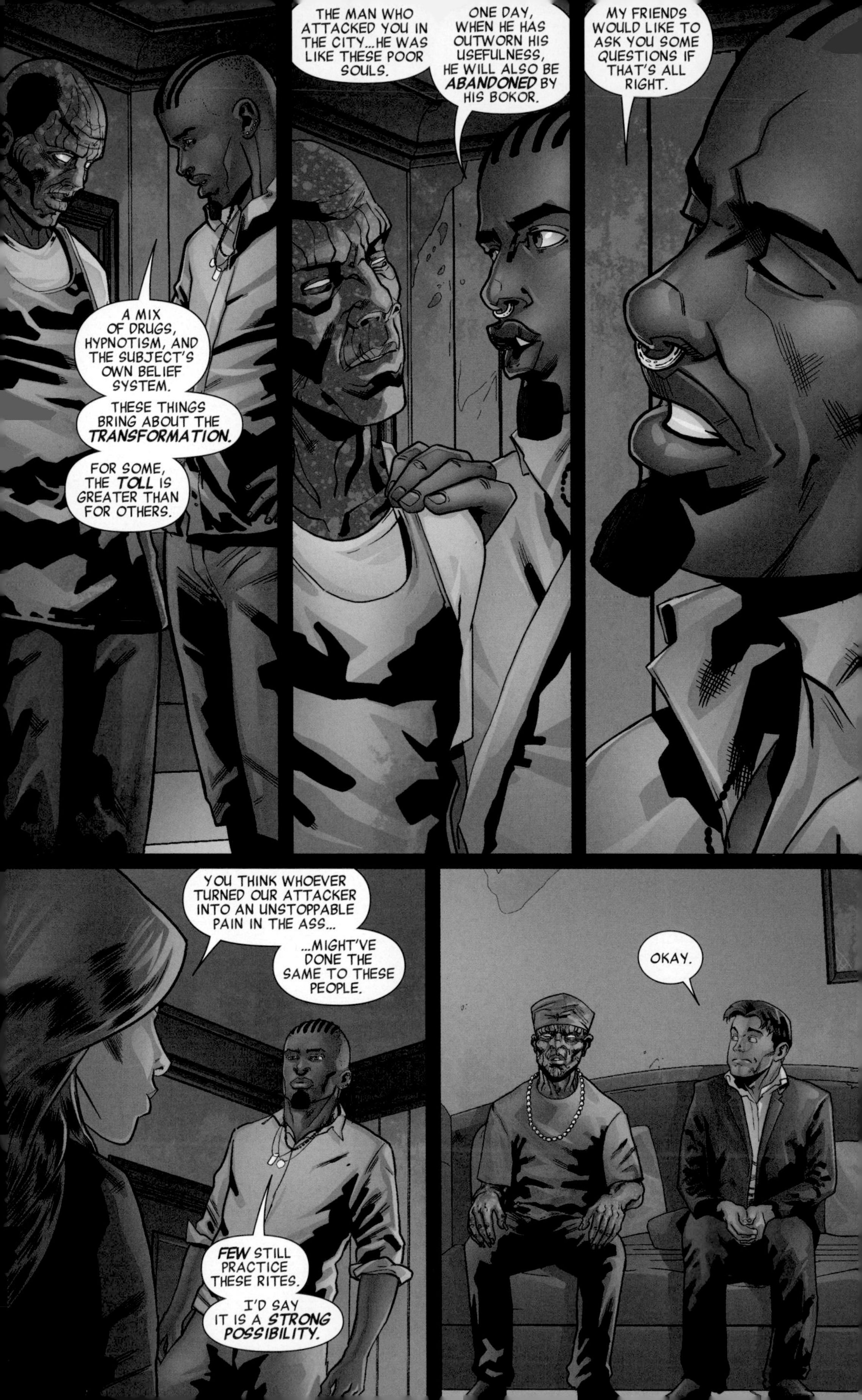
A MIX OF DRUGS, HYPNOTISM, AND THE SUBJECT'S OWN BELIEF SYSTEM.
THESE THINGS BRING ABOUT THE TRANSFORMATION.
FOR SOME, THE TOLL IS GREATER THAN FOR OTHERS.
THE MAN WHO ATTACKED YOU IN THE CITY...HE WAS LIKE THESE POOR SOULS.
ONE DAY, WHEN HE HAS OUTWORN HIS USEFULNESS, HE WILL ALSO BE ABANDONED BY HIS BOKOR.
MY FRIENDS WOULD LIKE TO ASK YOU SOME QUESTIONS IF THAT'S ALL RIGHT.
YOU THINK WHOEVER TURNED OUR ATTACKER INTO AN UNSTOPPABLE PAIN IN THE ASS...
...MIGHT'VE DONE THE SAME TO THESE PEOPLE.
FEW STILL PRACTICE THESE RITES.
I'D SAY IT IS A STRONG POSSIBILITY.
OKAY.

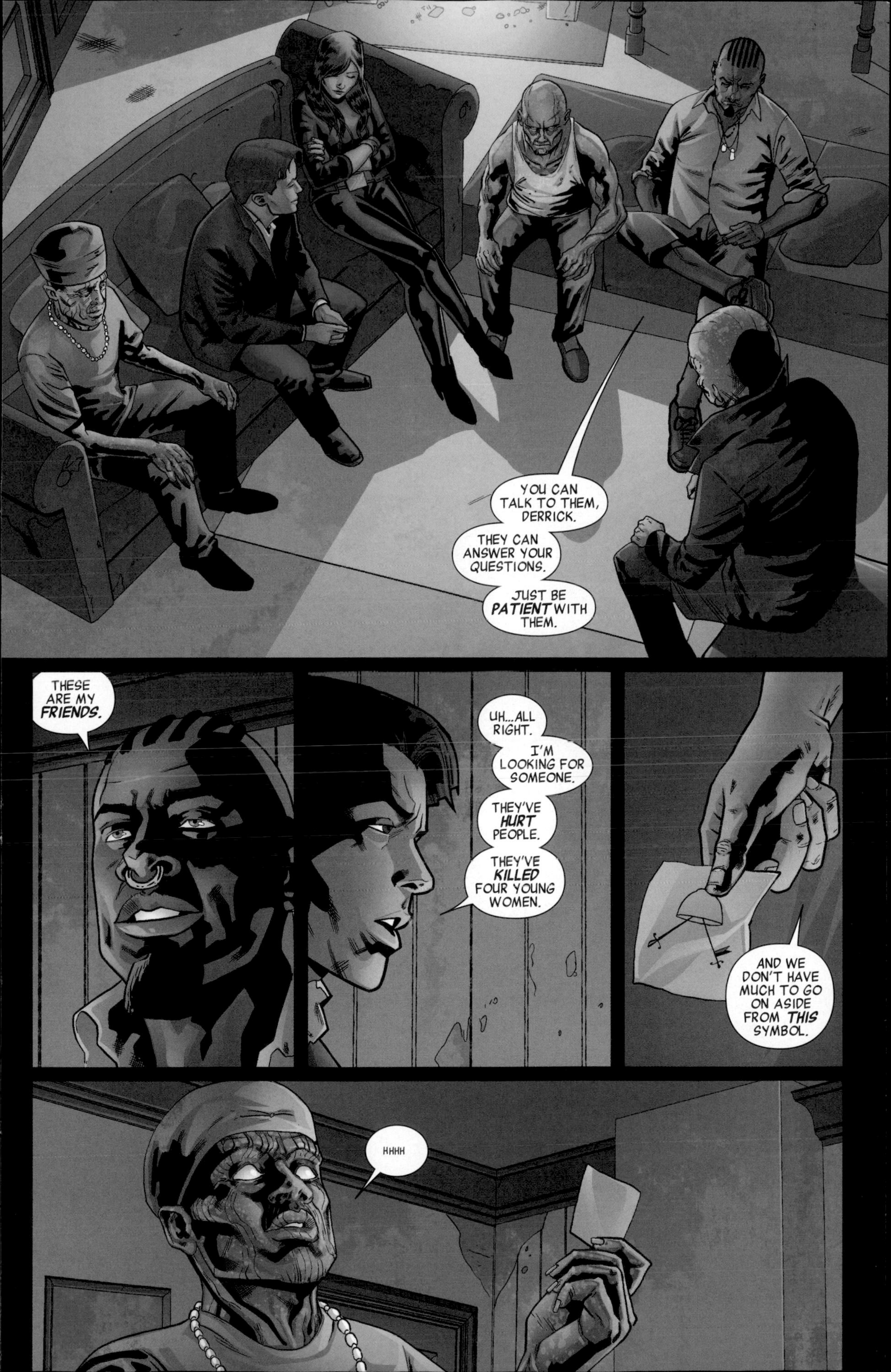
YOU CAN TALK TO THEM, DERRICK.
THEY CAN ANSWER YOUR QUESTIONS.
JUST BE PATIENT WITH THEM.
THESE ARE MY FRIENDS.
UH...ALL RIGHT.
I'M LOOKING FOR SOMEONE.
THEY'VE HURT PEOPLE.
THEY'VE KILLED FOUR YOUNG WOMEN.
AND WE DON'T HAVE MUCH TO GO ON ASIDE FROM THIS SYMBOL.
HHHH

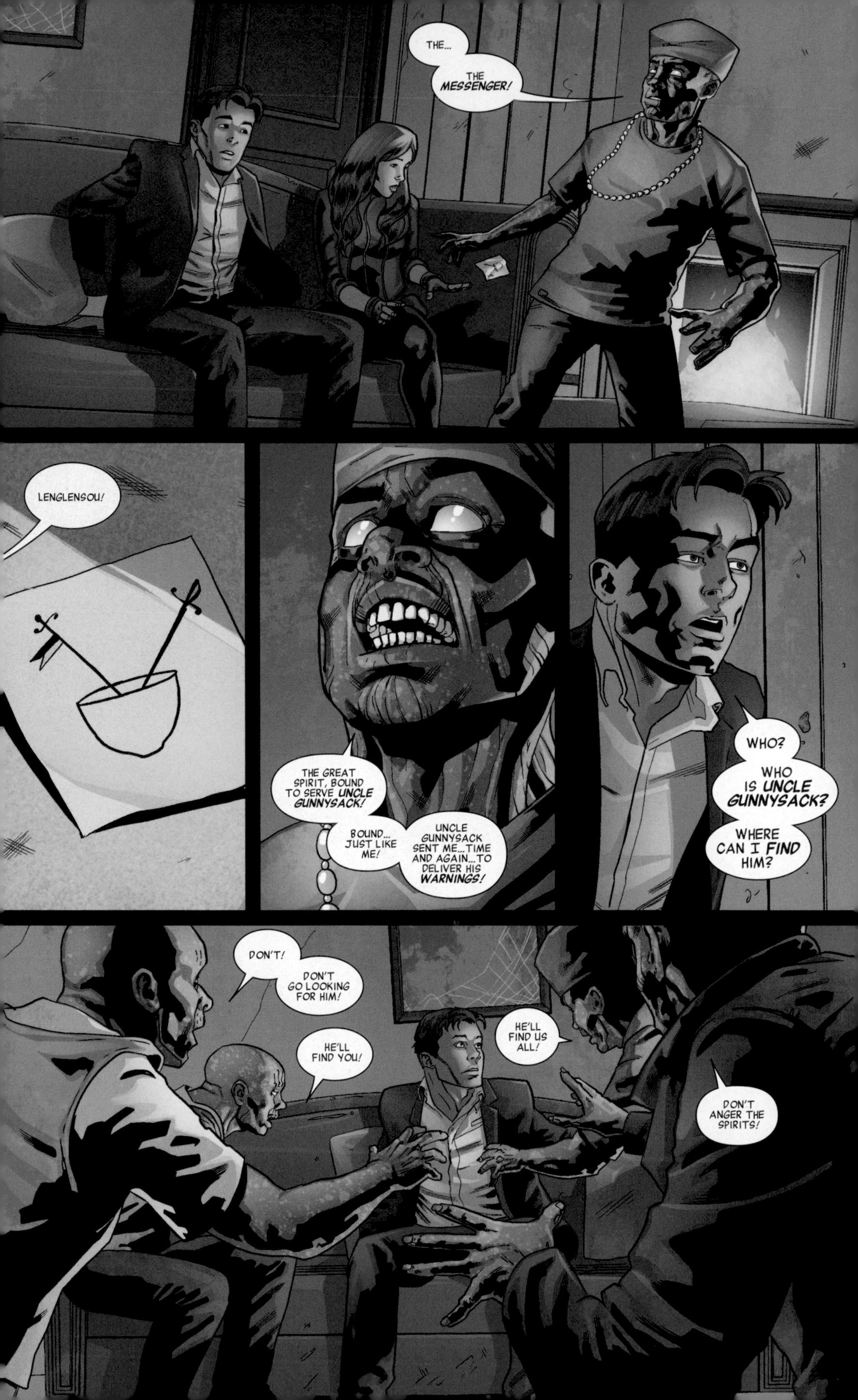
THE...
THE MESSENGER!
LENGLENSOU!
THE GREAT SPIRIT, BOUND TO SERVE UNCLE GUNNYSACK!
BOUND... JUST LIKE ME!
UNCLE GUNNYSACK SENT ME...TIME AND AGAIN...TO DELIVER HIS WARNINGS!
WHO?
WHO IS UNCLE GUNNYSACK?
WHERE CAN I FIND HIM?
DON'T!
DON'T GO LOOKING FOR HIM!
HE'LL FIND YOU!
HE'LL FIND US ALL!
DON'T ANGER THE SPIRITS!

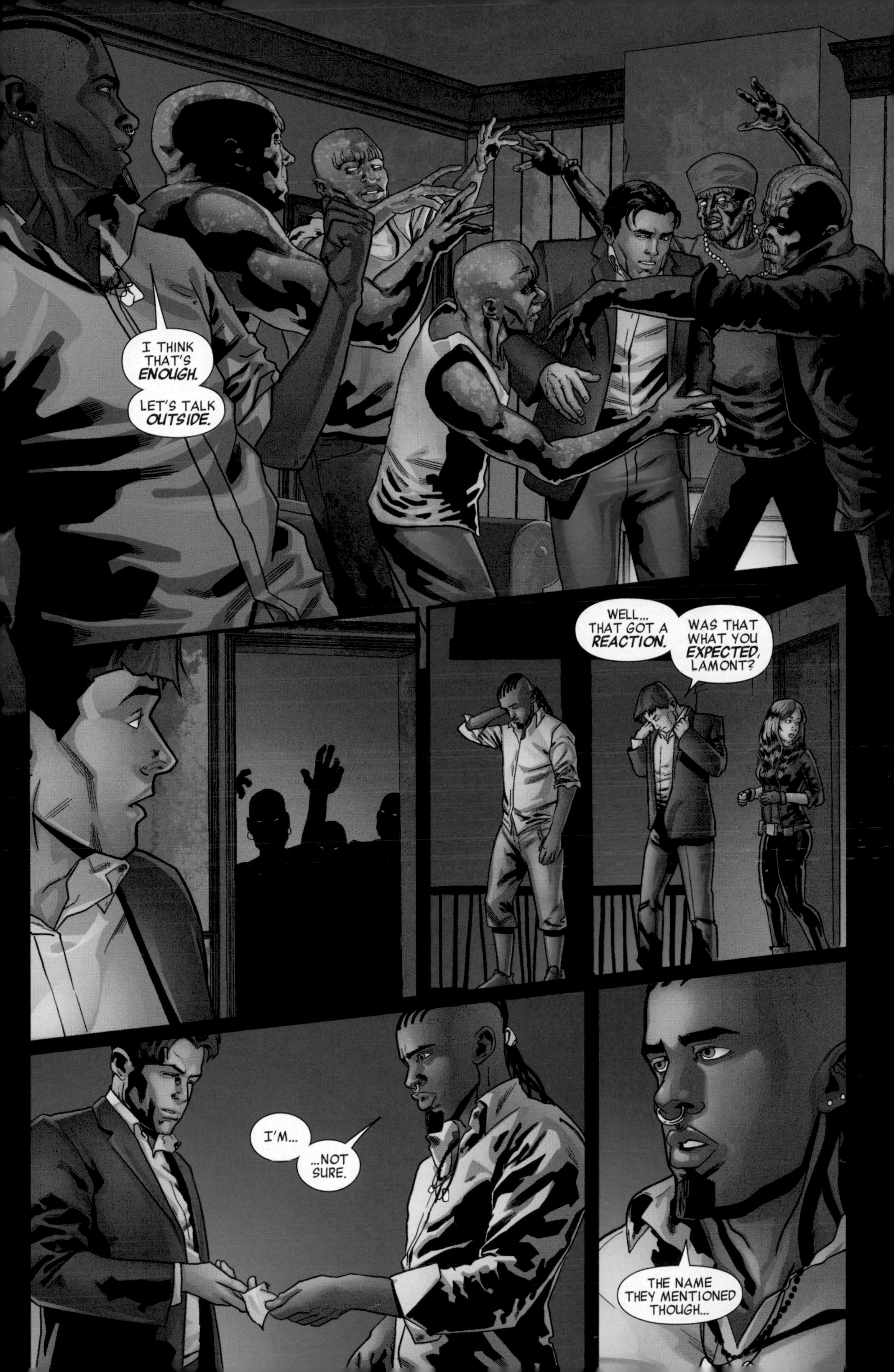
I THINK THAT'S ENOUGH.
LET'S TALK OUTSIDE.
WELL... THAT GOT A REACTION.
WAS THAT WHAT YOU EXPECTED, LAMONT?
I'M...
...NOT SURE.
THE NAME THEY MENTIONED THOUGH...

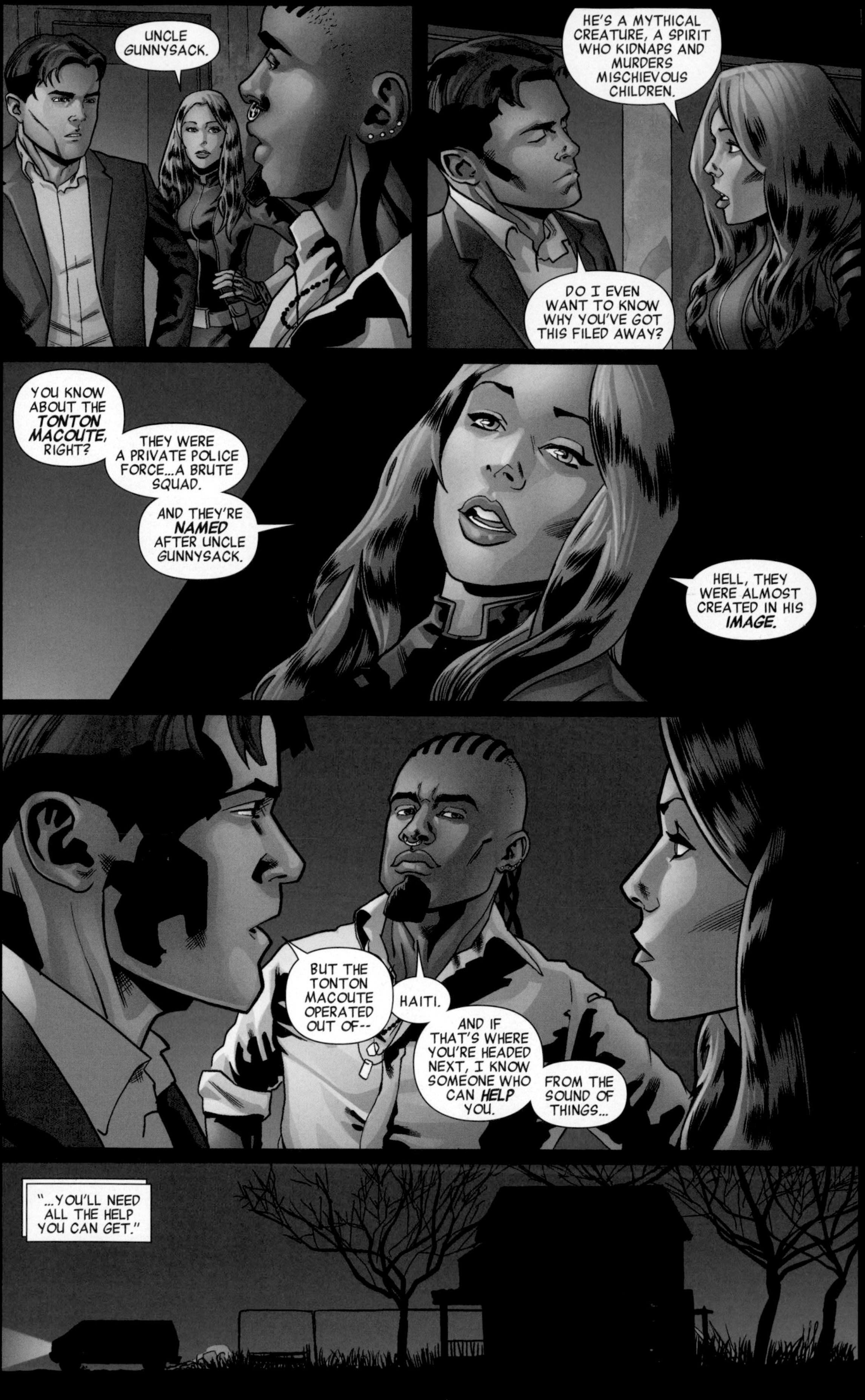
UNCLE GUNNYSACK.
HE'S A MYTHICAL CREATURE, A SPIRIT WHO KIDNAPS AND MURDERS MISCHIEVOUS CHILDREN.
DO I EVEN WANT TO KNOW WHY YOU'VE GOT THIS FILED AWAY?
YOU KNOW ABOUT THE TONTON MACOUTE, RIGHT?
THEY WERE A PRIVATE POLICE FORCE...A BRUTE SQUAD.
AND THEY'RE NAMED AFTER UNCLE GUNNYSACK.
HELL, THEY WERE ALMOST CREATED IN HIS IMAGE.
BUT THE TONTON MACOUTE OPERATED OUT OF--
HAITI.
AND IF THAT'S WHERE YOU'RE HEADED NEXT, I KNOW SOMEONE WHO CAN HELP YOU.
FROM THE SOUND OF THINGS...
"...YOU'LL NEED ALL THE HELP YOU CAN GET."

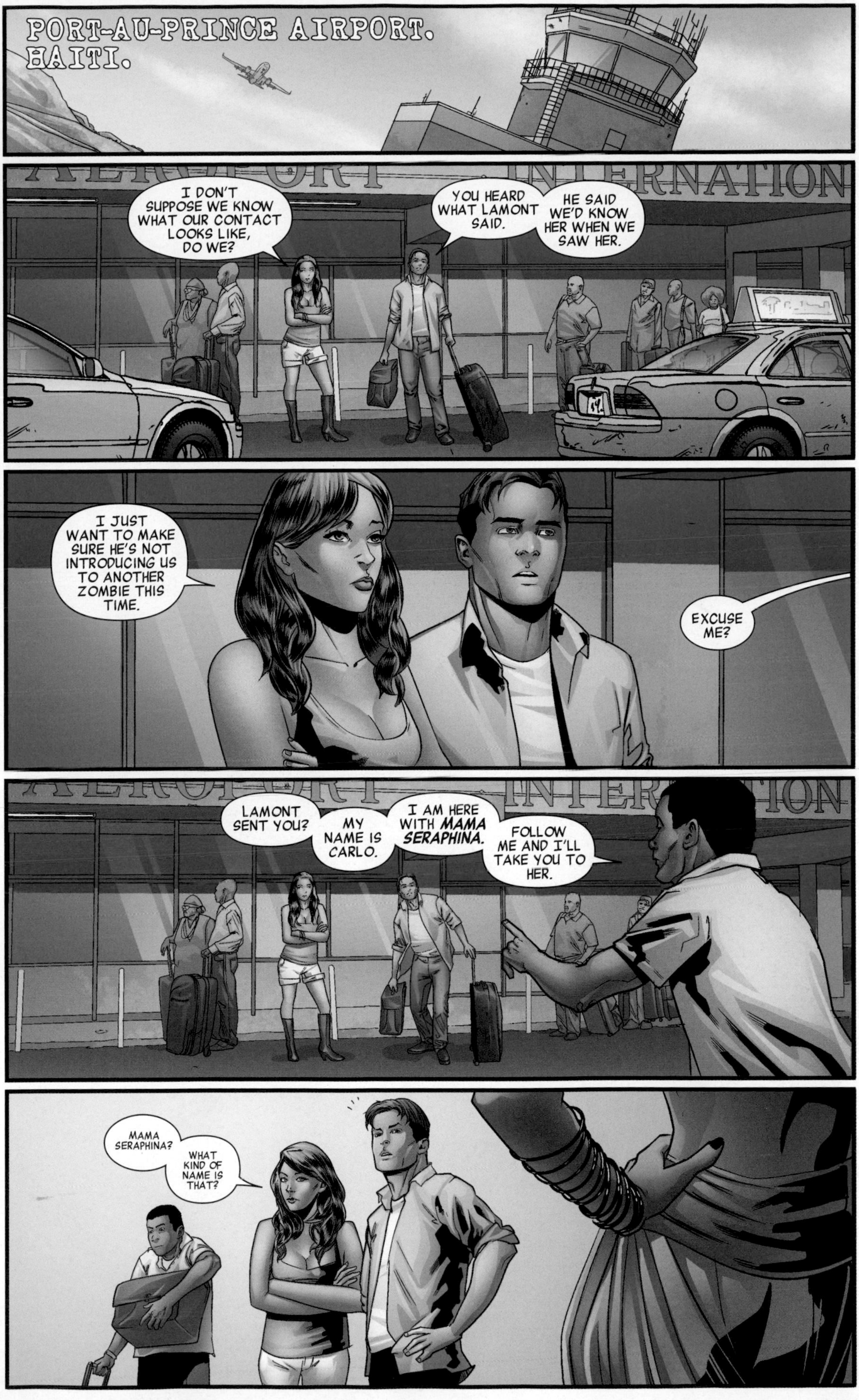
PORT-AU-PRINCE AIRPORT. HAITI.
I DON'T SUPPOSE WE KNOW WHAT OUR CONTACT LOOKS LIKE, DO WE?
YOU HEARD WHAT LAMONT SAID.
HE SAID WE'D KNOW HER WHEN WE SAW HER.
I JUST WANT TO MAKE SURE HE'S NOT INTRODUCING US TO ANOTHER ZOMBIE THIS TIME.
EXCUSE ME?
LAMONT SENT YOU?
MY NAME IS CARLO.
I AM HERE WITH MAMA SERAPHINA.
FOLLOW ME AND I'LL TAKE YOU TO HER.
MAMA SERAPHINA?
WHAT KIND OF NAME IS THAT?

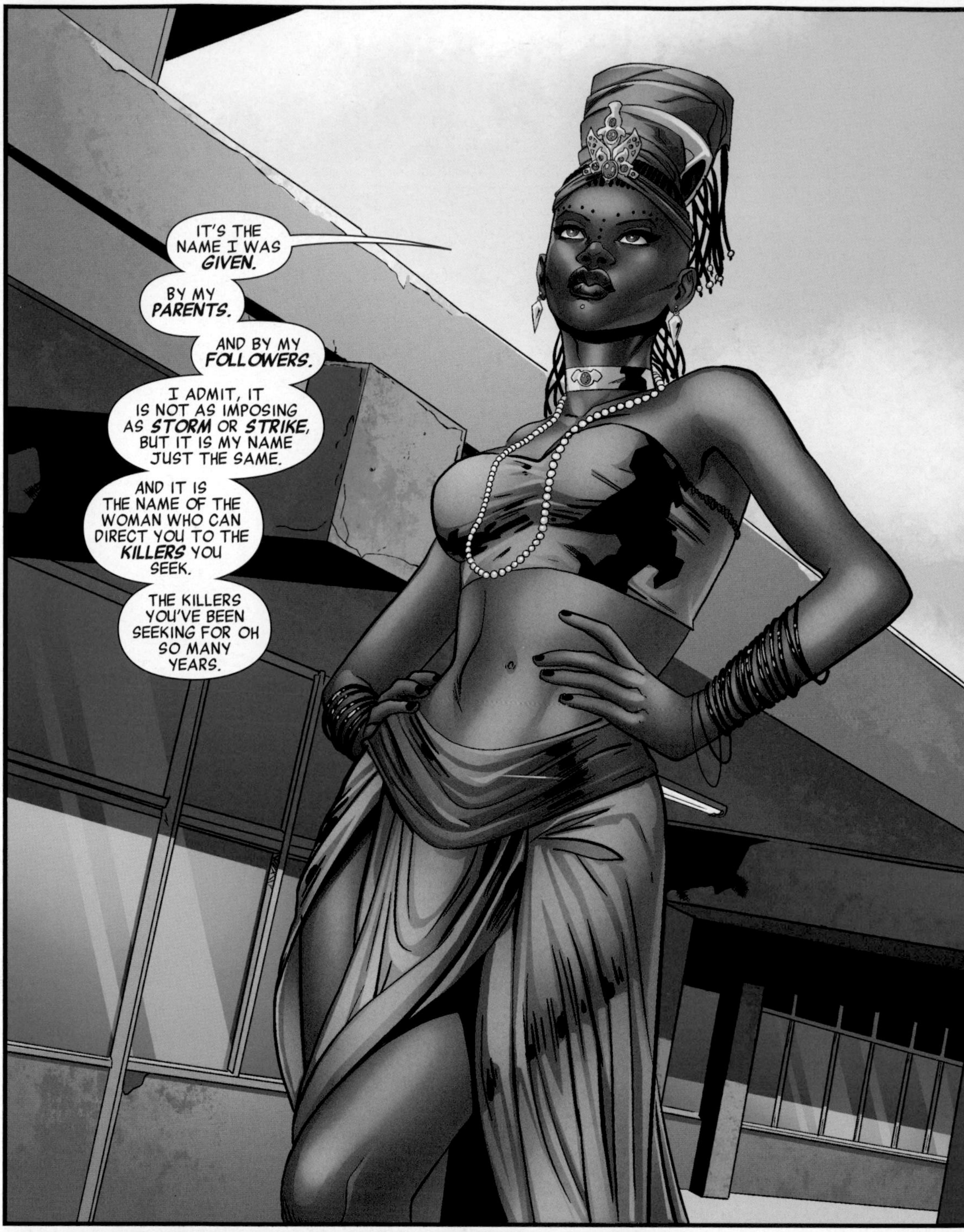
IT'S THE NAME I WAS GIVEN.
BY MY PARENTS.
AND BY MY FOLLOWERS.
I ADMIT, IT IS NOT AS IMPOSING AS STORM OR STRIKE, BUT IT IS MY NAME JUST THE SAME.
AND IT IS THE NAME OF THE WOMAN WHO CAN DIRECT YOU TO THE KILLERS YOU SEEK.
THE KILLERS YOU'VE BEEN SEEKING FOR OH SO MANY YEARS.
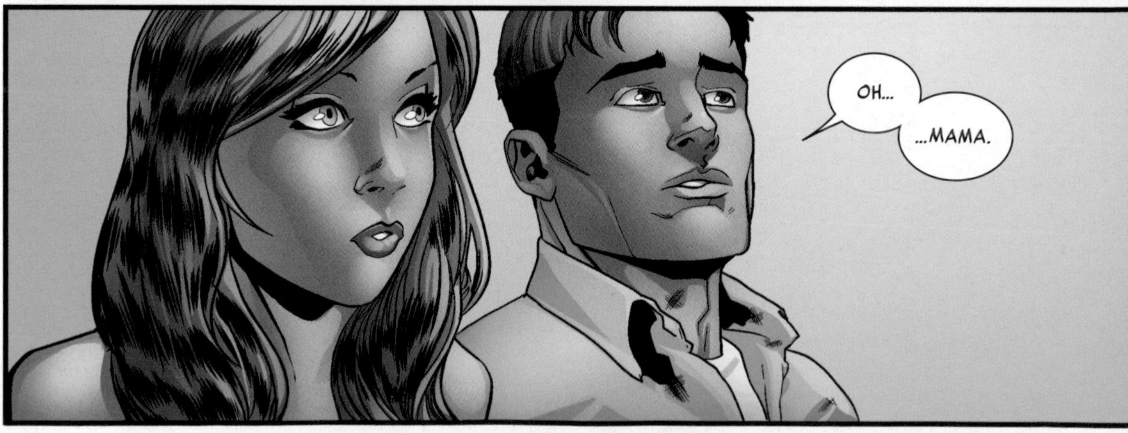
OH...
...MAMA.

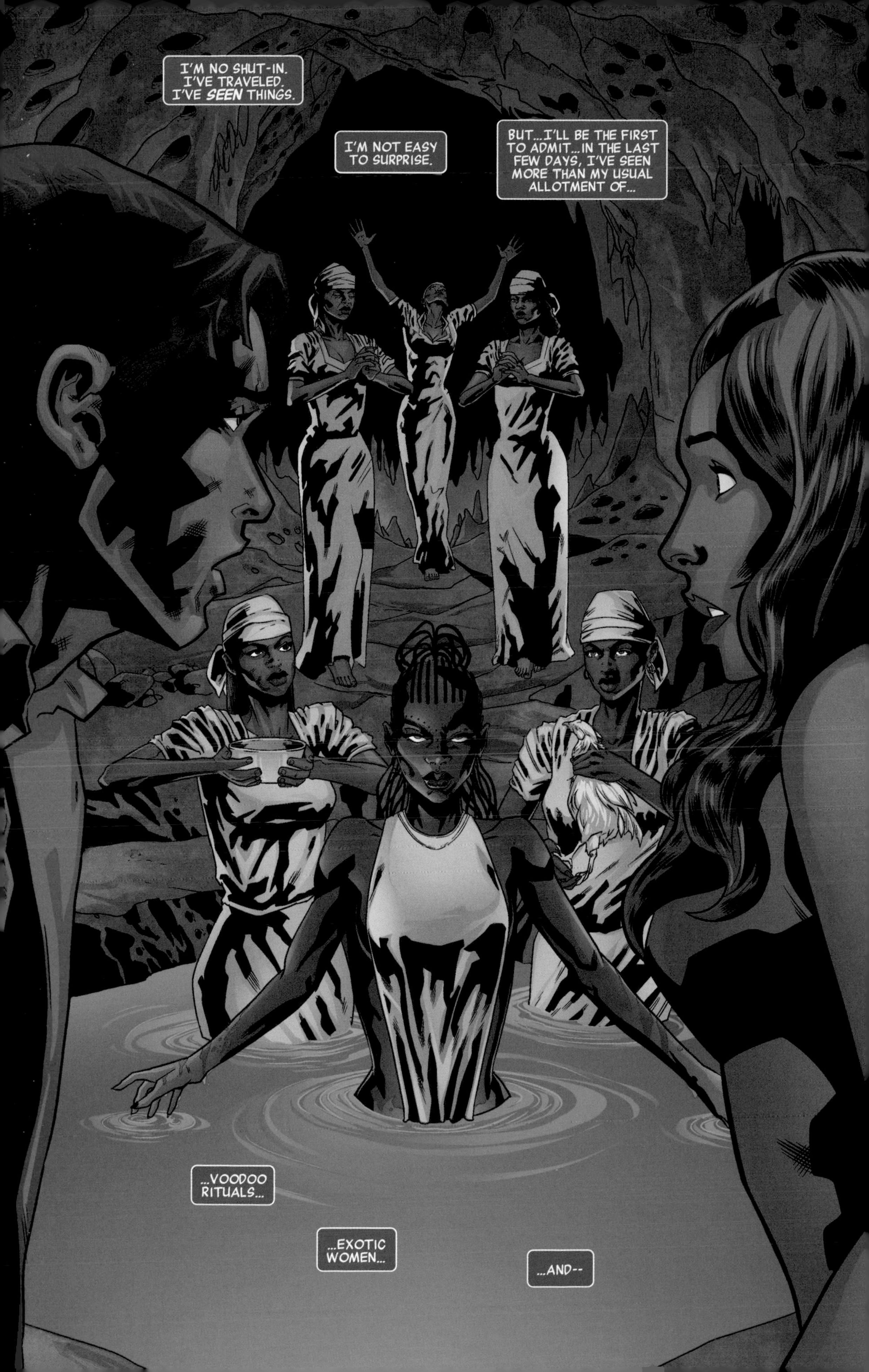
I'M NO SHUT-IN. I'VE TRAVELED. I'VE SEEN THINGS.
I'M NOT EASY TO SURPRISE.
BUT...I'LL BE THE FIRST TO ADMIT...IN THE LAST FEW DAYS, I'VE SEEN MORE THAN MY USUAL ALLOTMENT OF...
...VOODOO RITUALS...
...EXOTIC WOMEN...
...AND--

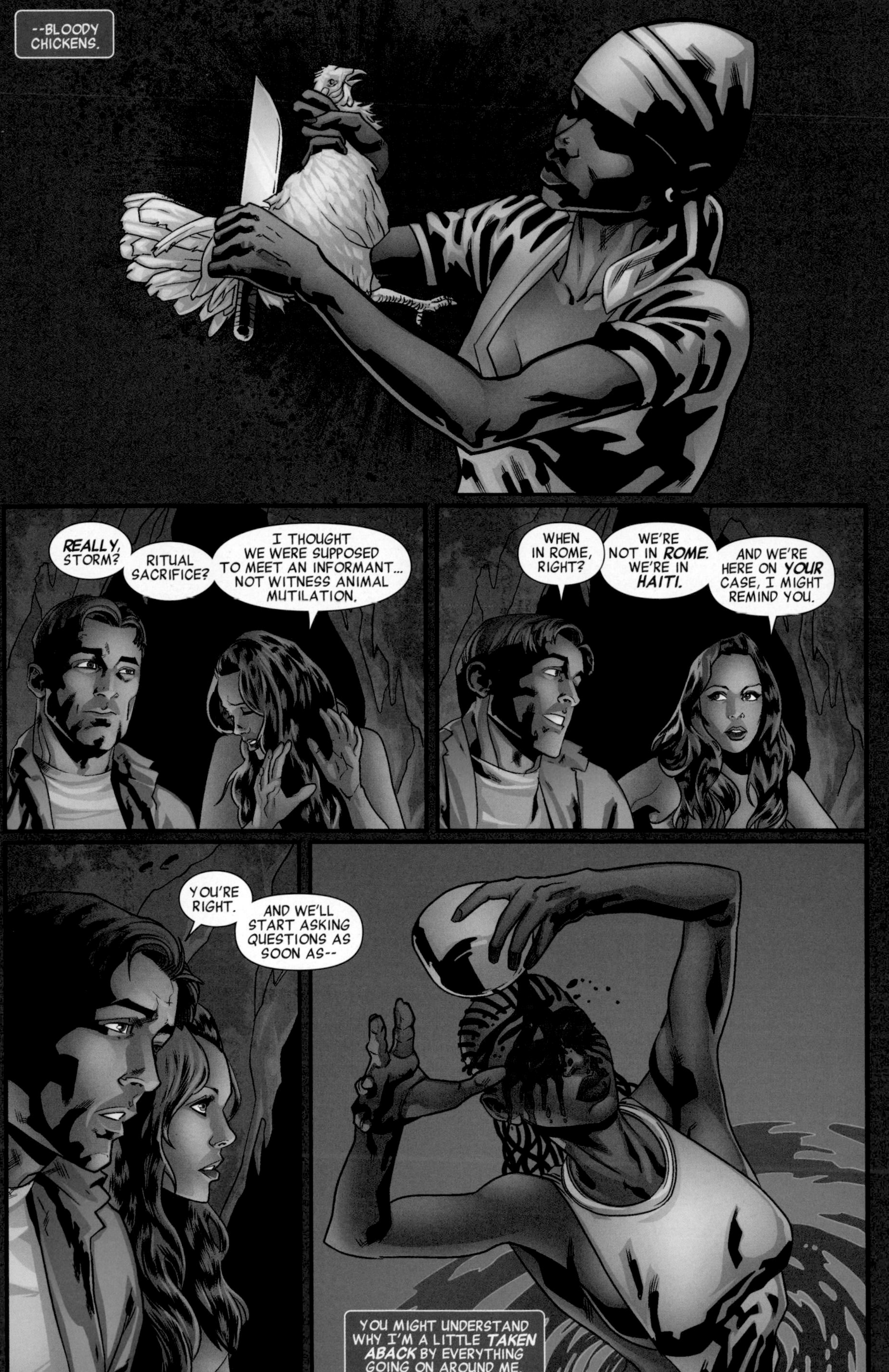
--BLOODY CHICKENS.
REALLY, STORM?
RITUAL SACRIFICE?
I THOUGHT WE WERE SUPPOSED TO MEET AN INFORMANT... NOT WITNESS ANIMAL MUTILATION.
WHEN IN ROME, RIGHT?
WE'RE NOT IN ROME. WE'RE IN HAITI.
AND WE'RE HERE ON YOUR CASE, I MIGHT REMIND YOU.
YOU'RE RIGHT.
AND WE'LL START ASKING QUESTIONS AS SOON AS--
YOU MIGHT UNDERSTAND WHY I'M A LITTLE TAKEN ABACK BY EVERYTHING GOING ON AROUND ME.

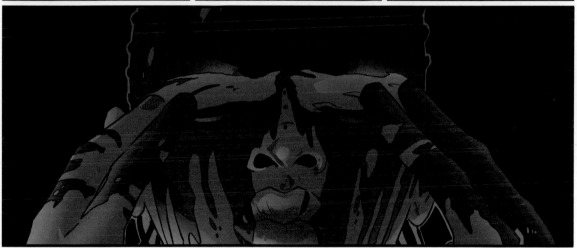

SO...WE SHOULD TALK ABOUT *MURDER*, YES?

UH...

I CAN HELP YOU FIND THE DEVILS YOU SEEK.

BUT I SUPPOSE I SHOULD START--

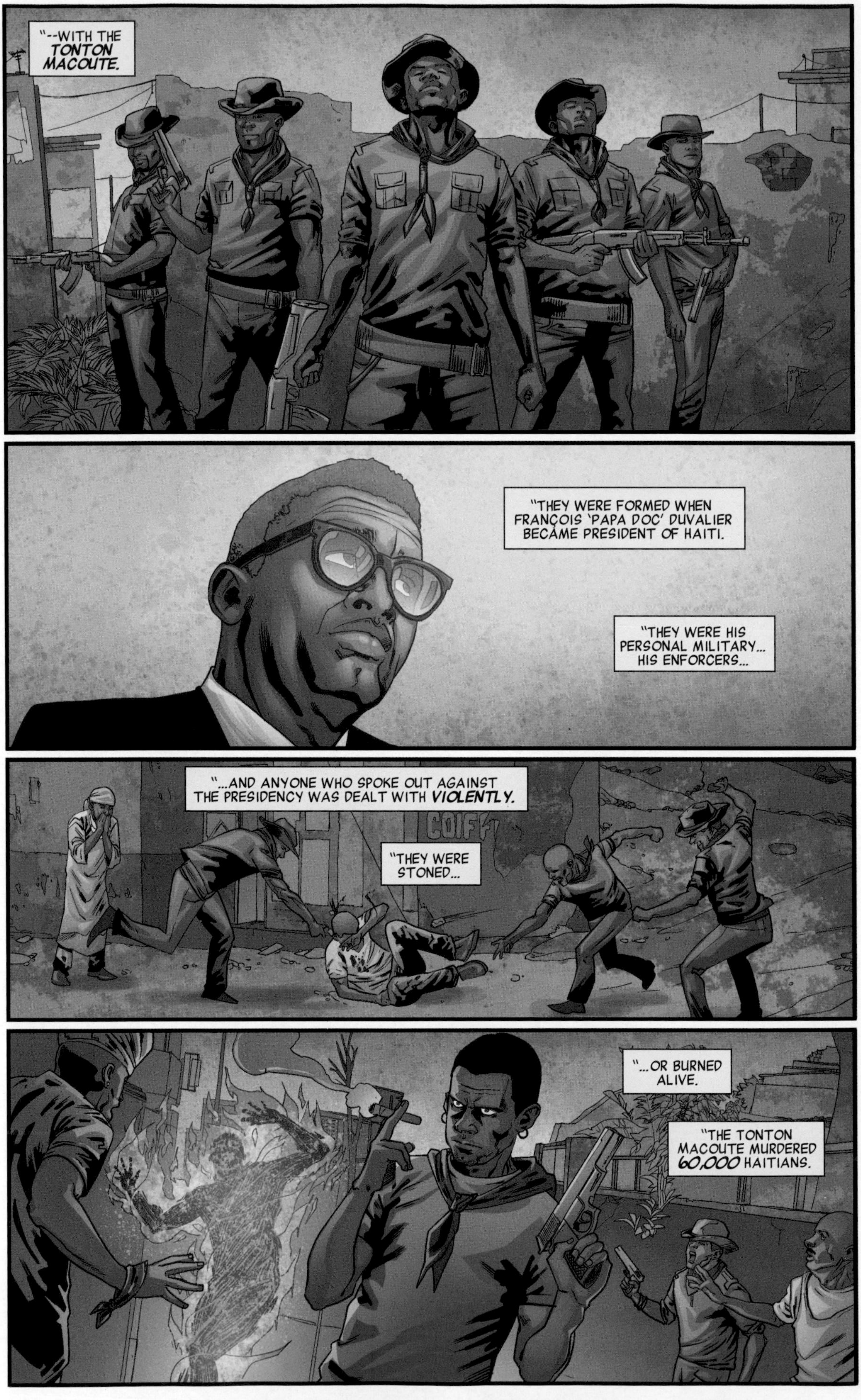
"--WITH THE TONTON MACOUTE.
"THEY WERE FORMED WHEN FRANÇOIS 'PAPA DOC' DUVALIER BECAME PRESIDENT OF HAITI.
"THEY WERE HIS PERSONAL MILITARY... HIS ENFORCERS...
"...AND ANYONE WHO SPOKE OUT AGAINST THE PRESIDENCY WAS DEALT WITH VIOLENTLY.
"THEY WERE STONED...
COIFF
"...OR BURNED ALIVE.
"THE TONTON MACOUTE MURDERED 60,000 HAITIANS.

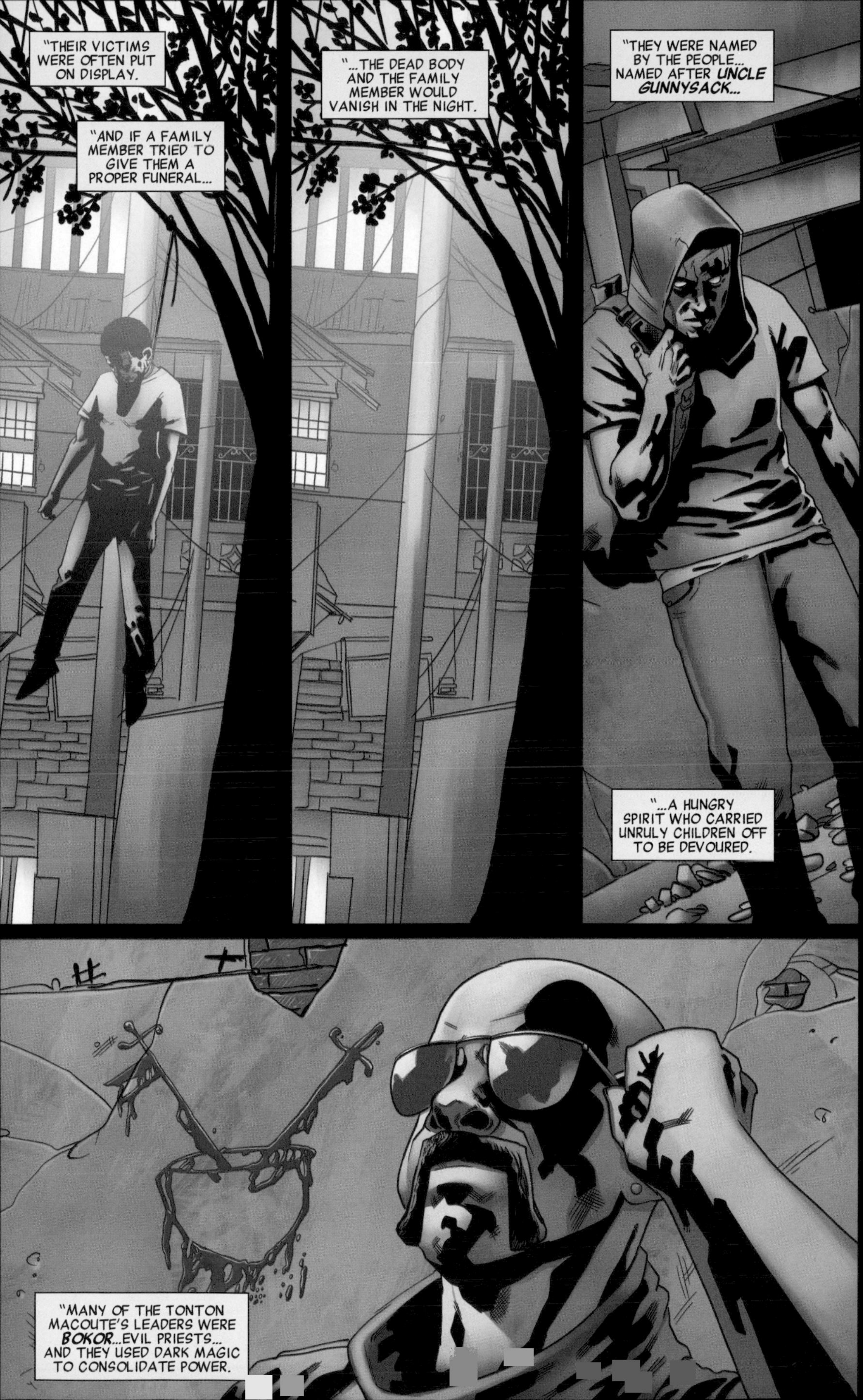
"THEIR VICTIMS WERE OFTEN PUT ON DISPLAY.
"AND IF A FAMILY MEMBER TRIED TO GIVE THEM A PROPER FUNERAL...
"...THE DEAD BODY AND THE FAMILY MEMBER WOULD VANISH IN THE NIGHT.
"THEY WERE NAMED BY THE PEOPLE... NAMED AFTER UNCLE GUNNYSACK...
"...A HUNGRY SPIRIT WHO CARRIED UNRULY CHILDREN OFF TO BE DEVOURED.
"MANY OF THE TONTON MACOUTE'S LEADERS WERE BOKOR...EVIL PRIESTS... AND THEY USED DARK MAGIC TO CONSOLIDATE POWER.

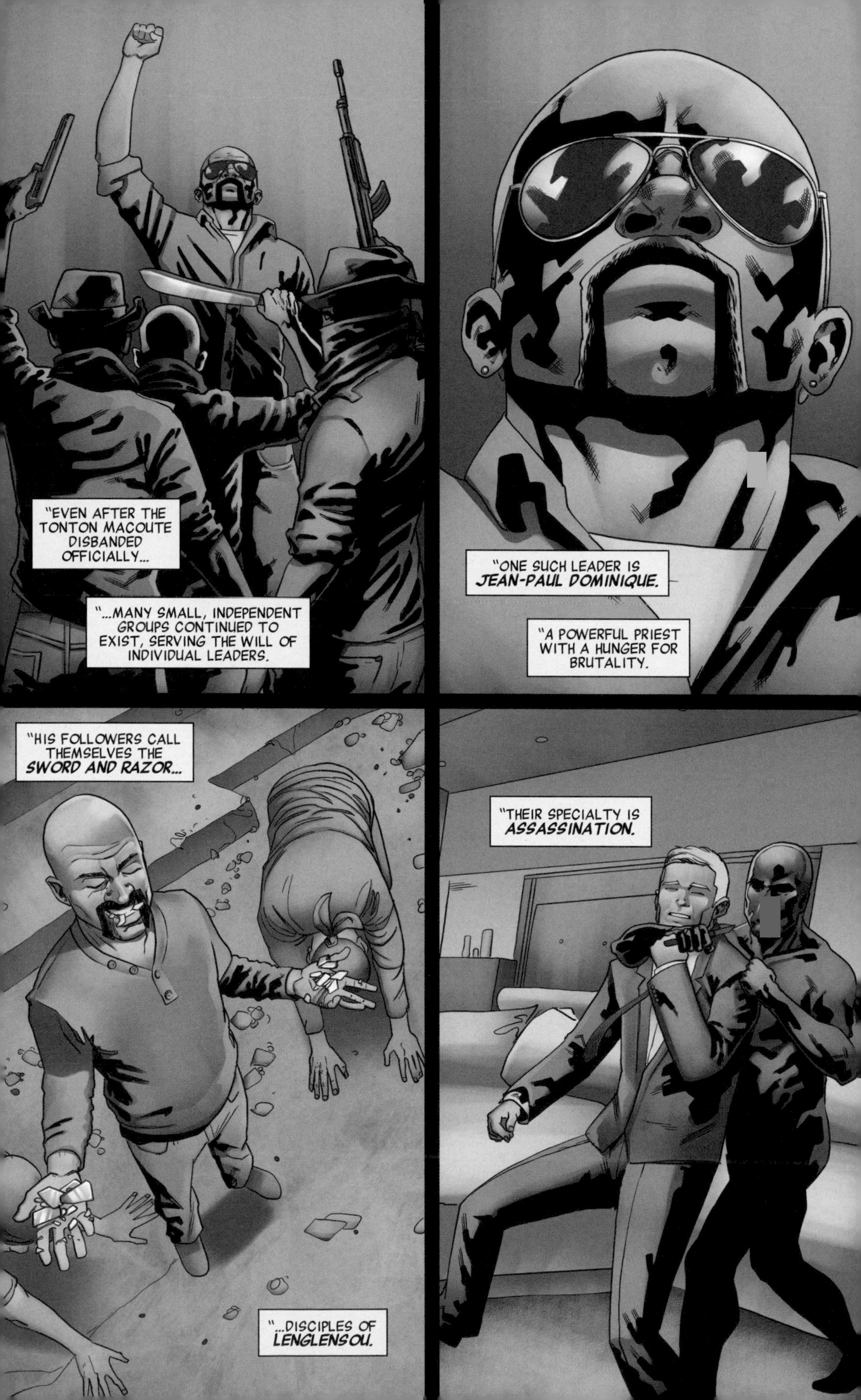
"EVEN AFTER THE TONTON MACOUTE DISBANDED OFFICIALLY...
"...MANY SMALL, INDEPENDENT GROUPS CONTINUED TO EXIST, SERVING THE WILL OF INDIVIDUAL LEADERS.
"ONE SUCH LEADER IS JEAN-PAUL DOMINIQUE.
"A POWERFUL PRIEST WITH A HUNGER FOR BRUTALITY.
"HIS FOLLOWERS CALL THEMSELVES THE SWORD AND RAZOR...
"...DISCIPLES OF LENGLENSOU.
"THEIR SPECIALTY IS ASSASSINATION.

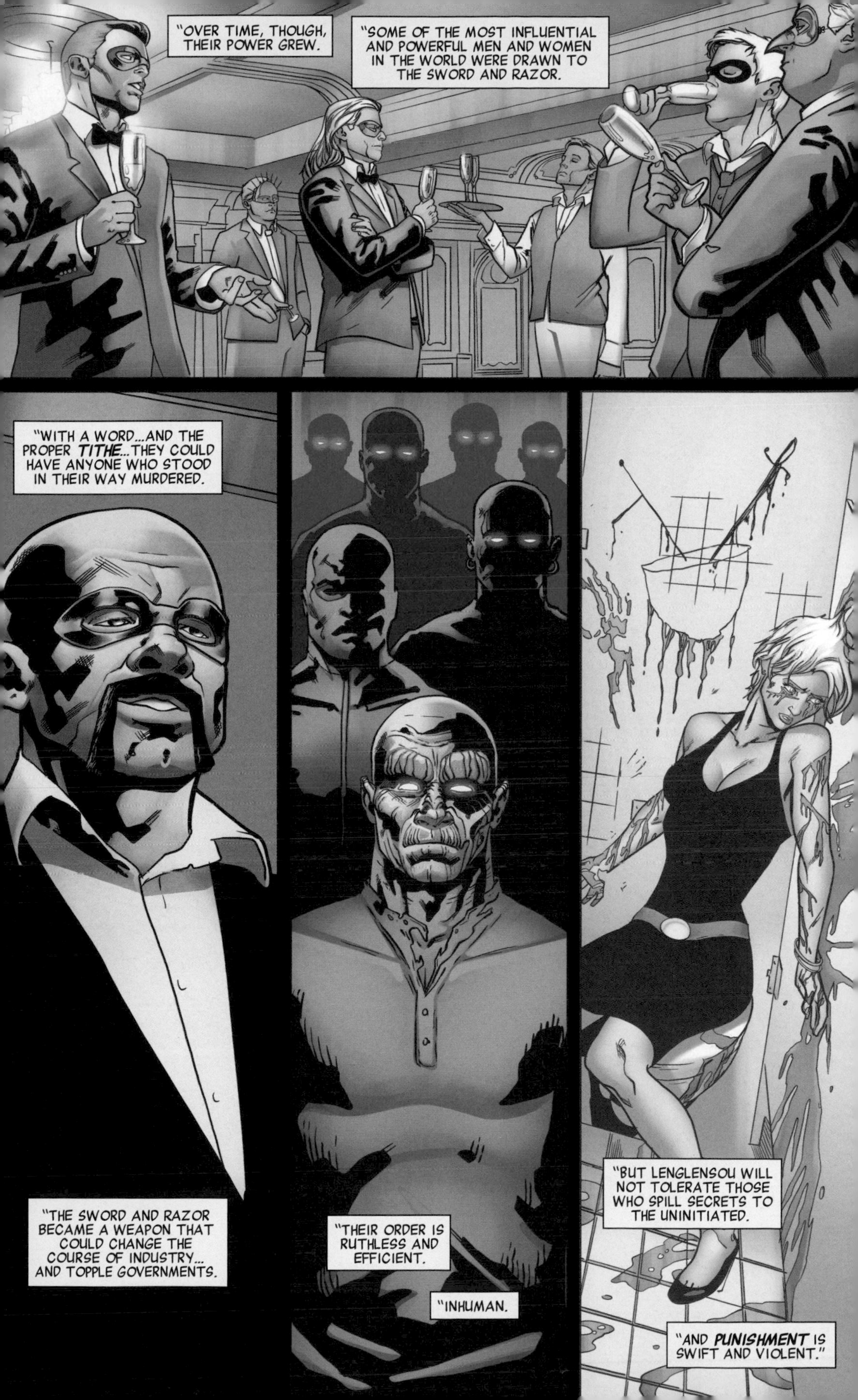
"OVER TIME, THOUGH, THEIR POWER GREW.
"SOME OF THE MOST INFLUENTIAL AND POWERFUL MEN AND WOMEN IN THE WORLD WERE DRAWN TO THE SWORD AND RAZOR.
"WITH A WORD...AND THE PROPER TITHE...THEY COULD HAVE ANYONE WHO STOOD IN THEIR WAY MURDERED.
"THE SWORD AND RAZOR BECAME A WEAPON THAT COULD CHANGE THE COURSE OF INDUSTRY... AND TOPPLE GOVERNMENTS.
"THEIR ORDER IS RUTHLESS AND EFFICIENT.
"INHUMAN.
"BUT LENGLENSOU WILL NOT TOLERATE THOSE WHO SPILL SECRETS TO THE UNINITIATED.
"AND PUNISHMENT IS SWIFT AND VIOLENT."

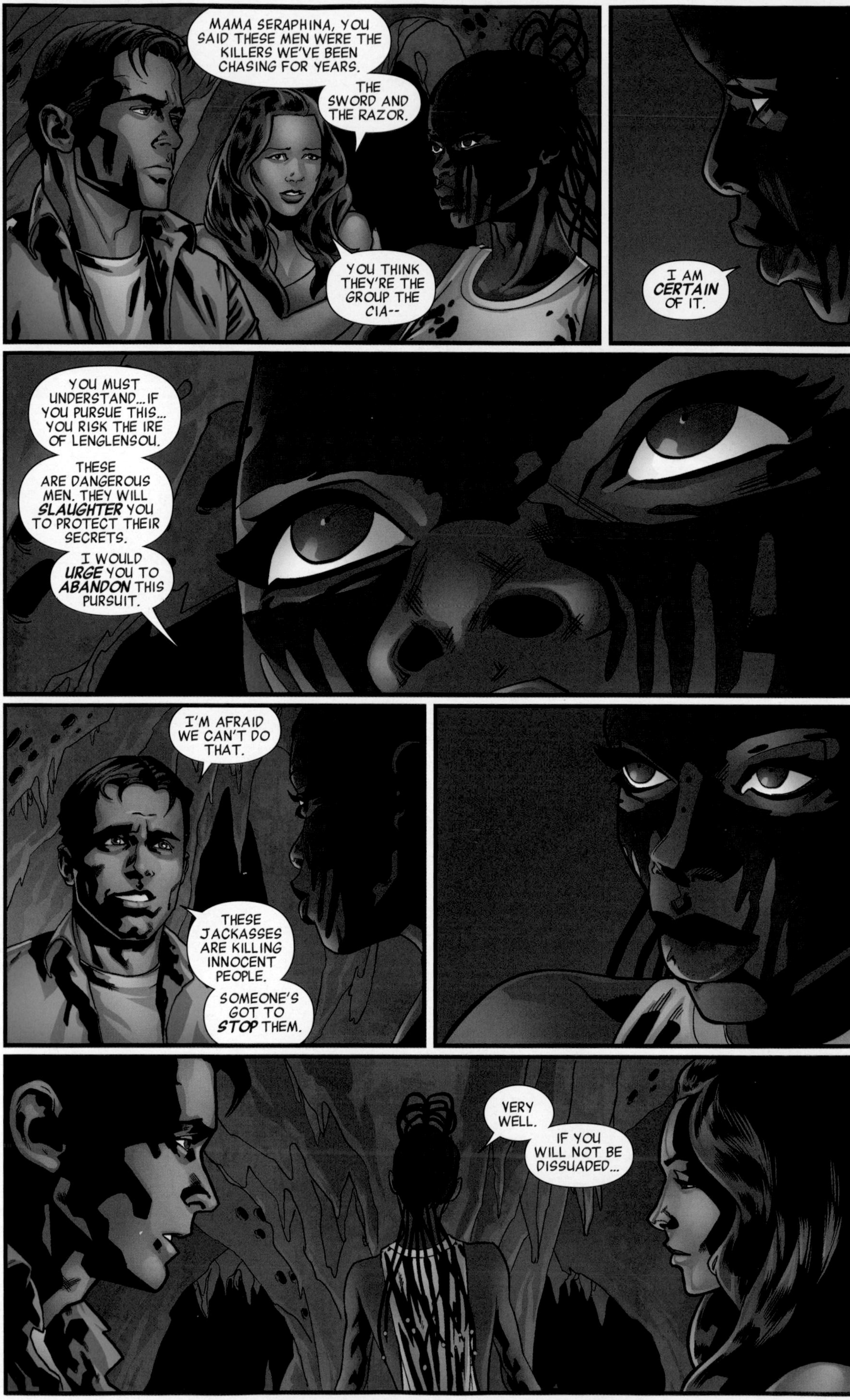
MAMA SERAPHINA, YOU SAID THESE MEN WERE THE KILLERS WE'VE BEEN CHASING FOR YEARS.
THE SWORD AND THE RAZOR.
YOU THINK THEY'RE THE GROUP THE CIA--
I AM CERTAIN OF IT.
YOU MUST UNDERSTAND... IF YOU PURSUE THIS... YOU RISK THE IRE OF LENGLENSOU.
THESE ARE DANGEROUS MEN. THEY WILL SLAUGHTER YOU TO PROTECT THEIR SECRETS.
I WOULD URGE YOU TO ABANDON THIS PURSUIT.
I'M AFRAID WE CAN'T DO THAT.
THESE JACKASSES ARE KILLING INNOCENT PEOPLE.
SOMEONE'S GOT TO STOP THEM.
VERY WELL.
IF YOU WILL NOT BE DISSUADED...

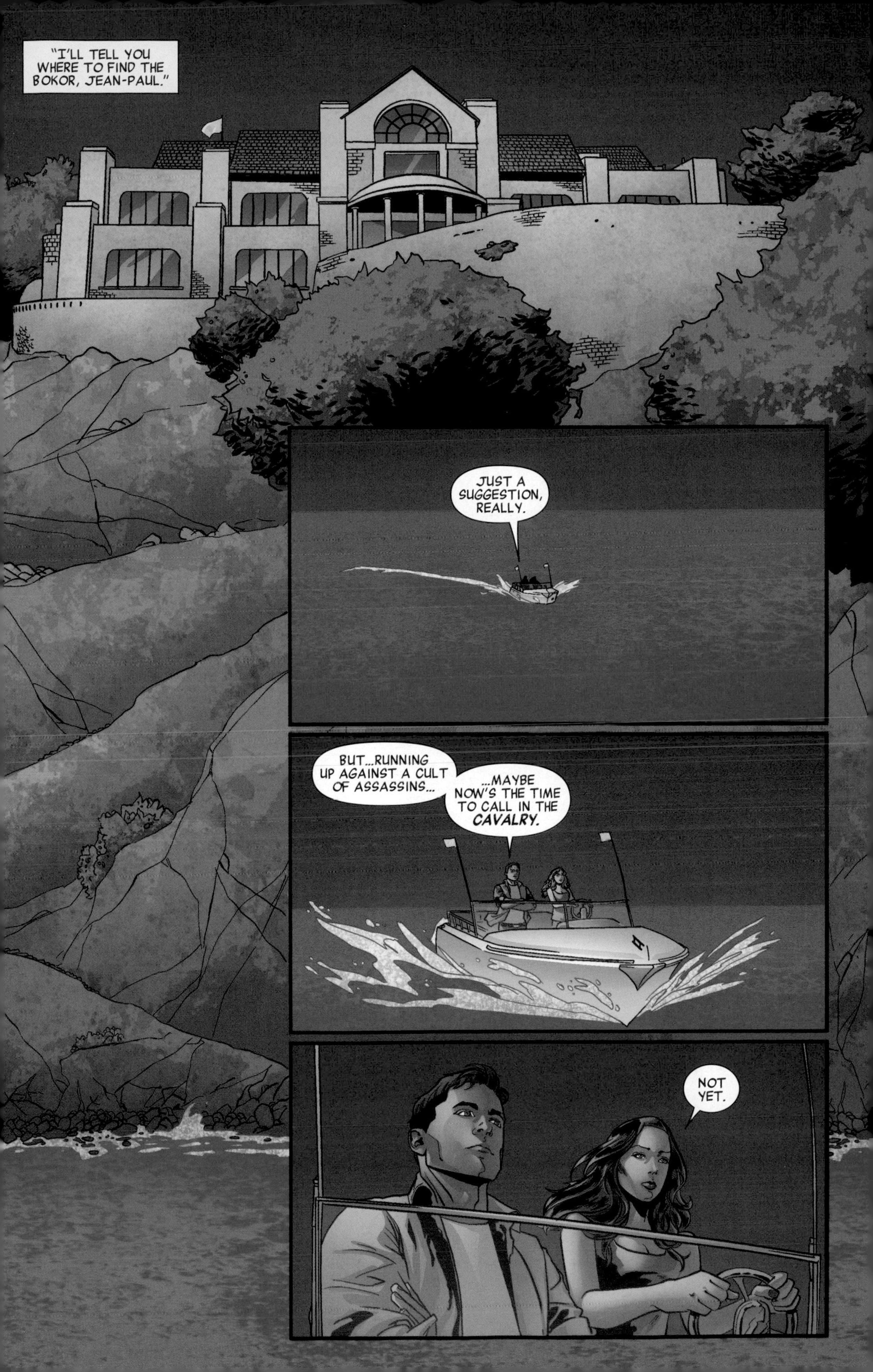
"I'LL TELL YOU WHERE TO FIND THE BOKOR, JEAN-PAUL."
JUST A SUGGESTION, REALLY.
BUT...RUNNING UP AGAINST A CULT OF ASSASSINS...
...MAYBE NOW'S THE TIME TO CALL IN THE CAVALRY.
NOT YET.

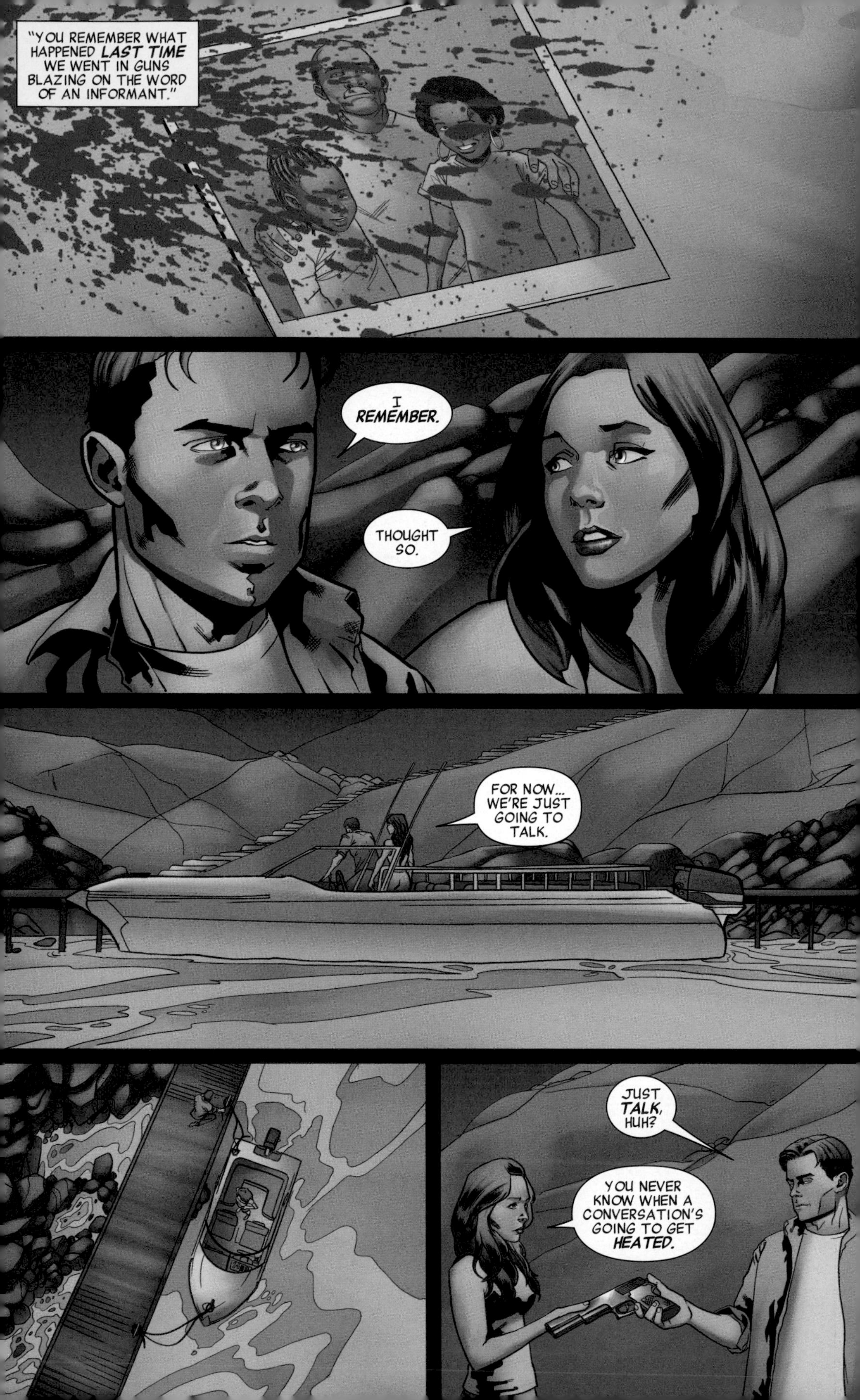
"YOU REMEMBER WHAT HAPPENED LAST TIME WE WENT IN GUNS BLAZING ON THE WORD OF AN INFORMANT."
I REMEMBER.
THOUGHT SO.
FOR NOW... WE'RE JUST GOING TO TALK.
JUST TALK, HUH?
YOU NEVER KNOW WHEN A CONVERSATION'S GOING TO GET HEATED.

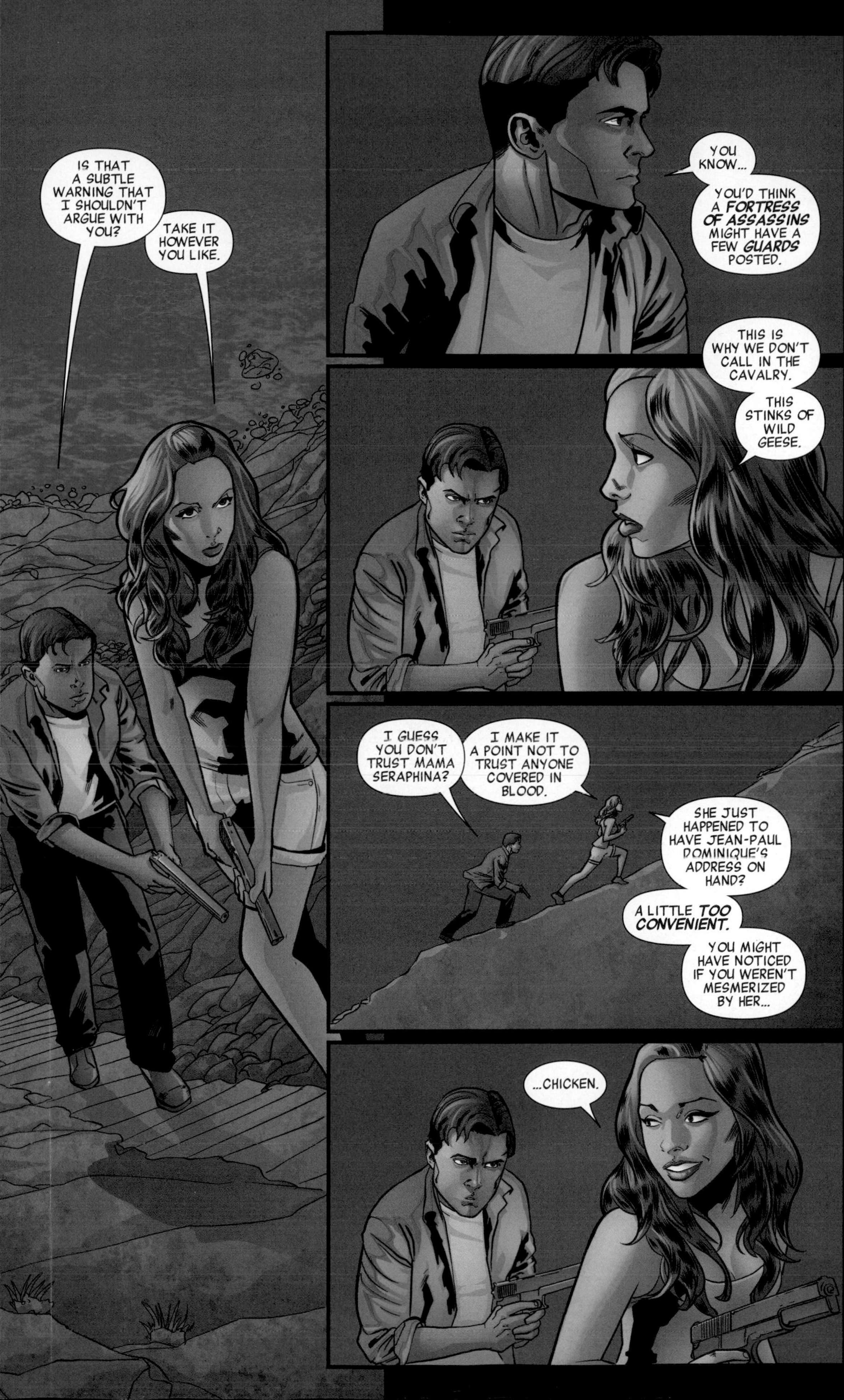

IS THAT A SUBTLE WARNING THAT I SHOULDN'T ARGUE WITH YOU?
TAKE IT HOWEVER YOU LIKE.
YOU KNOW...
YOU'D THINK A FORTRESS OF ASSASSINS MIGHT HAVE A FEW GUARDS POSTED.
THIS IS WHY WE DON'T CALL IN THE CAVALRY.
THIS STINKS OF WILD GEESE.
I GUESS YOU DON'T TRUST MAMA SERAPHINA?
I MAKE IT A POINT NOT TO TRUST ANYONE COVERED IN BLOOD.
SHE JUST HAPPENED TO HAVE JEAN-PAUL DOMINIQUE'S ADDRESS ON HAND?
A LITTLE TOO CONVENIENT.
YOU MIGHT HAVE NOTICED IF YOU WEREN'T MESMERIZED BY HER...
...CHICKEN.

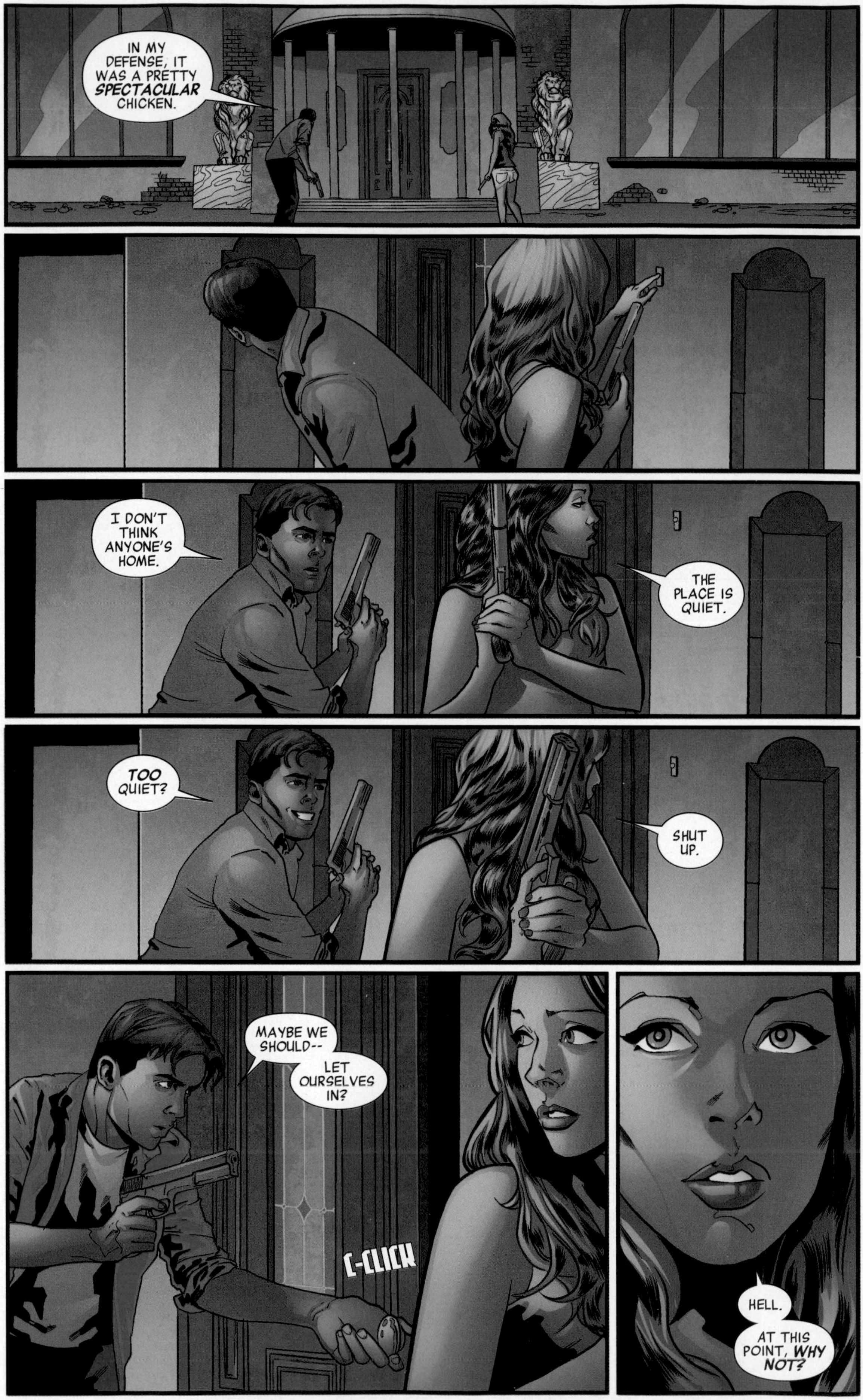
IN MY DEFENSE, IT WAS A PRETTY SPECTACULAR CHICKEN.
I DON'T THINK ANYONE'S HOME.
THE PLACE IS QUIET.
TOO QUIET?
SHUT UP.
MAYBE WE SHOULD--
LET OURSELVES IN?
C-CLICK
HELL.
AT THIS POINT, WHY NOT?

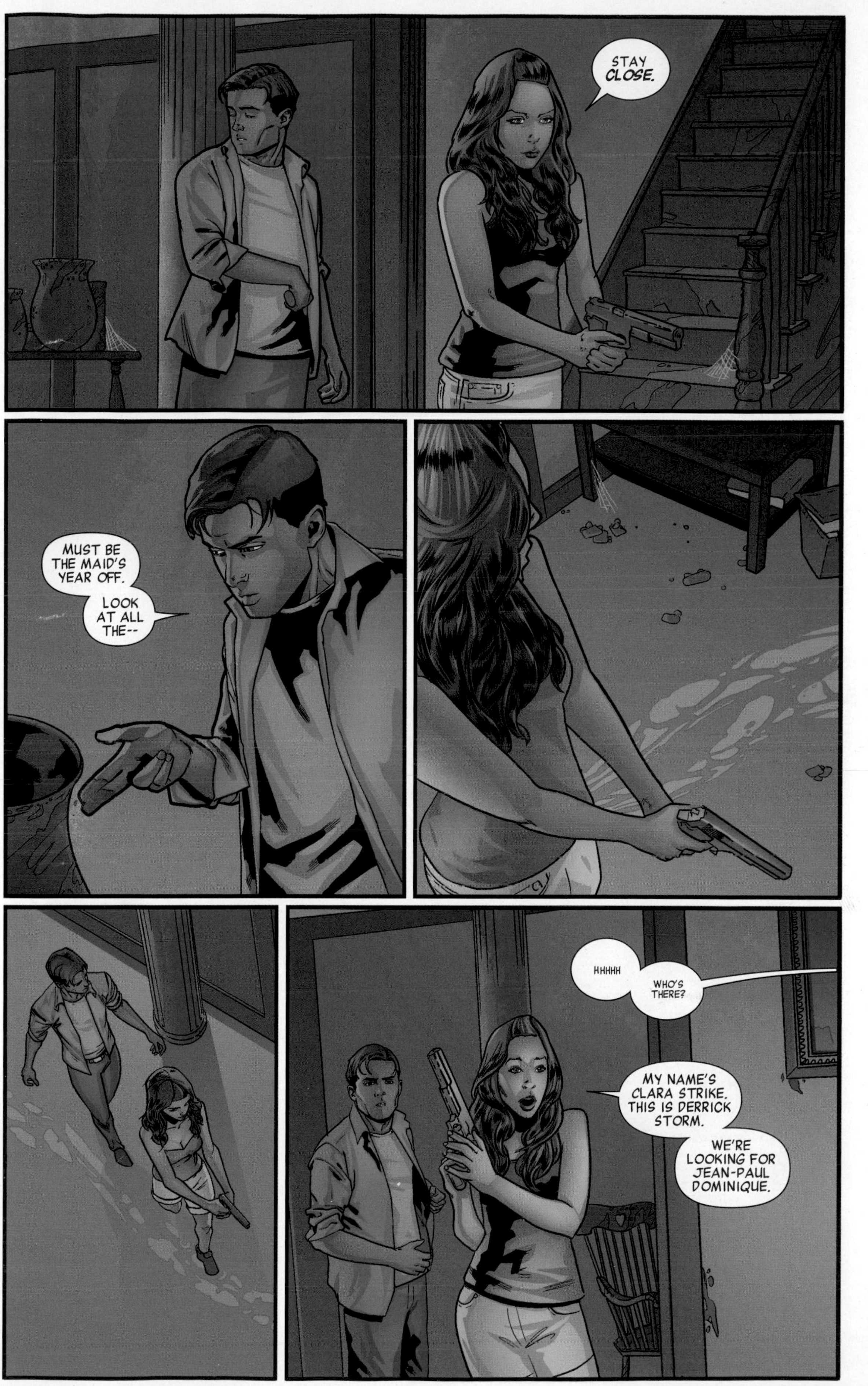
STAY CLOSE.
MUST BE THE MAID'S YEAR OFF.
LOOK AT ALL THE--
HHHHH
WHO'S THERE?
MY NAME'S CLARA STRIKE. THIS IS DERRICK STORM.
WE'RE LOOKING FOR JEAN-PAUL DOMINIQUE.

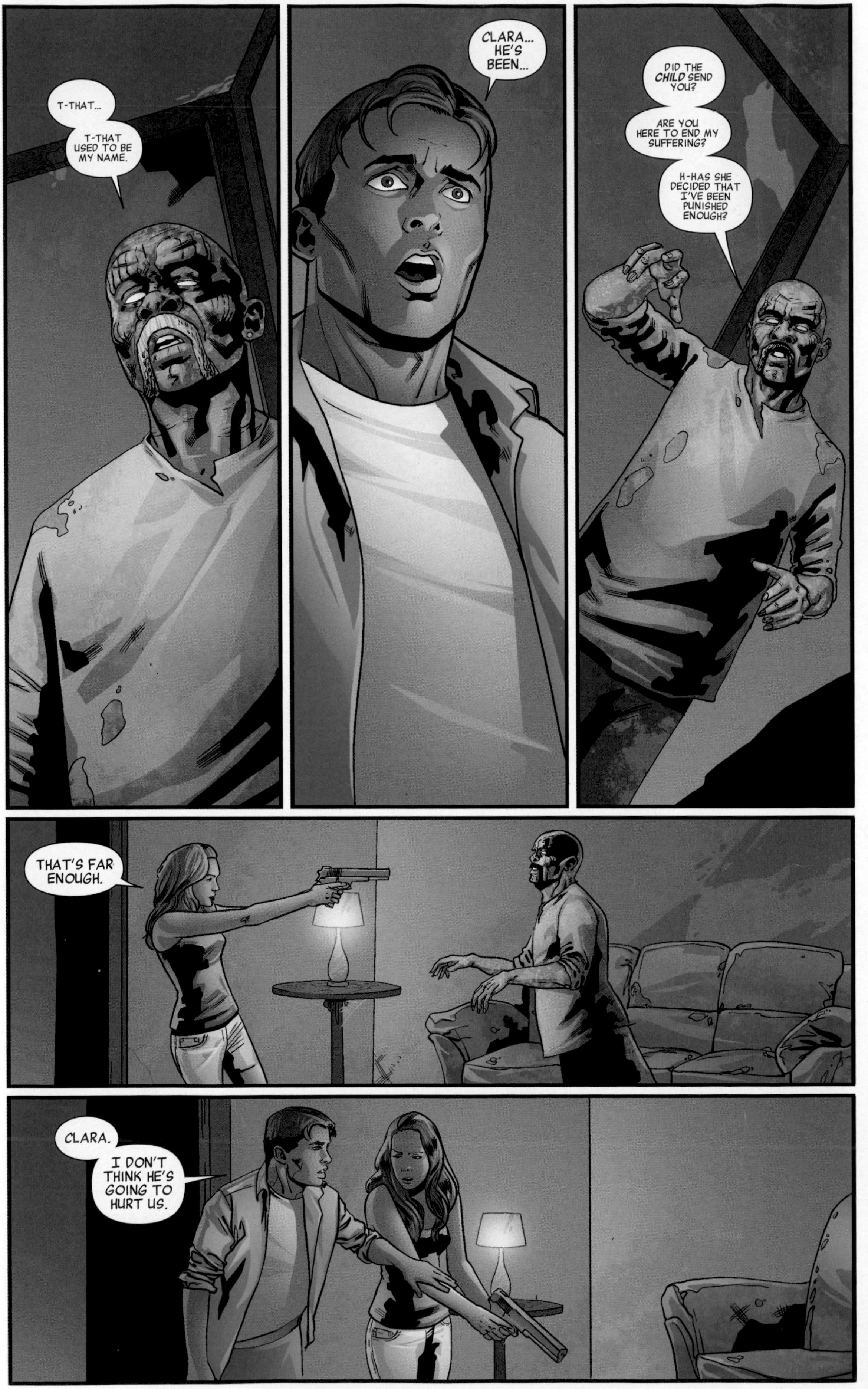
T-THAT...
T-THAT USED TO BE MY NAME.
CLARA... HE'S BEEN...
DID THE CHILD SEND YOU?
ARE YOU HERE TO END MY SUFFERING?
H-HAS SHE DECIDED THAT I'VE BEEN PUNISHED ENOUGH?
THAT'S FAR ENOUGH.
CLARA.
I DON'T THINK HE'S GOING TO HURT US.

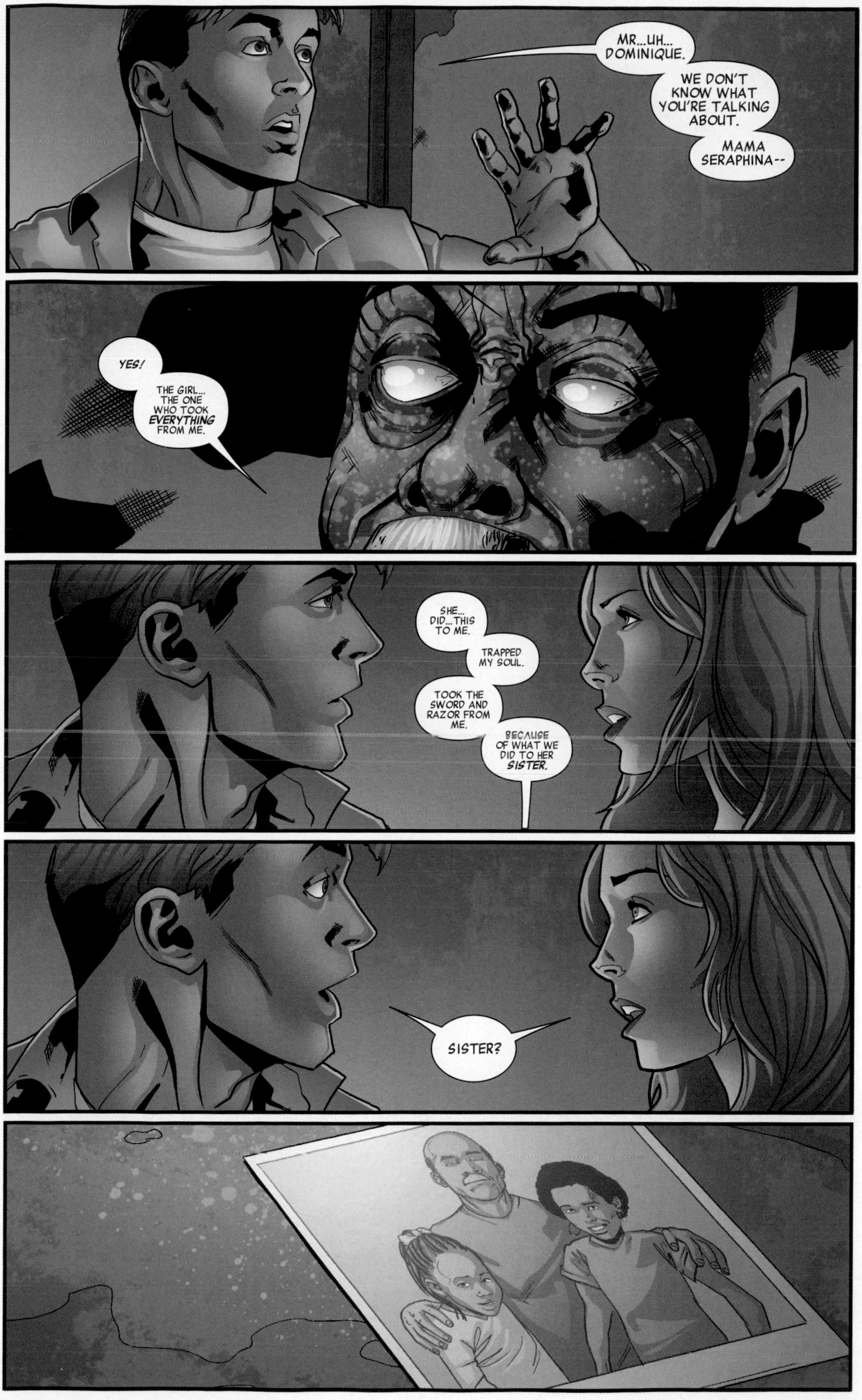
MR...UH... DOMINIQUE.
WE DON'T KNOW WHAT YOU'RE TALKING ABOUT.
MAMA SERAPHINA--
YES!
THE GIRL... THE ONE WHO TOOK EVERYTHING FROM ME.
SHE... DID...THIS TO ME.
TRAPPED MY SOUL.
TOOK THE SWORD AND RAZOR FROM ME.
BECAUSE OF WHAT WE DID TO HER SISTER.
SISTER?

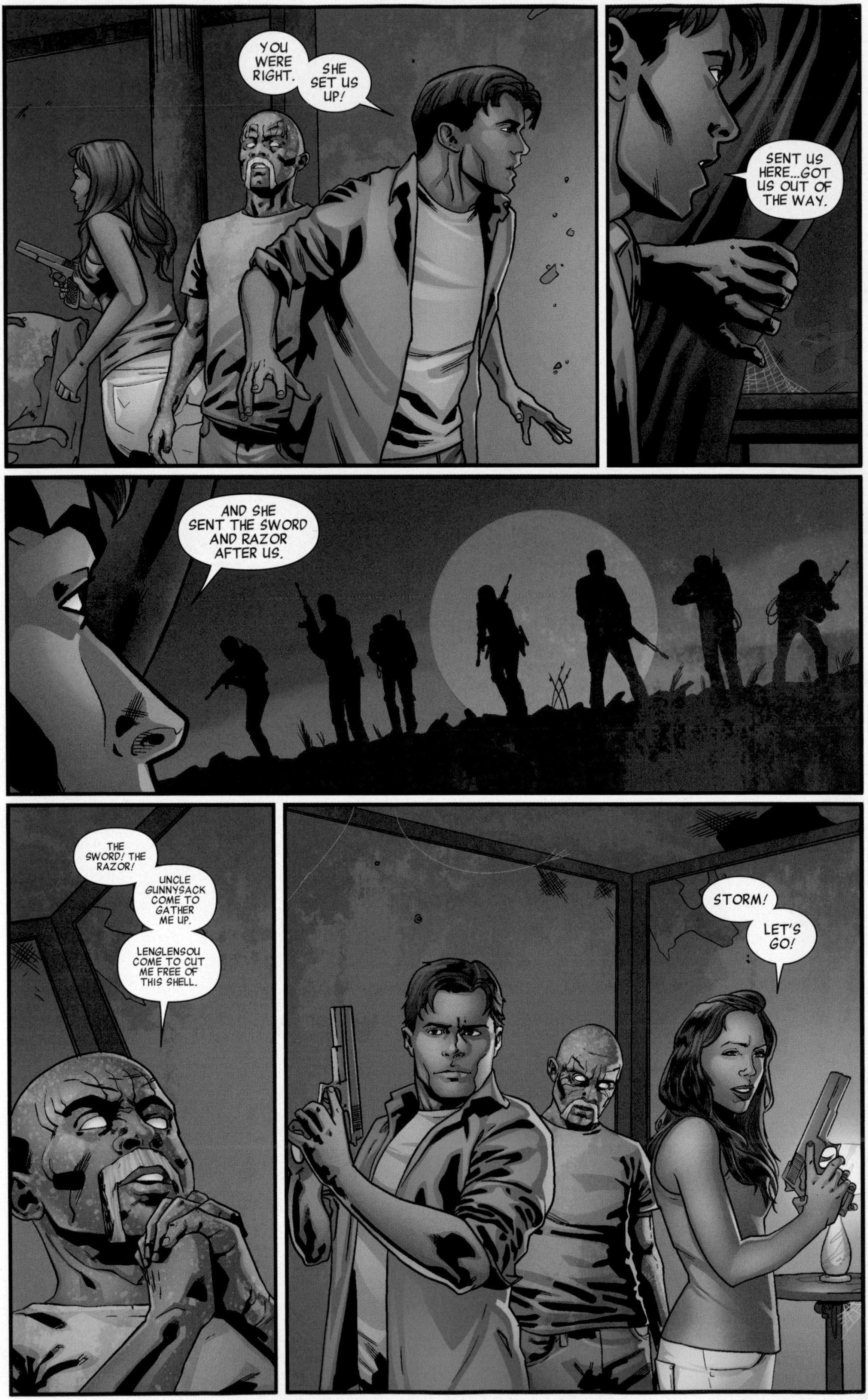
YOU WERE RIGHT.
SHE SET US UP!
SENT US HERE...GOT US OUT OF THE WAY.
AND SHE SENT THE SWORD AND RAZOR AFTER US.
THE SWORD! THE RAZOR!
UNCLE GUNNYSACK COME TO GATHER ME UP.
LENGLENSOU COME TO CUT ME FREE OF THIS SHELL.
STORM!
LET'S GO!

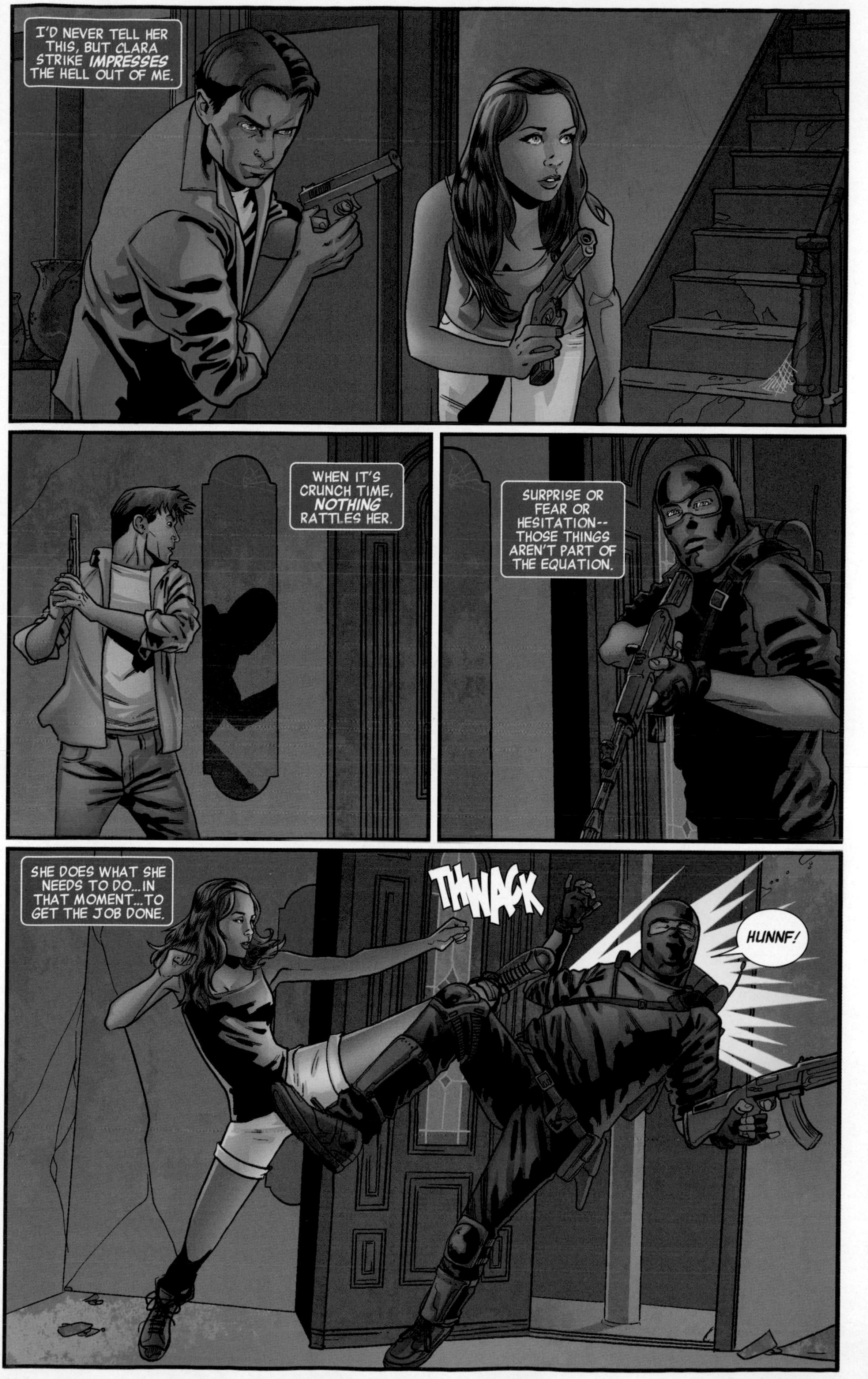
I'D NEVER TELL HER THIS, BUT CLARA STRIKE IMPRESSES THE HELL OUT OF ME.
WHEN IT'S CRUNCH TIME, NOTHING RATTLES HER.
SURPRISE OR FEAR OR HESITATION-- THOSE THINGS AREN'T PART OF THE EQUATION.
SHE DOES WHAT SHE NEEDS TO DO... IN THAT MOMENT... TO GET THE JOB DONE.
THWACK
HUNNF!

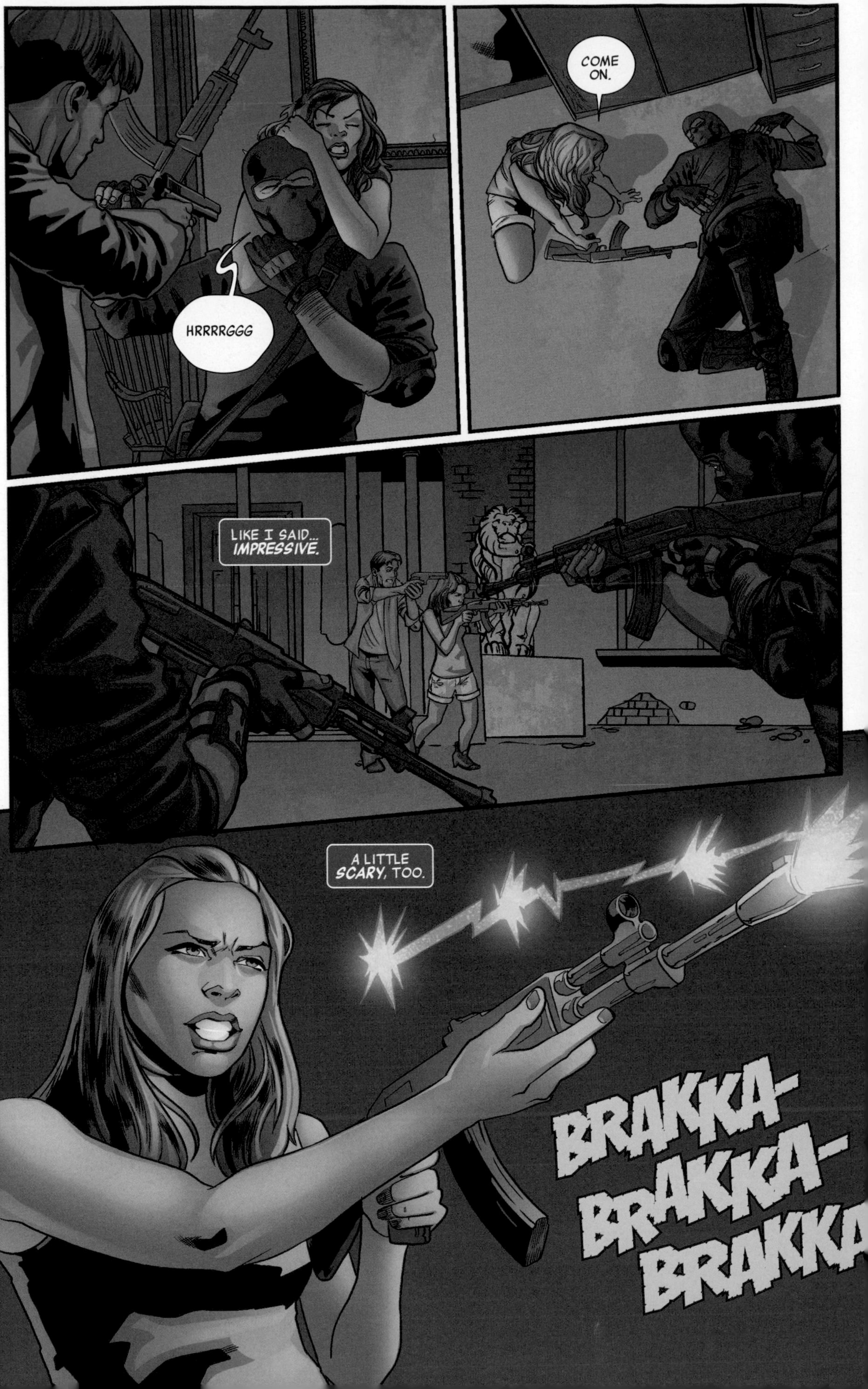

HRRRRGGG
COME ON.
LIKE I SAID... IMPRESSIVE.
A LITTLE SCARY, TOO.
BRAKKA-BRAKKA-BRAKKA

BRAKKA-BRAKKA-BRAKKA-BRAKKA

THEY'RE RIGHT BEHIND US!

GET TO THE BOAT! GET IT STARTED!

BRAKKA-BRAKKA-BRAKKA-BRAKKA

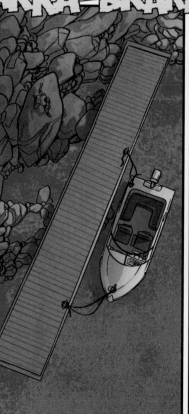

C'MON, CLARA.

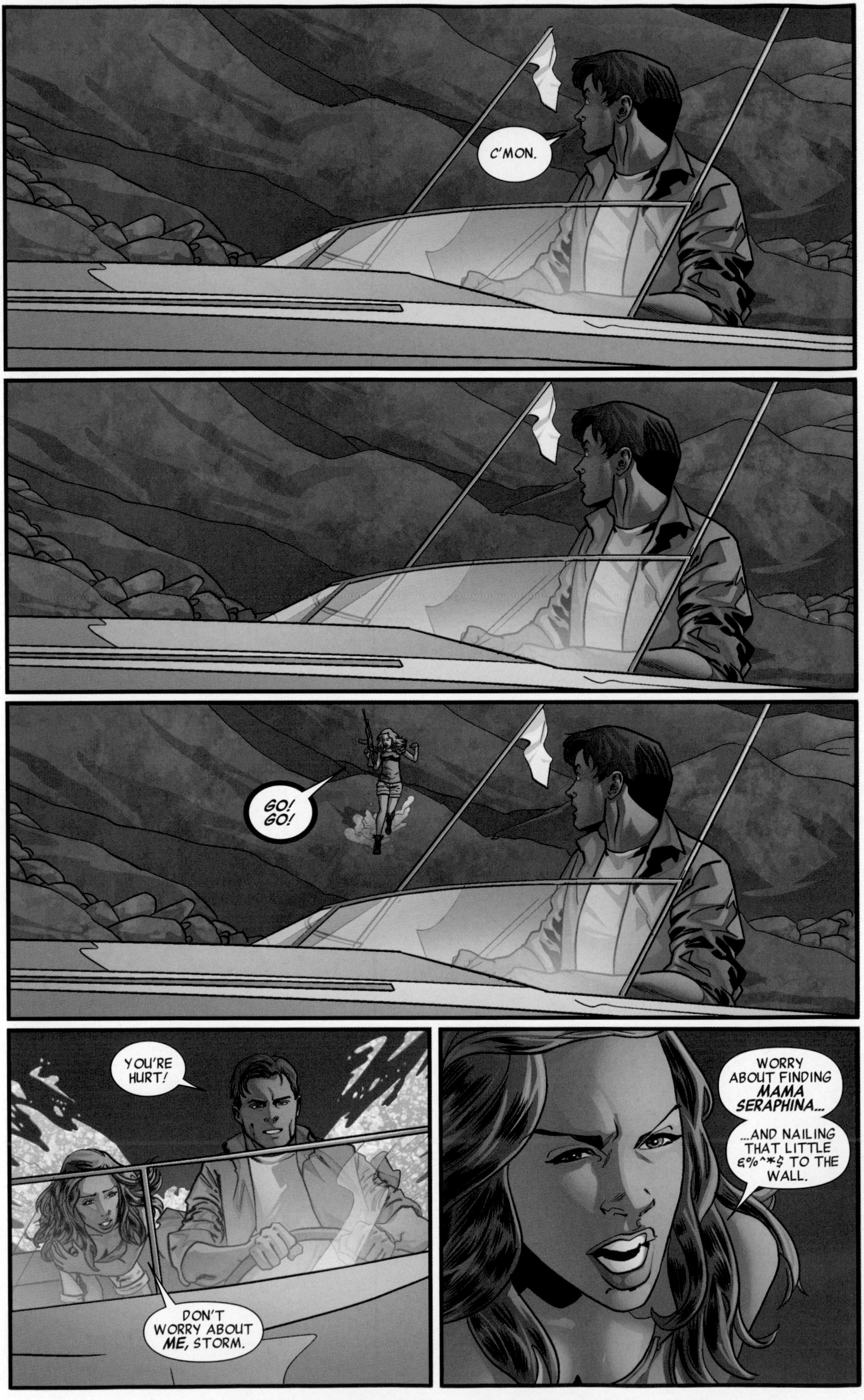
C'MON.
GO! GO!
YOU'RE HURT!
DON'T WORRY ABOUT ME, STORM.
WORRY ABOUT FINDING MAMA SERAPHINA...
...AND NAILING THAT LITTLE &%^*$ TO THE WALL.

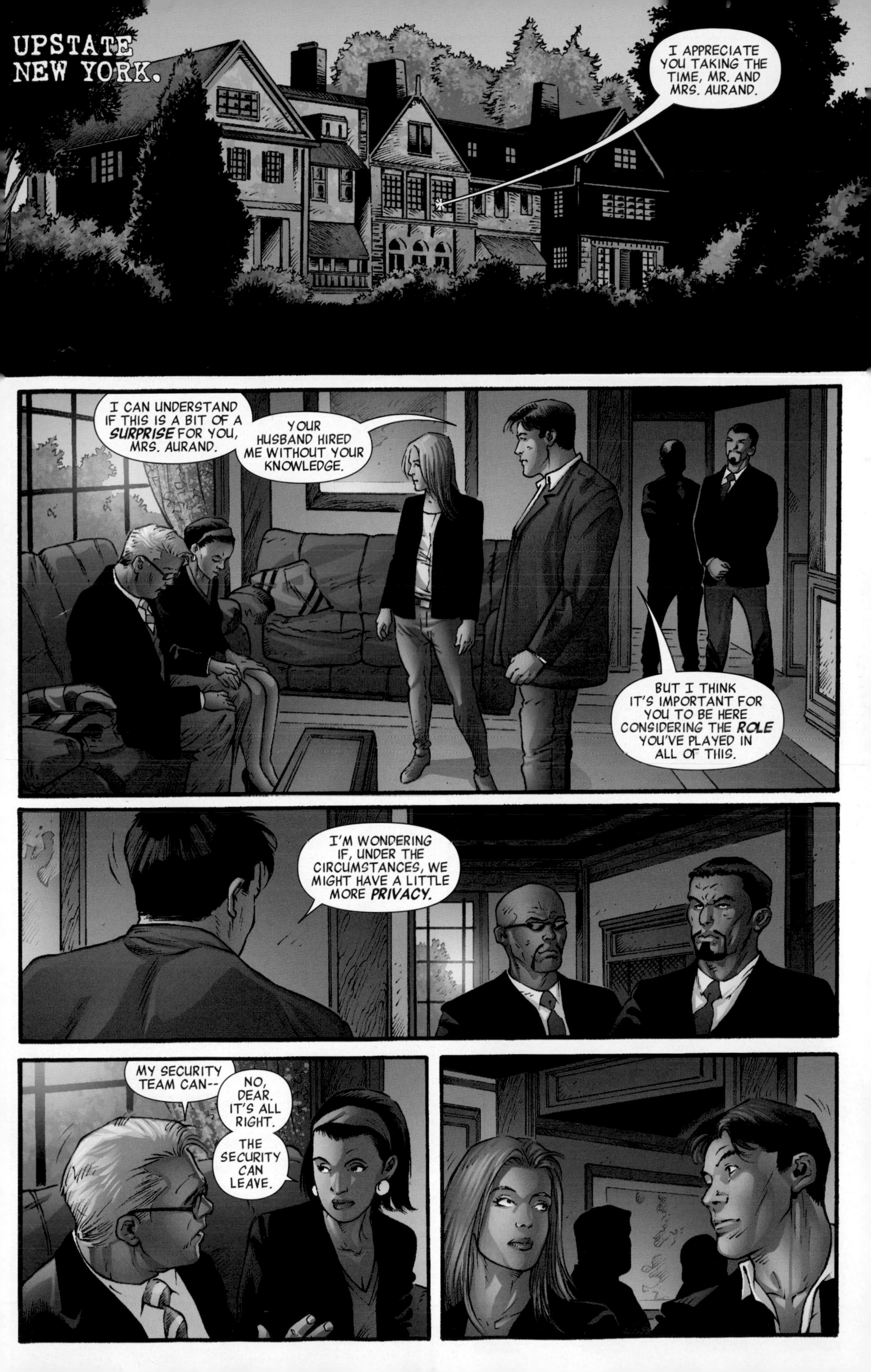

UPSTATE NEW YORK.
I APPRECIATE YOU TAKING THE TIME, MR. AND MRS. AURAND.
I CAN UNDERSTAND IF THIS IS A BIT OF A SURPRISE FOR YOU, MRS. AURAND.
YOUR HUSBAND HIRED ME WITHOUT YOUR KNOWLEDGE.
BUT I THINK IT'S IMPORTANT FOR YOU TO BE HERE CONSIDERING THE ROLE YOU'VE PLAYED IN ALL OF THIS.
I'M WONDERING IF, UNDER THE CIRCUMSTANCES, WE MIGHT HAVE A LITTLE MORE PRIVACY.
MY SECURITY TEAM CAN--
NO, DEAR. IT'S ALL RIGHT.
THE SECURITY CAN LEAVE.

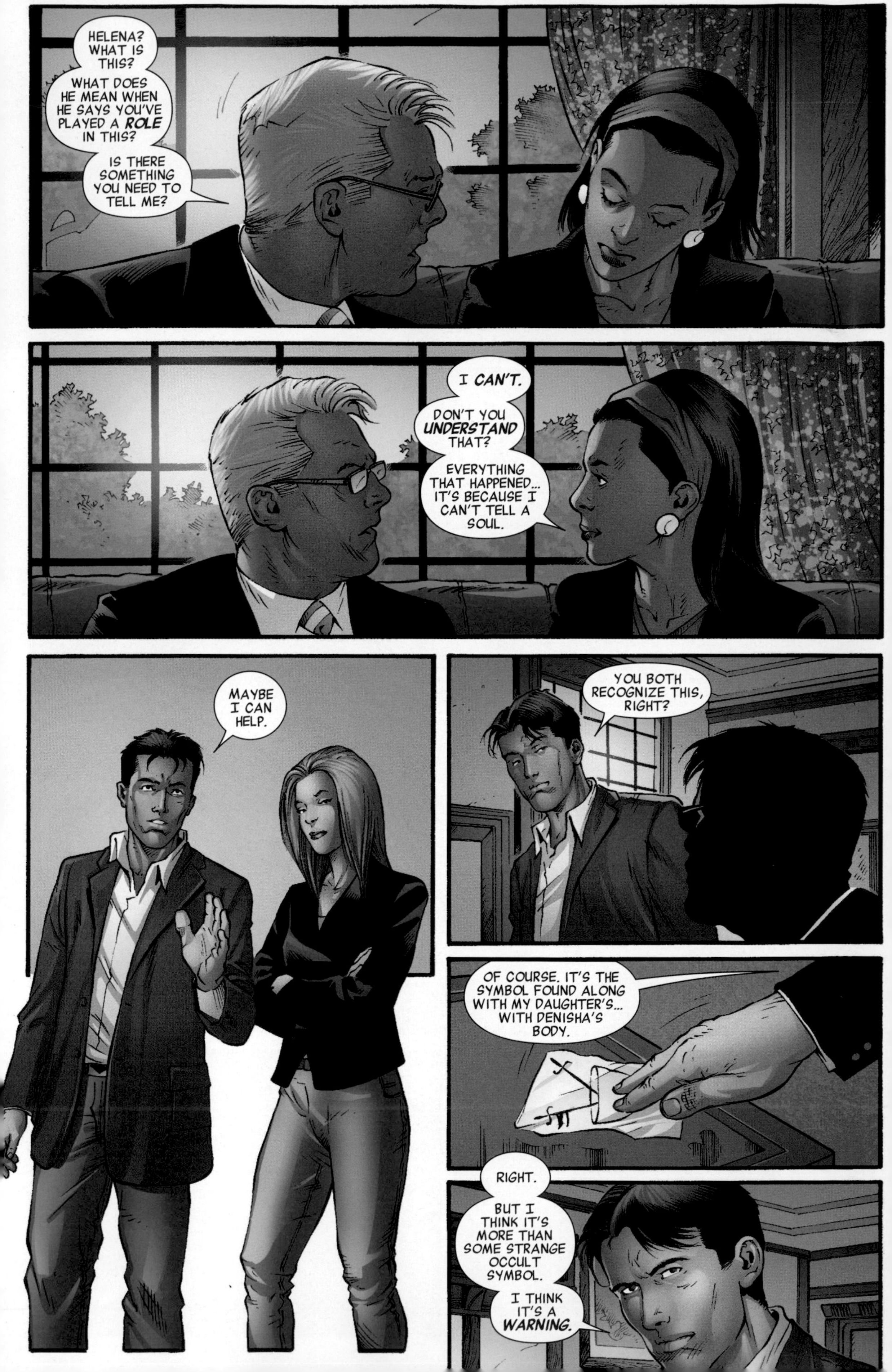
HELENA? WHAT IS THIS?
WHAT DOES HE MEAN WHEN HE SAYS YOU'VE PLAYED A ROLE IN THIS?
IS THERE SOMETHING YOU NEED TO TELL ME?
I CAN'T.
DON'T YOU UNDERSTAND THAT?
EVERYTHING THAT HAPPENED... IT'S BECAUSE I CAN'T TELL A SOUL.
MAYBE I CAN HELP.
YOU BOTH RECOGNIZE THIS, RIGHT?
OF COURSE. IT'S THE SYMBOL FOUND ALONG WITH MY DAUGHTER'S... WITH DENISHA'S BODY.
RIGHT.
BUT I THINK IT'S MORE THAN SOME STRANGE OCCULT SYMBOL.
I THINK IT'S A WARNING.

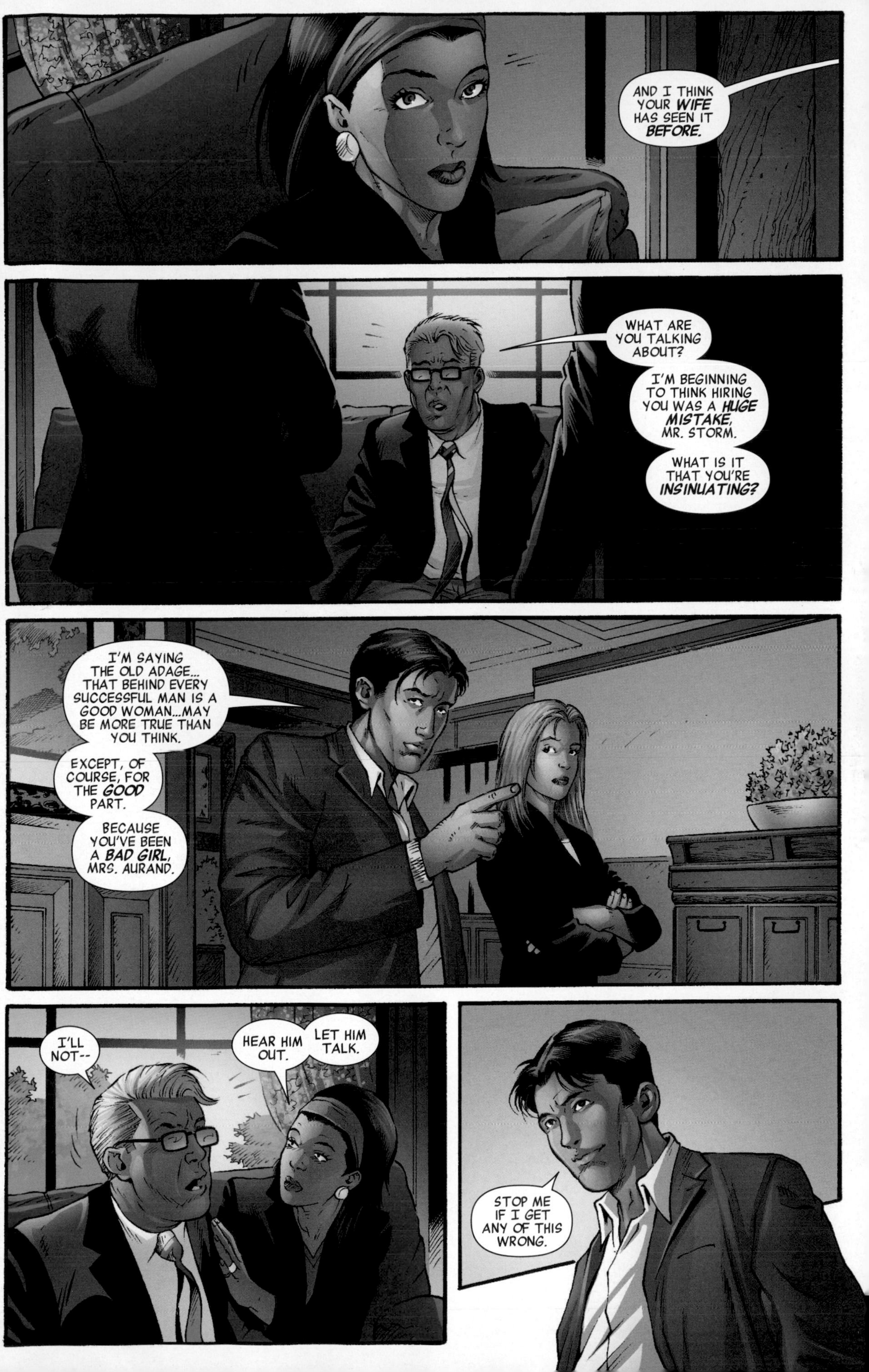
AND I THINK YOUR WIFE HAS SEEN IT BEFORE.
WHAT ARE YOU TALKING ABOUT?
I'M BEGINNING TO THINK HIRING YOU WAS A HUGE MISTAKE, MR. STORM.
WHAT IS IT THAT YOU'RE INSINUATING?
I'M SAYING THE OLD ADAGE... THAT BEHIND EVERY SUCCESSFUL MAN IS A GOOD WOMAN...MAY BE MORE TRUE THAN YOU THINK.
EXCEPT, OF COURSE, FOR THE GOOD PART.
BECAUSE YOU'VE BEEN A BAD GIRL, MRS. AURAND.
I'LL NOT--
HEAR HIM OUT.
LET HIM TALK.
STOP ME IF I GET ANY OF THIS WRONG.

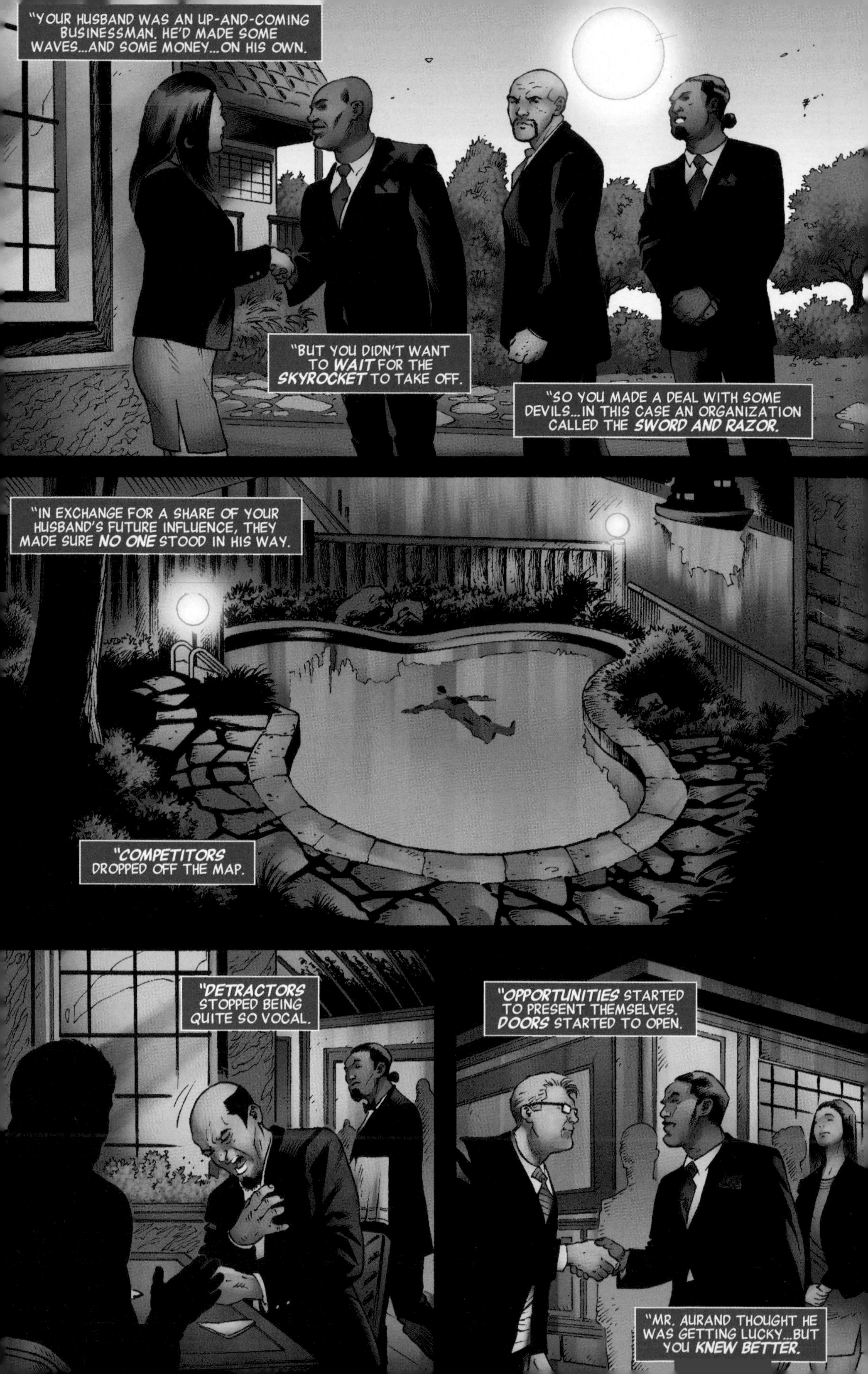
"YOUR HUSBAND WAS AN UP-AND-COMING BUSINESSMAN. HE'D MADE SOME WAVES...AND SOME MONEY...ON HIS OWN.
"BUT YOU DIDN'T WANT TO WAIT FOR THE SKYROCKET TO TAKE OFF.
"SO YOU MADE A DEAL WITH SOME DEVILS...IN THIS CASE AN ORGANIZATION CALLED THE SWORD AND RAZOR.
"IN EXCHANGE FOR A SHARE OF YOUR HUSBAND'S FUTURE INFLUENCE, THEY MADE SURE NO ONE STOOD IN HIS WAY.
"COMPETITORS DROPPED OFF THE MAP.
"DETRACTORS STOPPED BEING QUITE SO VOCAL.
"OPPORTUNITIES STARTED TO PRESENT THEMSELVES. DOORS STARTED TO OPEN.
"MR. AURAND THOUGHT HE WAS GETTING LUCKY...BUT YOU KNEW BETTER.

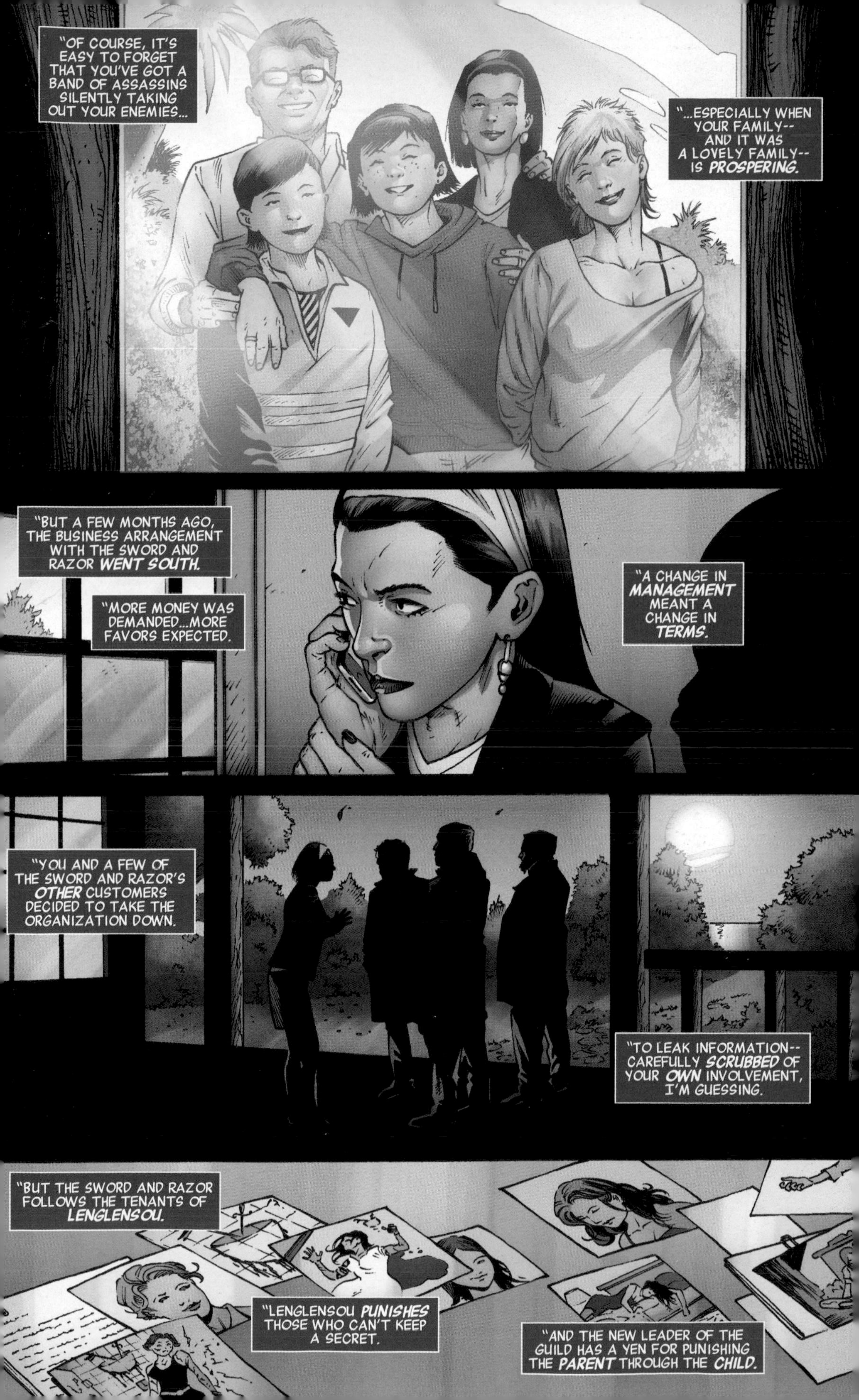

"OF COURSE, IT'S EASY TO FORGET THAT YOU'VE GOT A BAND OF ASSASSINS SILENTLY TAKING OUT YOUR ENEMIES...
"...ESPECIALLY WHEN YOUR FAMILY-- AND IT WAS A LOVELY FAMILY-- IS PROSPERING.
"BUT A FEW MONTHS AGO, THE BUSINESS ARRANGEMENT WITH THE SWORD AND RAZOR WENT SOUTH.
"MORE MONEY WAS DEMANDED...MORE FAVORS EXPECTED.
"A CHANGE IN MANAGEMENT MEANT A CHANGE IN TERMS.
"YOU AND A FEW OF THE SWORD AND RAZOR'S OTHER CUSTOMERS DECIDED TO TAKE THE ORGANIZATION DOWN.
"TO LEAK INFORMATION-- CAREFULLY SCRUBBED OF YOUR OWN INVOLVEMENT, I'M GUESSING.
"BUT THE SWORD AND RAZOR FOLLOWS THE TENANTS OF LENGLENSOU.
"LENGLENSOU PUNISHES THOSE WHO CAN'T KEEP A SECRET.
"AND THE NEW LEADER OF THE GUILD HAS A YEN FOR PUNISHING THE PARENT THROUGH THE CHILD.

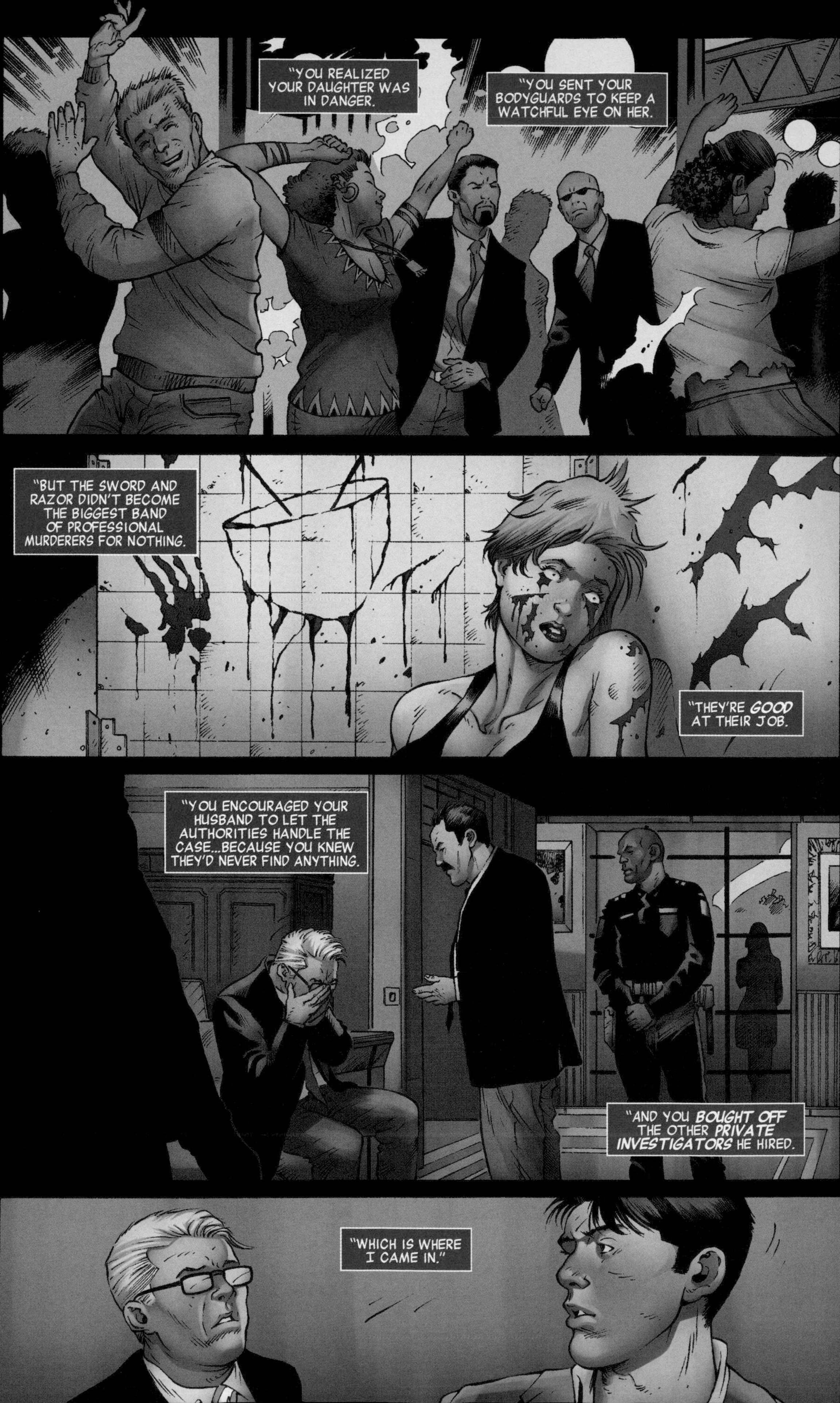
"YOU REALIZED YOUR DAUGHTER WAS IN DANGER.
"YOU SENT YOUR BODYGUARDS TO KEEP A WATCHFUL EYE ON HER.
"BUT THE SWORD AND RAZOR DIDN'T BECOME THE BIGGEST BAND OF PROFESSIONAL MURDERERS FOR NOTHING.
"THEY'RE *GOOD* AT THEIR JOB.
"YOU ENCOURAGED YOUR HUSBAND TO LET THE AUTHORITIES HANDLE THE CASE...BECAUSE YOU KNEW THEY'D NEVER FIND ANYTHING.
"AND YOU *BOUGHT OFF* THE OTHER *PRIVATE INVESTIGATORS* HE HIRED.
"WHICH IS WHERE I CAME IN."

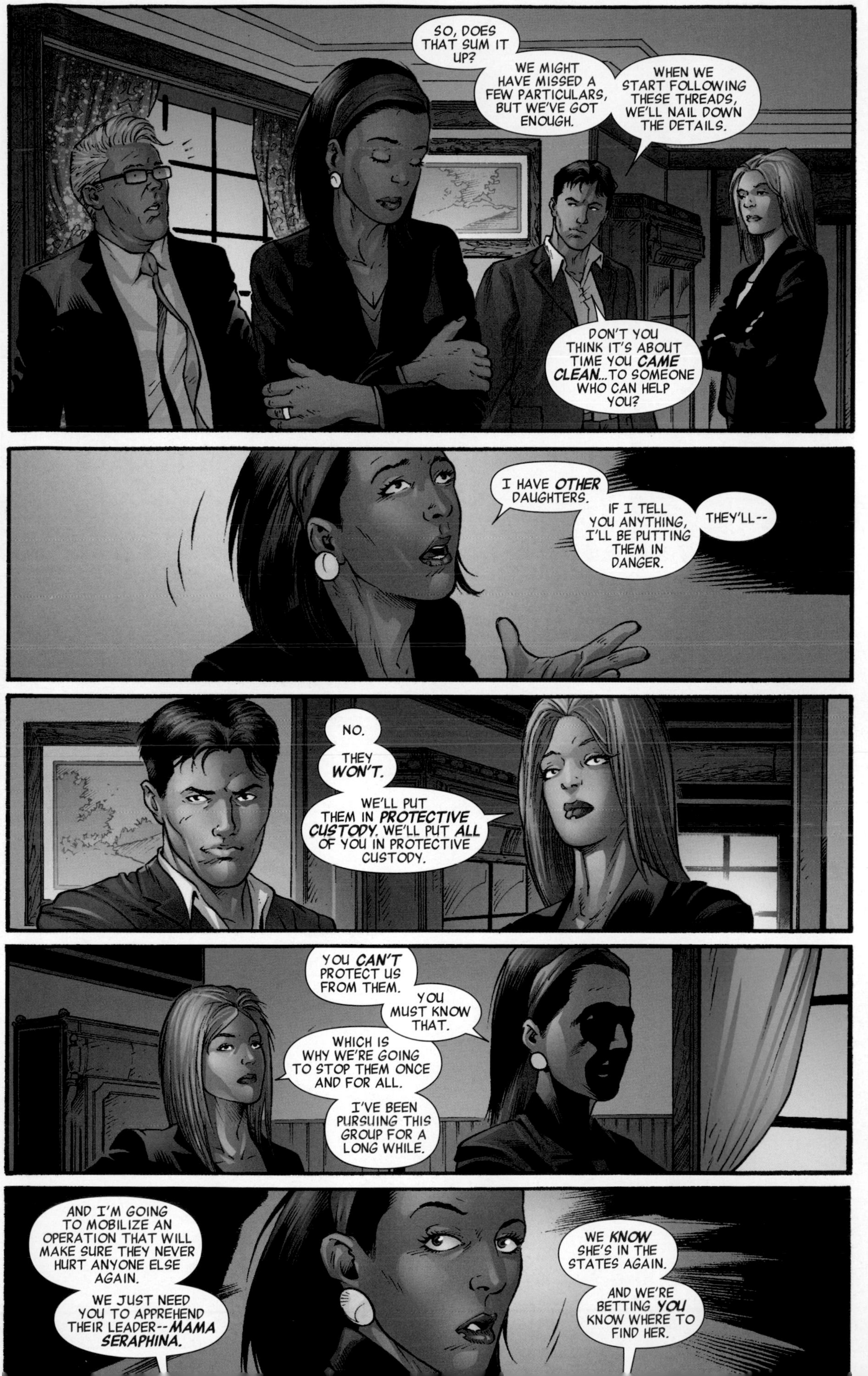

SO, DOES THAT SUM IT UP?
WE MIGHT HAVE MISSED A FEW PARTICULARS, BUT WE'VE GOT ENOUGH.
WHEN WE START FOLLOWING THESE THREADS, WE'LL NAIL DOWN THE DETAILS.
DON'T YOU THINK IT'S ABOUT TIME YOU **CAME CLEAN**...TO SOMEONE WHO CAN HELP YOU?
I HAVE **OTHER** DAUGHTERS.
IF I TELL YOU ANYTHING, I'LL BE PUTTING THEM IN DANGER.
THEY'LL--
NO.
THEY **WON'T.**
WE'LL PUT THEM IN **PROTECTIVE CUSTODY.** WE'LL PUT **ALL** OF YOU IN PROTECTIVE CUSTODY.
YOU **CAN'T** PROTECT US FROM THEM.
YOU MUST KNOW THAT.
WHICH IS WHY WE'RE GOING TO STOP THEM ONCE AND FOR ALL.
I'VE BEEN PURSUING THIS GROUP FOR A LONG WHILE.
AND I'M GOING TO MOBILIZE AN OPERATION THAT WILL MAKE SURE THEY NEVER HURT ANYONE ELSE AGAIN.
WE JUST NEED YOU TO APPREHEND THEIR LEADER--**MAMA SERAPHINA.**
WE **KNOW** SHE'S IN THE STATES AGAIN.
AND WE'RE BETTING **YOU** KNOW WHERE TO FIND HER.

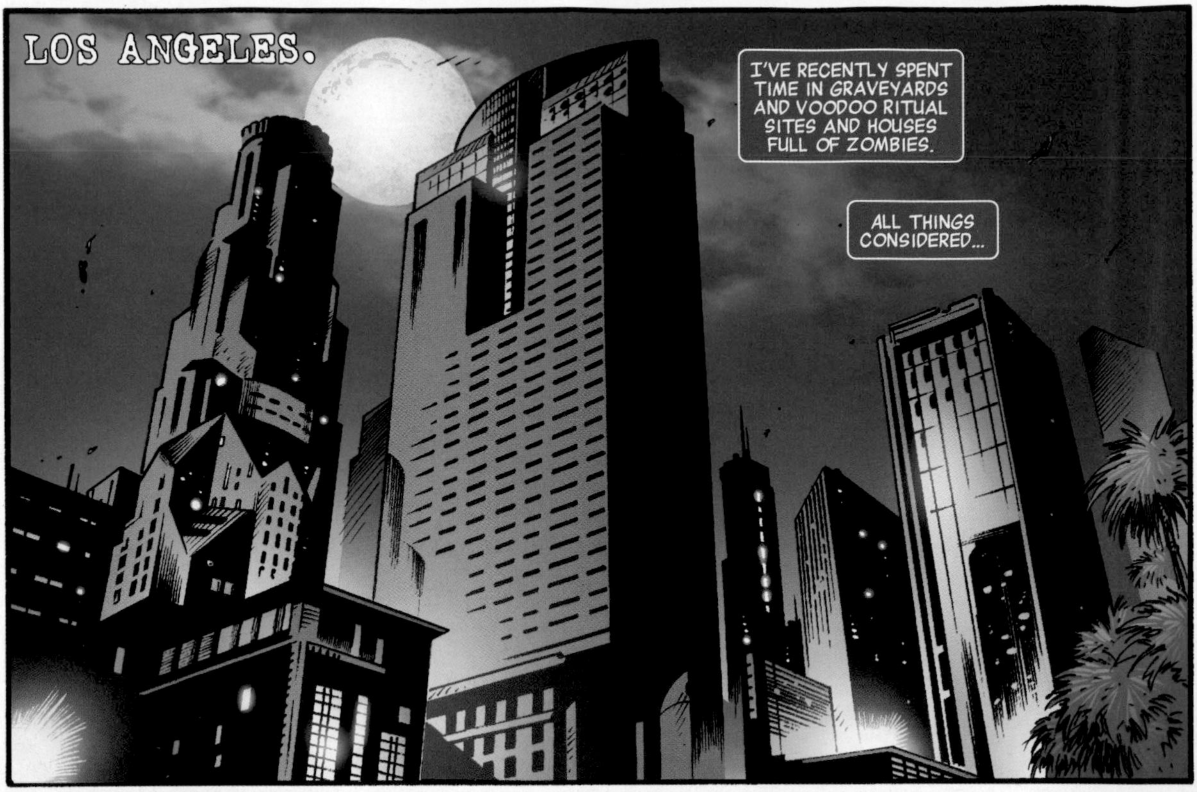
LOS ANGELES.
I'VE RECENTLY SPENT TIME IN GRAVEYARDS AND VOODOO RITUAL SITES AND HOUSES FULL OF ZOMBIES.
ALL THINGS CONSIDERED...

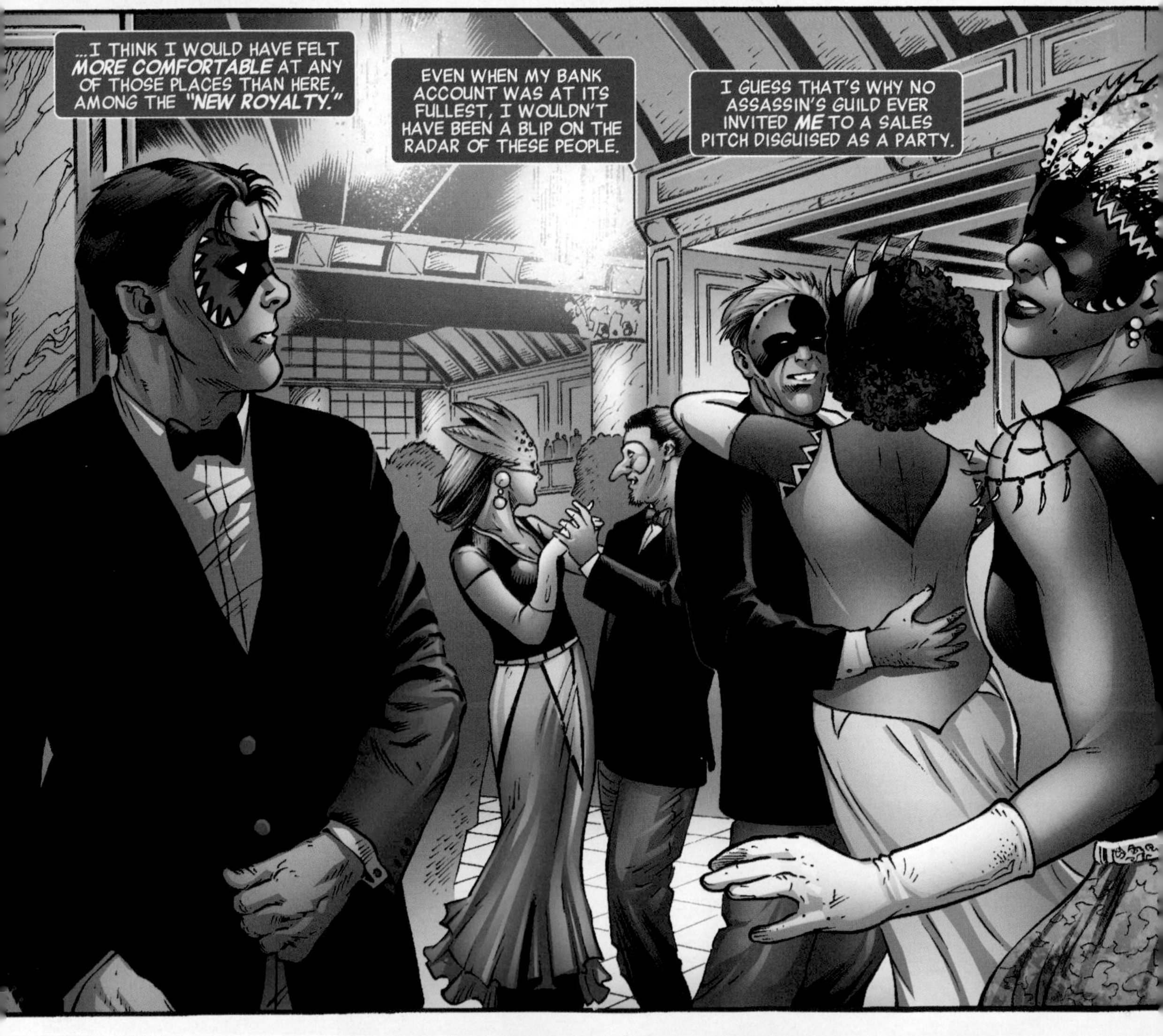
...I THINK I WOULD HAVE FELT *MORE COMFORTABLE* AT ANY OF THOSE PLACES THAN HERE, AMONG THE *"NEW ROYALTY."*
EVEN WHEN MY BANK ACCOUNT WAS AT ITS FULLEST, I WOULDN'T HAVE BEEN A BLIP ON THE RADAR OF THESE PEOPLE.
I GUESS THAT'S WHY NO ASSASSIN'S GUILD EVER INVITED *ME* TO A SALES PITCH DISGUISED AS A PARTY.

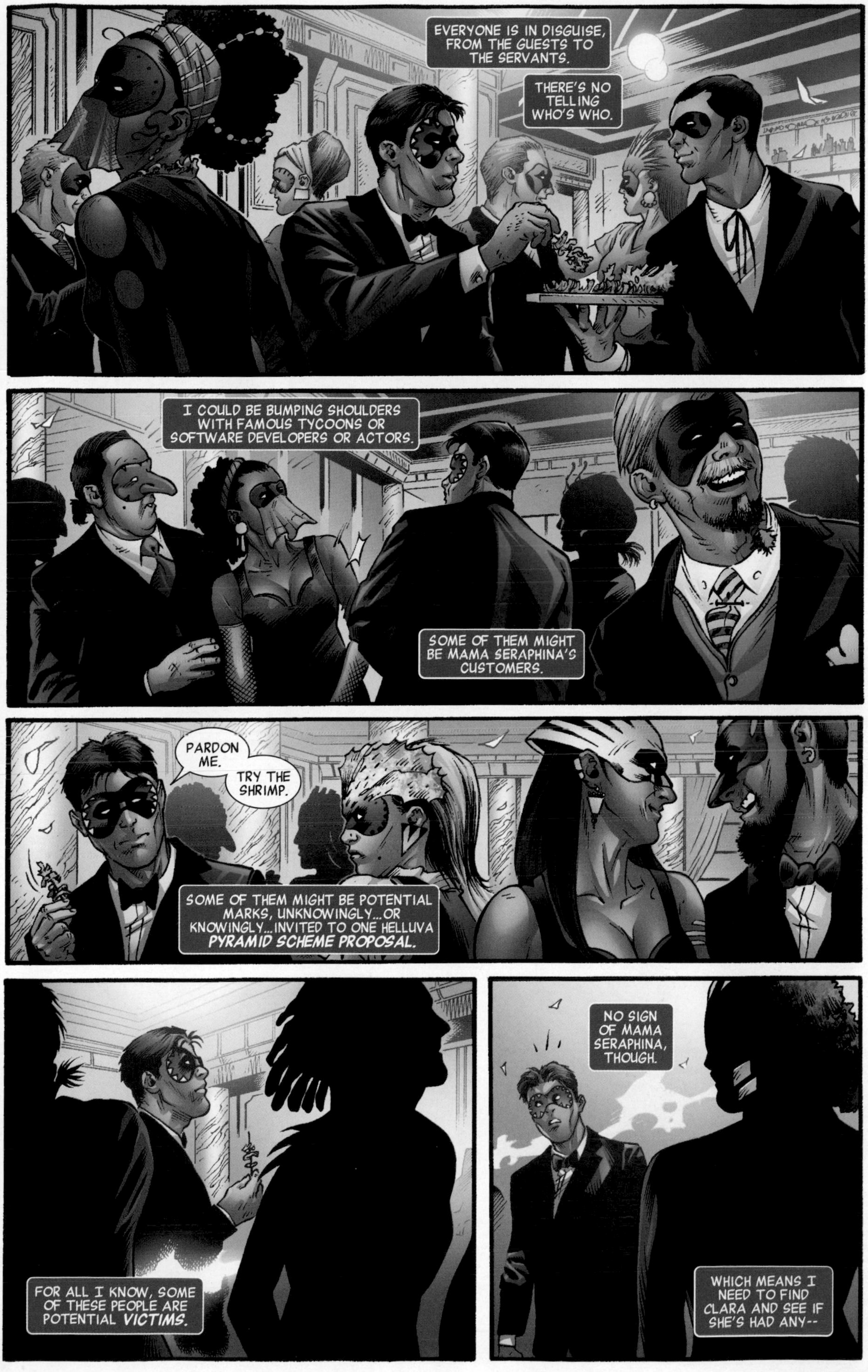
EVERYONE IS IN DISGUISE, FROM THE GUESTS TO THE SERVANTS.
THERE'S NO TELLING WHO'S WHO.
I COULD BE BUMPING SHOULDERS WITH FAMOUS TYCOONS OR SOFTWARE DEVELOPERS OR ACTORS.
SOME OF THEM MIGHT BE MAMA SERAPHINA'S CUSTOMERS.
PARDON ME.
TRY THE SHRIMP.
SOME OF THEM MIGHT BE POTENTIAL MARKS, UNKNOWINGLY...OR KNOWINGLY...INVITED TO ONE HELLUVA *PYRAMID SCHEME PROPOSAL.*
FOR ALL I KNOW, SOME OF THESE PEOPLE ARE POTENTIAL *VICTIMS.*
NO SIGN OF MAMA SERAPHINA, THOUGH.
WHICH MEANS I NEED TO FIND CLARA AND SEE IF SHE'S HAD ANY--

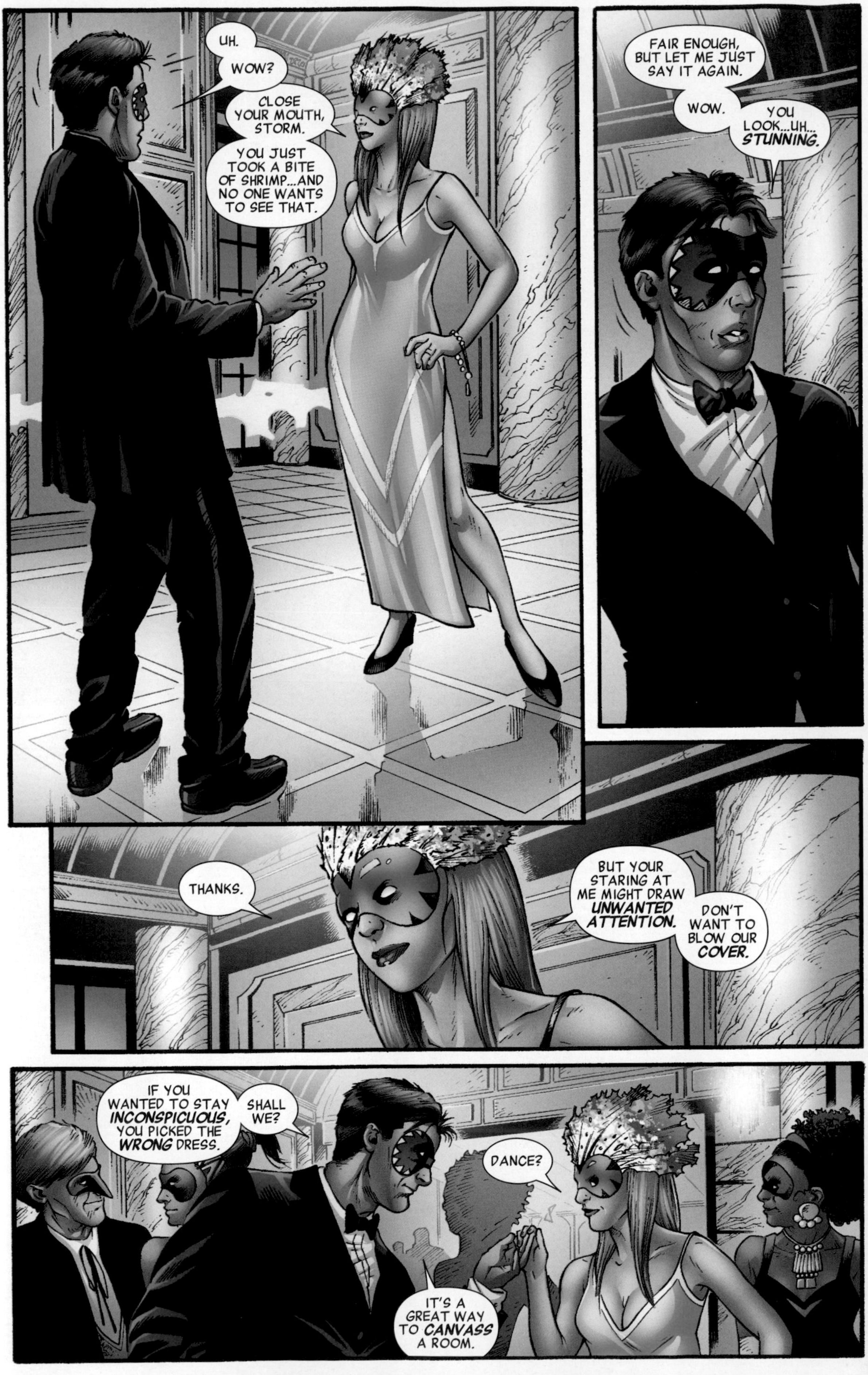
UH.
WOW?
CLOSE YOUR MOUTH, STORM.
YOU JUST TOOK A BITE OF SHRIMP...AND NO ONE WANTS TO SEE THAT.
FAIR ENOUGH, BUT LET ME JUST SAY IT AGAIN.
WOW.
YOU LOOK...UH... STUNNING.
THANKS.
BUT YOUR STARING AT ME MIGHT DRAW UNWANTED ATTENTION.
DON'T WANT TO BLOW OUR COVER.
IF YOU WANTED TO STAY INCONSPICUOUS, YOU PICKED THE WRONG DRESS.
SHALL WE?
DANCE?
IT'S A GREAT WAY TO CANVASS A ROOM.

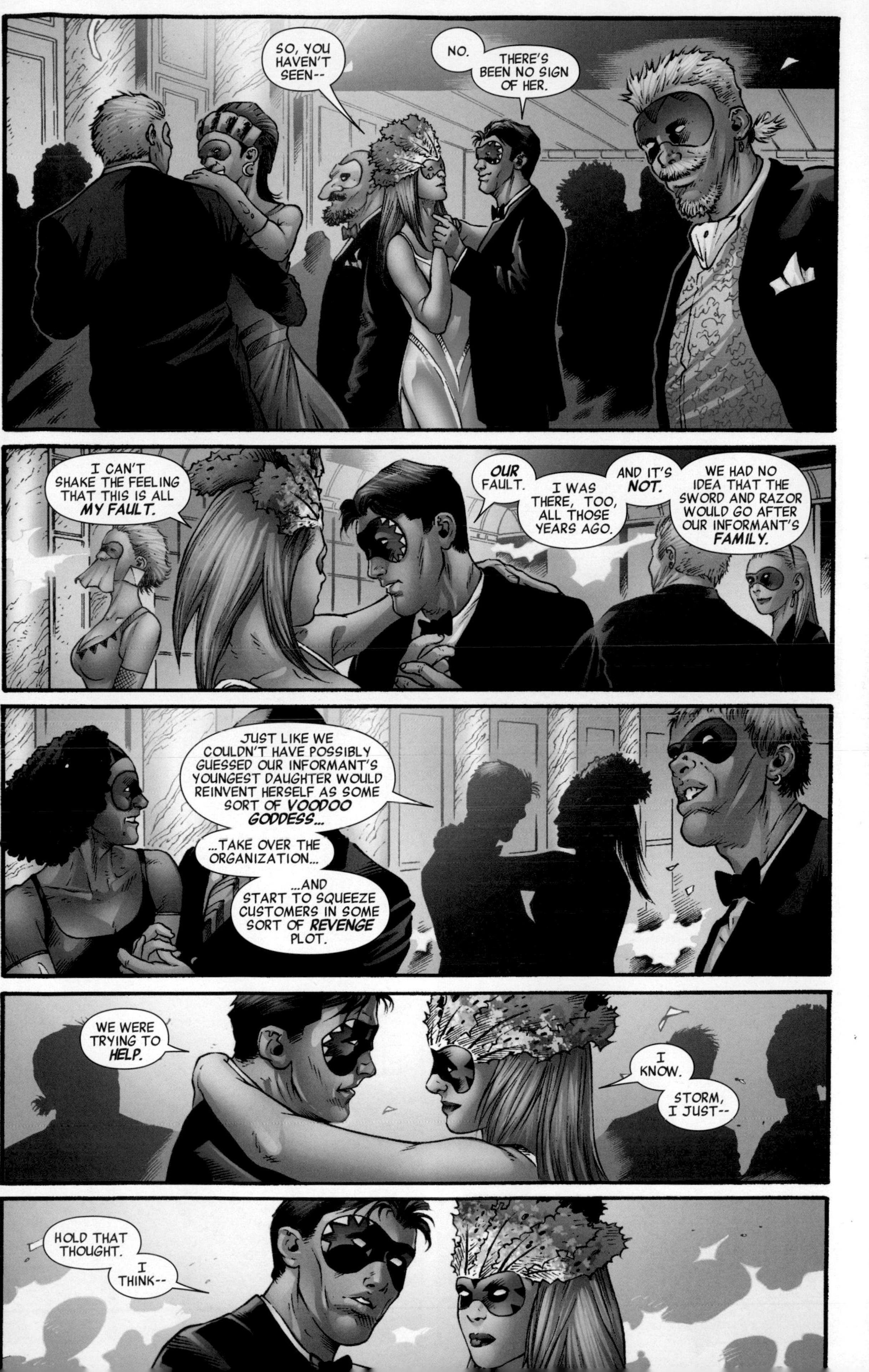
SO, YOU HAVEN'T SEEN--
NO.
THERE'S BEEN NO SIGN OF HER.
I CAN'T SHAKE THE FEELING THAT THIS IS ALL MY FAULT.
OUR FAULT.
I WAS THERE, TOO, ALL THOSE YEARS AGO.
AND IT'S NOT.
WE HAD NO IDEA THAT THE SWORD AND RAZOR WOULD GO AFTER OUR INFORMANT'S FAMILY.
JUST LIKE WE COULDN'T HAVE POSSIBLY GUESSED OUR INFORMANT'S YOUNGEST DAUGHTER WOULD REINVENT HERSELF AS SOME SORT OF VOODOO GODDESS...
...TAKE OVER THE ORGANIZATION...
...AND START TO SQUEEZE CUSTOMERS IN SOME SORT OF REVENGE PLOT.
WE WERE TRYING TO HELP.
I KNOW.
STORM, I JUST--
HOLD THAT THOUGHT.
I THINK--

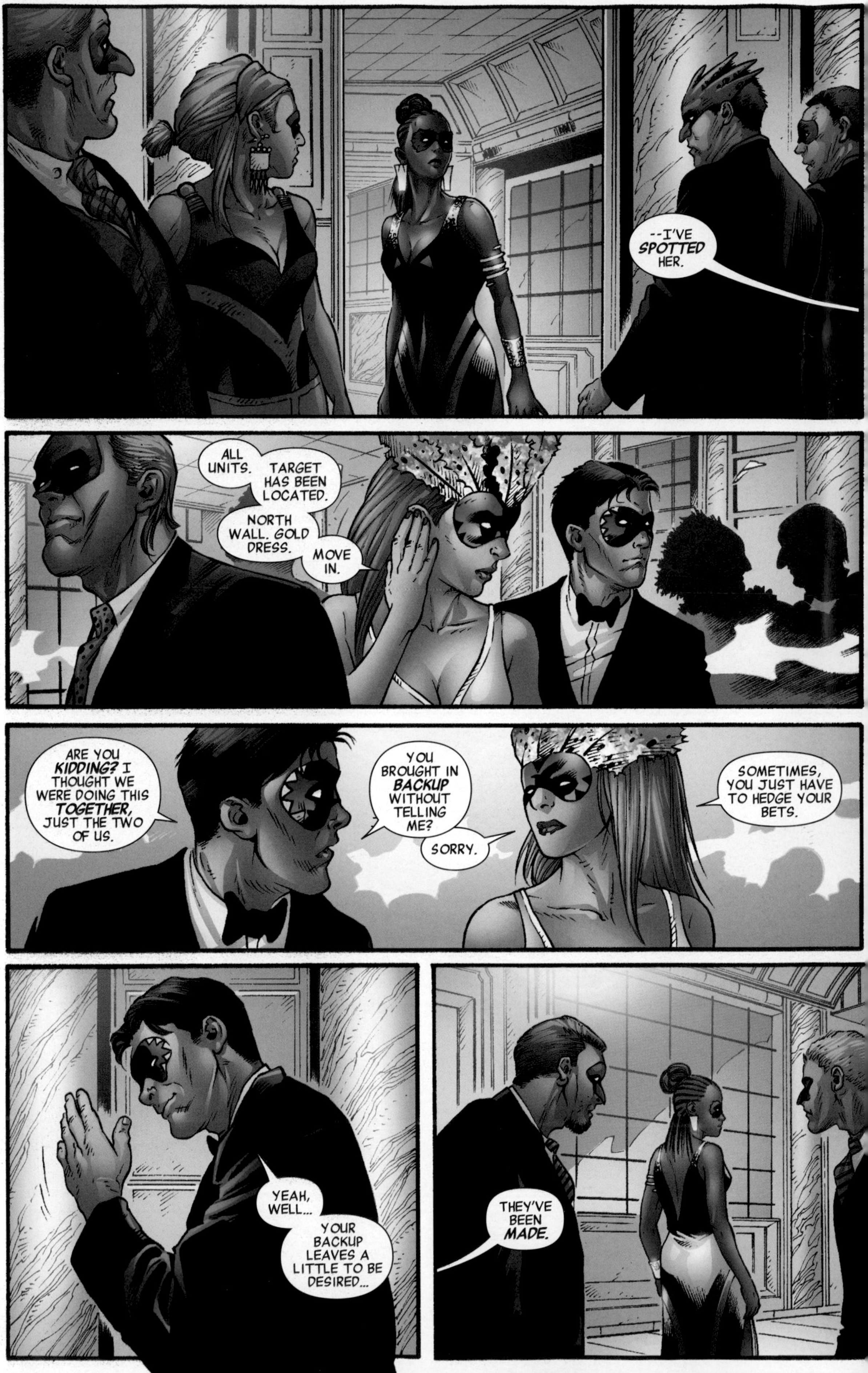
--I'VE SPOTTED HER.
ALL UNITS.
TARGET HAS BEEN LOCATED.
NORTH WALL. GOLD DRESS.
MOVE IN.
ARE YOU KIDDING? I THOUGHT WE WERE DOING THIS TOGETHER, JUST THE TWO OF US.
YOU BROUGHT IN BACKUP WITHOUT TELLING ME?
SORRY.
SOMETIMES, YOU JUST HAVE TO HEDGE YOUR BETS.
YEAH, WELL...
YOUR BACKUP LEAVES A LITTLE TO BE DESIRED...
THEY'VE BEEN MADE.

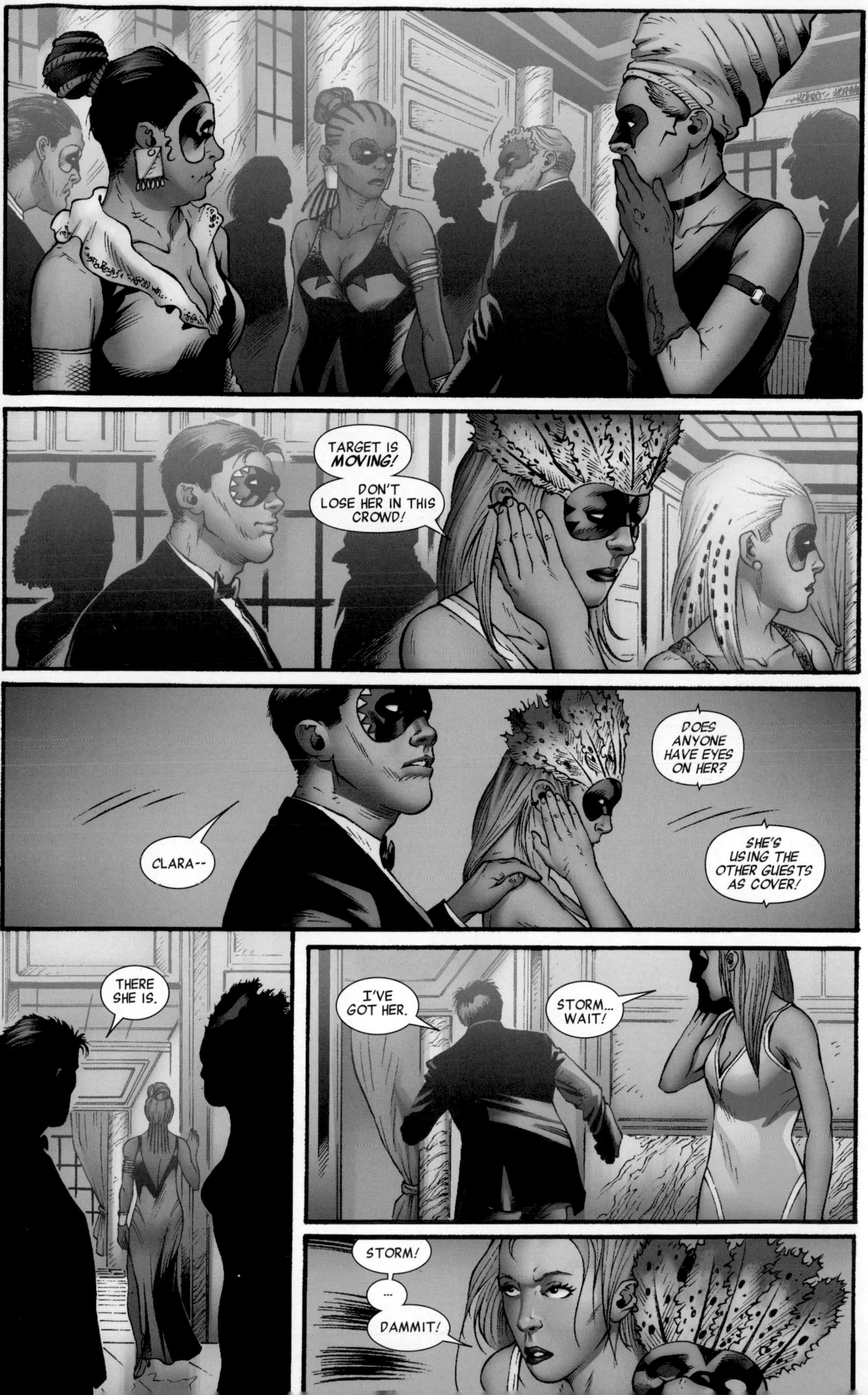
TARGET IS MOVING!
DON'T LOSE HER IN THIS CROWD!
CLARA--
DOES ANYONE HAVE EYES ON HER?
SHE'S USING THE OTHER GUESTS AS COVER!
THERE SHE IS.
I'VE GOT HER.
STORM... WAIT!
STORM!
...
DAMMIT!

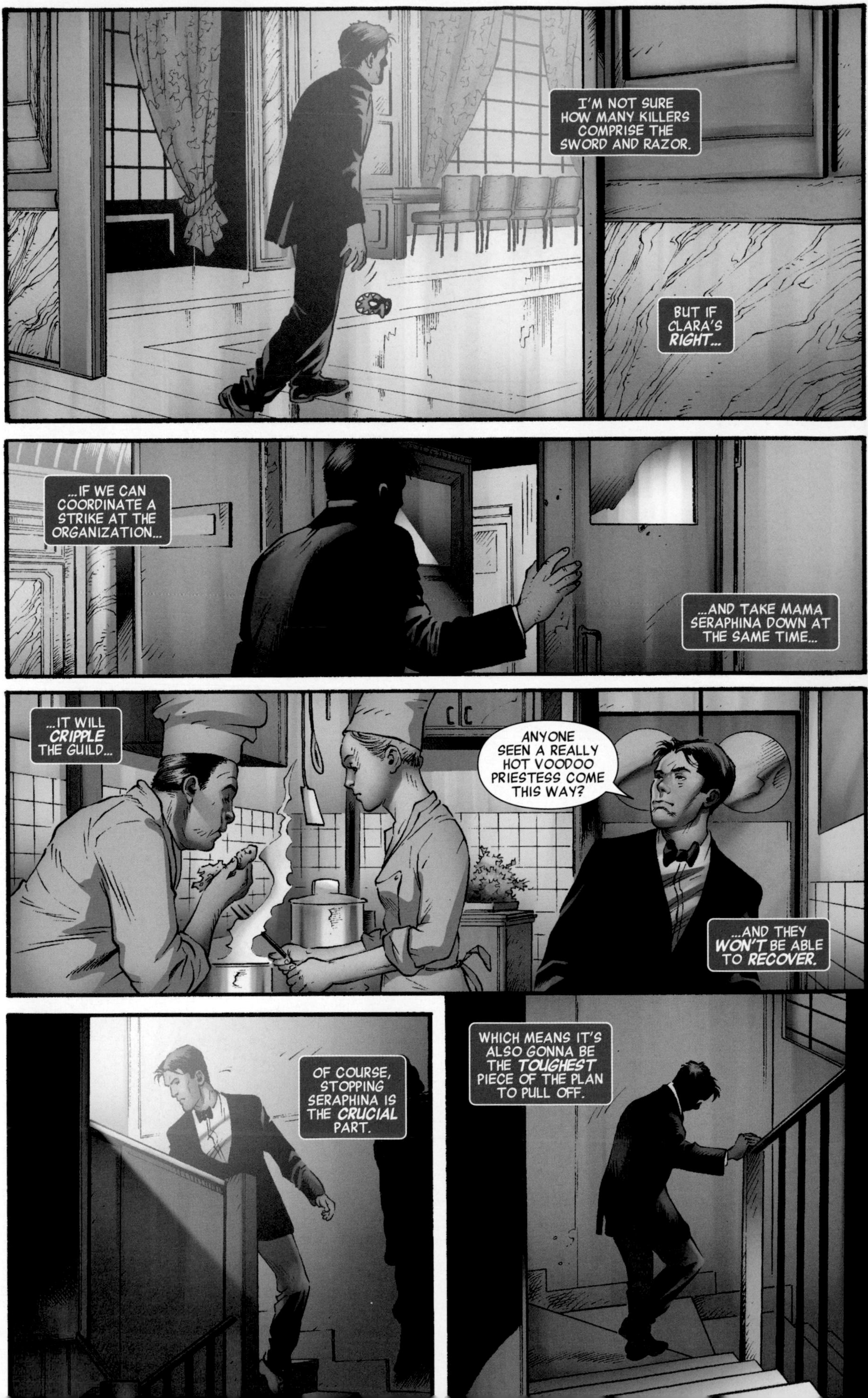
I'M NOT SURE HOW MANY KILLERS COMPRISE THE SWORD AND RAZOR.
BUT IF CLARA'S RIGHT...
...IF WE CAN COORDINATE A STRIKE AT THE ORGANIZATION...
...AND TAKE MAMA SERAPHINA DOWN AT THE SAME TIME...
...IT WILL CRIPPLE THE GUILD...
ANYONE SEEN A REALLY HOT VOODOO PRIESTESS COME THIS WAY?
...AND THEY WON'T BE ABLE TO RECOVER.
OF COURSE, STOPPING SERAPHINA IS THE CRUCIAL PART.
WHICH MEANS IT'S ALSO GONNA BE THE TOUGHEST PIECE OF THE PLAN TO PULL OFF.

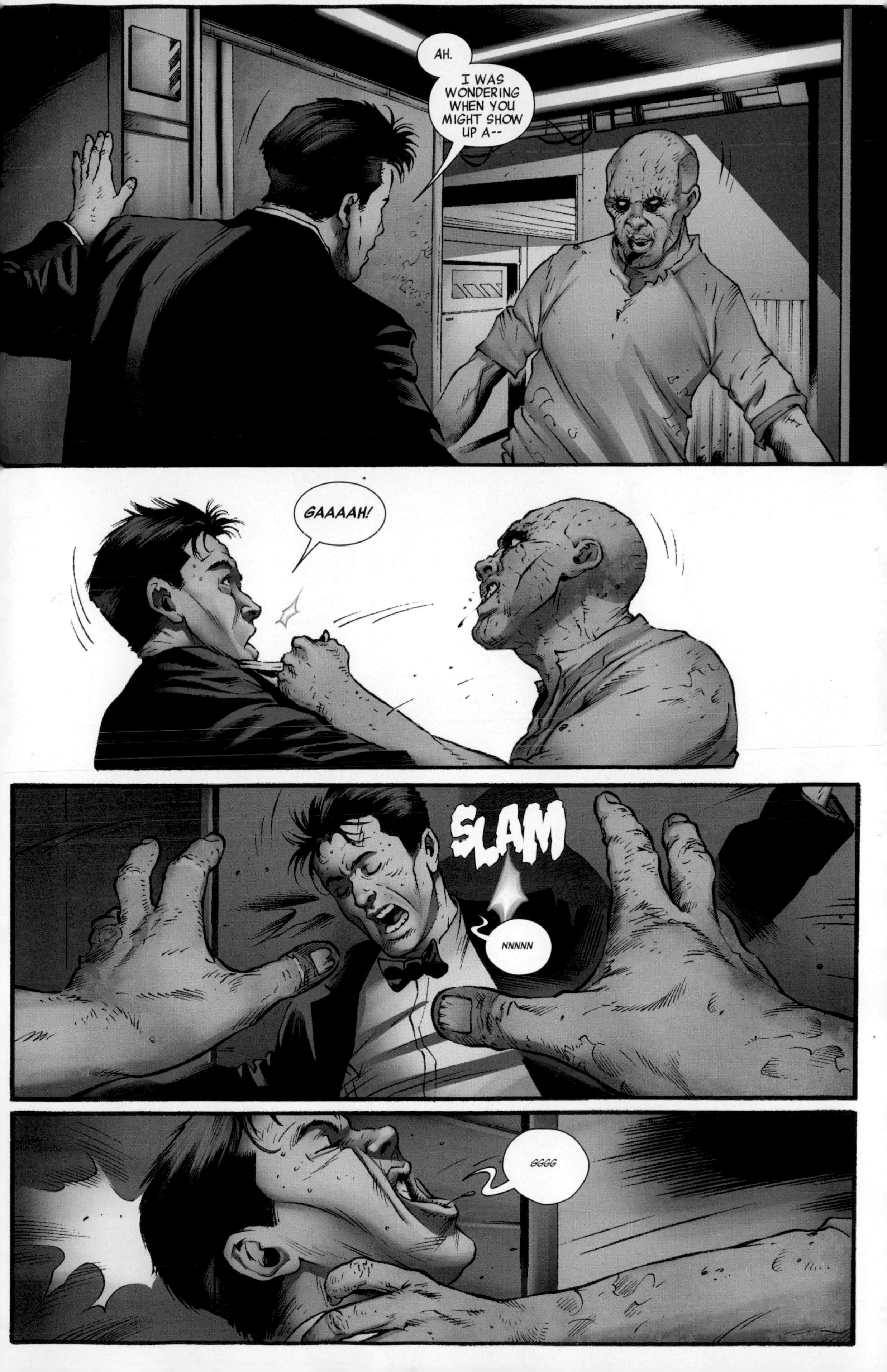
AH.
I WAS WONDERING WHEN YOU MIGHT SHOW UP A--
GAAAAH!
SLAM
NNNNN
GGGG

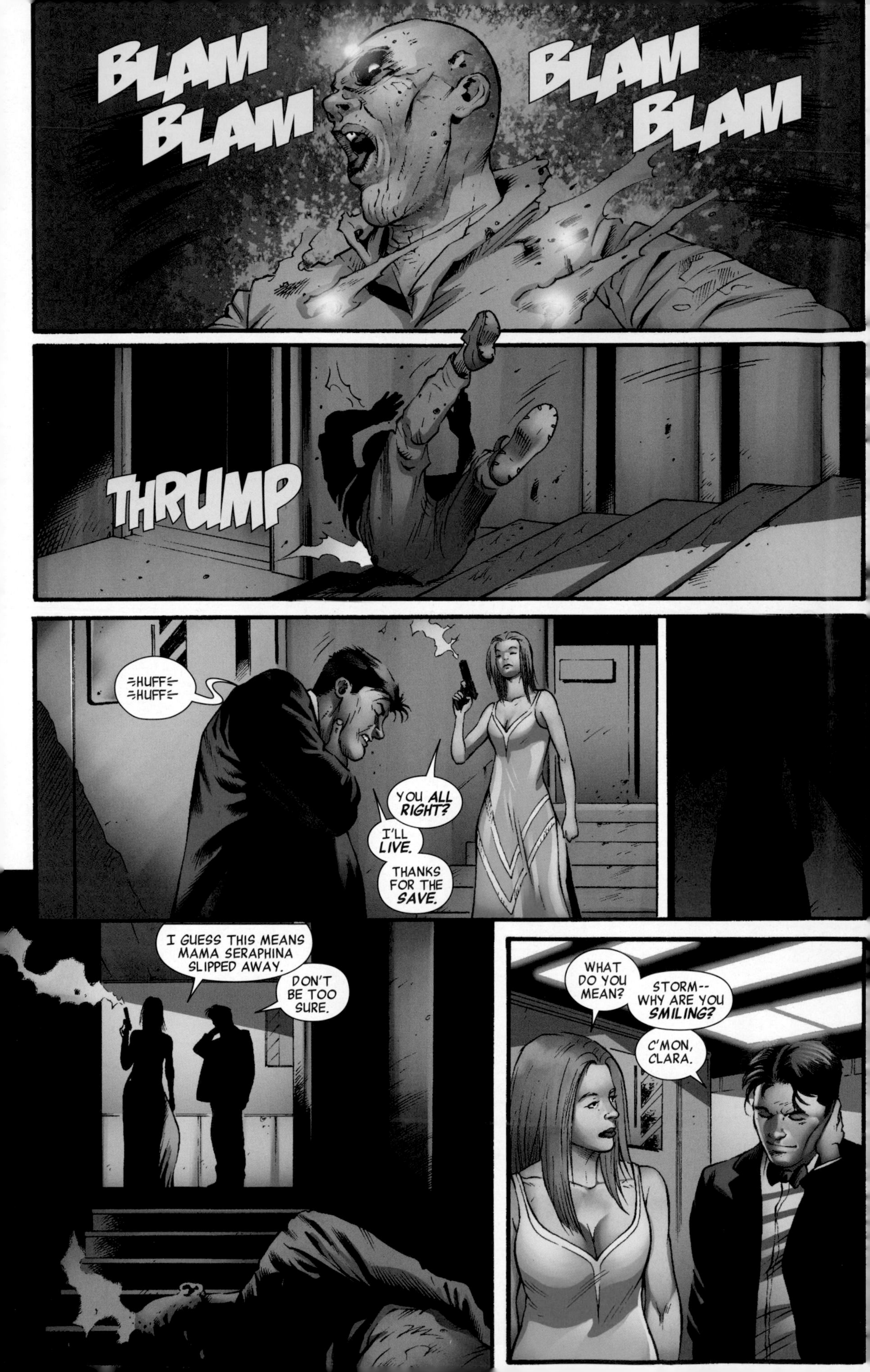
BLAM BLAM
BLAM BLAM
THRUMP
≈HUFF≈ ≈HUFF≈
YOU ALL RIGHT?
I'LL LIVE.
THANKS FOR THE SAVE.
I GUESS THIS MEANS MAMA SERAPHINA SLIPPED AWAY.
DON'T BE TOO SURE.
WHAT DO YOU MEAN?
STORM-- WHY ARE YOU SMILING?
C'MON, CLARA.

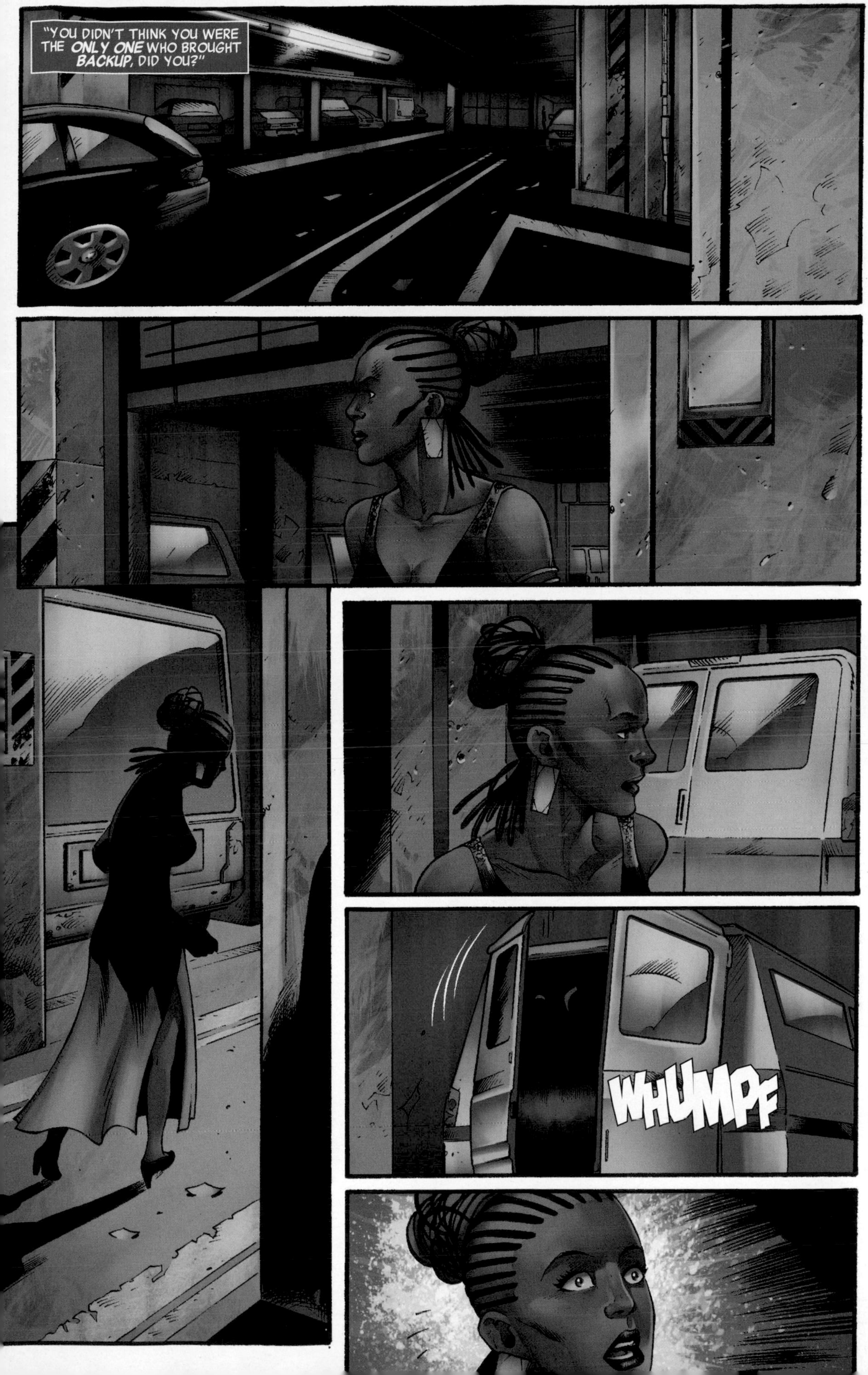
"YOU DIDN'T THINK YOU WERE THE ONLY ONE WHO BROUGHT BACKUP, DID YOU?"
WHUMPF

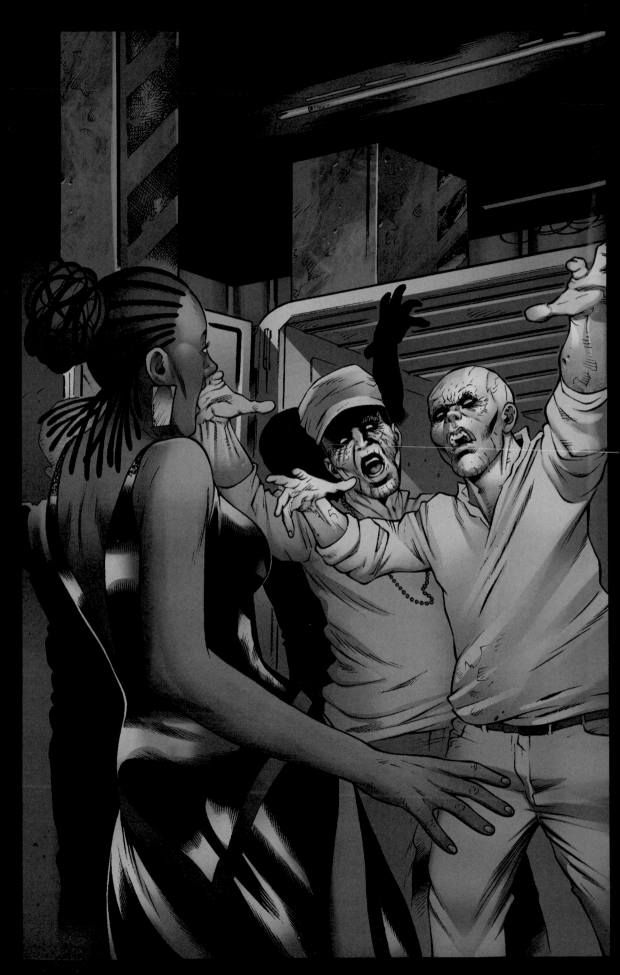

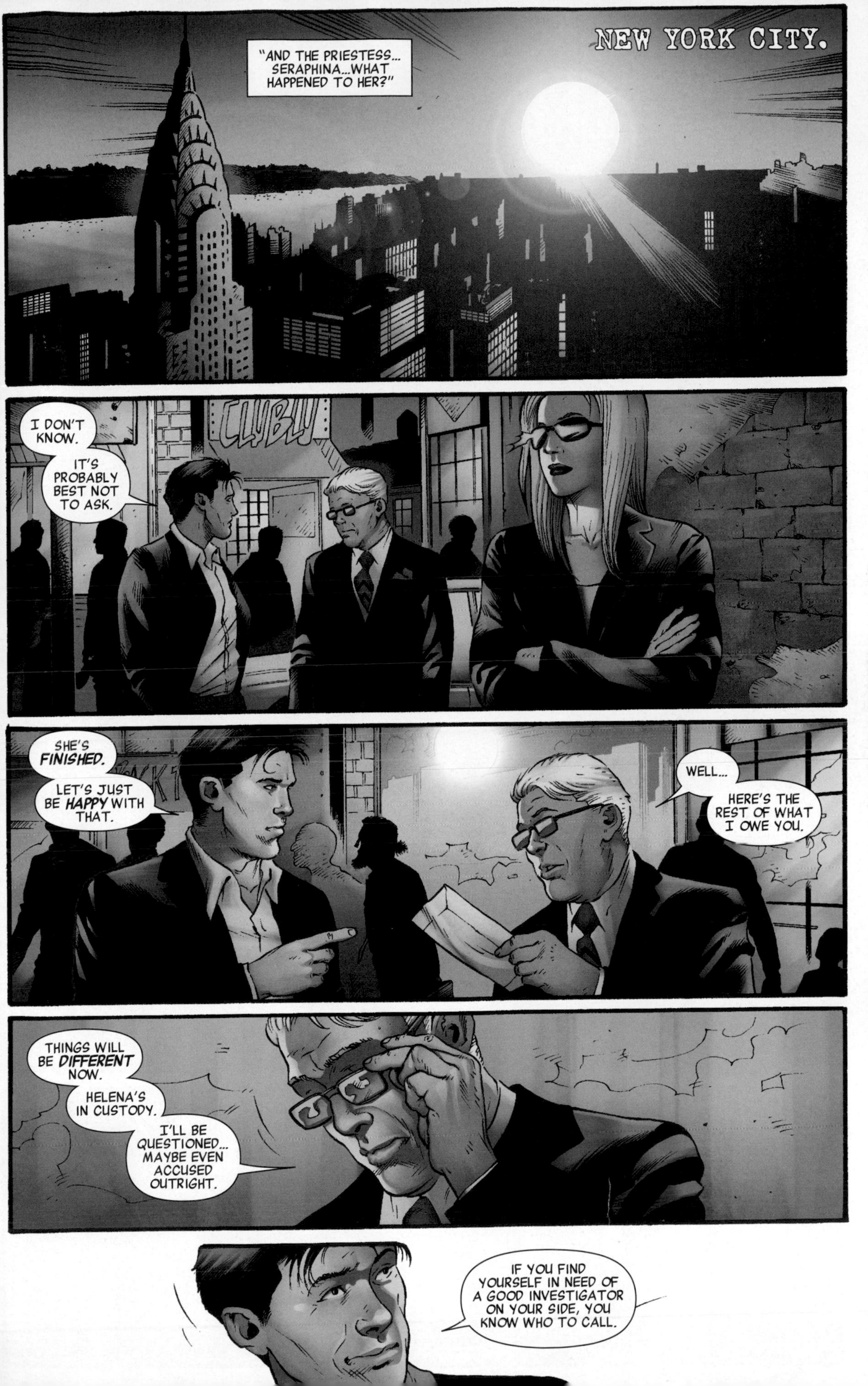
NEW YORK CITY.
"AND THE PRIESTESS... SERAPHINA...WHAT HAPPENED TO HER?"
CLUB
I DON'T KNOW.
IT'S PROBABLY BEST NOT TO ASK.
SHE'S *FINISHED.*
LET'S JUST BE *HAPPY* WITH THAT.
WELL...
HERE'S THE REST OF WHAT I OWE YOU.
THINGS WILL BE *DIFFERENT* NOW.
HELENA'S IN CUSTODY.
I'LL BE QUESTIONED... MAYBE EVEN ACCUSED OUTRIGHT.
IF YOU FIND YOURSELF IN NEED OF A GOOD INVESTIGATOR ON YOUR SIDE, YOU KNOW WHO TO CALL.

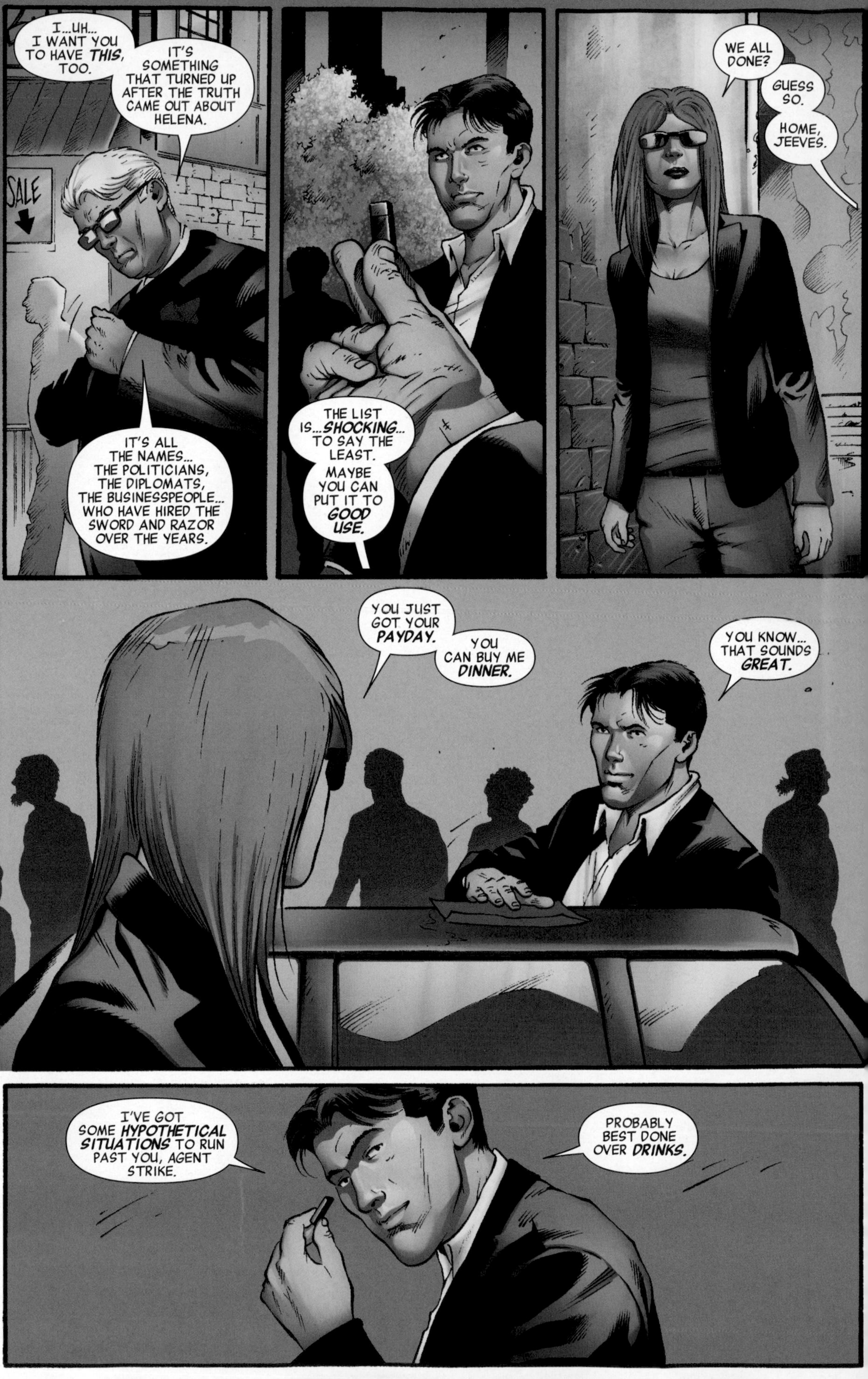

I...UH... I WANT YOU TO HAVE THIS, TOO.
IT'S SOMETHING THAT TURNED UP AFTER THE TRUTH CAME OUT ABOUT HELENA.
SALE
IT'S ALL THE NAMES... THE POLITICIANS, THE DIPLOMATS, THE BUSINESSPEOPLE... WHO HAVE HIRED THE SWORD AND RAZOR OVER THE YEARS.
THE LIST IS...SHOCKING... TO SAY THE LEAST.
MAYBE YOU CAN PUT IT TO GOOD USE.
WE ALL DONE?
GUESS SO.
HOME, JEEVES.
YOU JUST GOT YOUR PAYDAY.
YOU CAN BUY ME DINNER.
YOU KNOW... THAT SOUNDS GREAT.
I'VE GOT SOME HYPOTHETICAL SITUATIONS TO RUN PAST YOU, AGENT STRIKE.
PROBABLY BEST DONE OVER DRINKS.

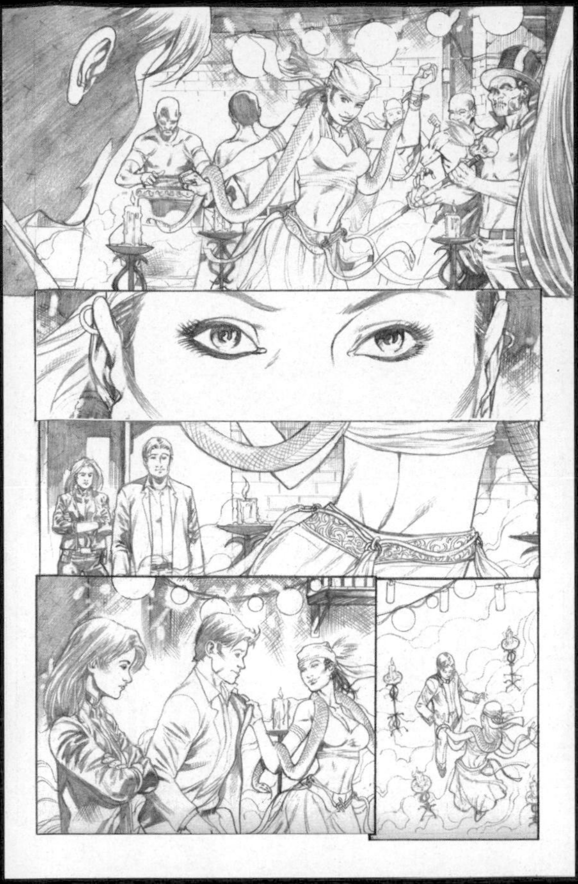

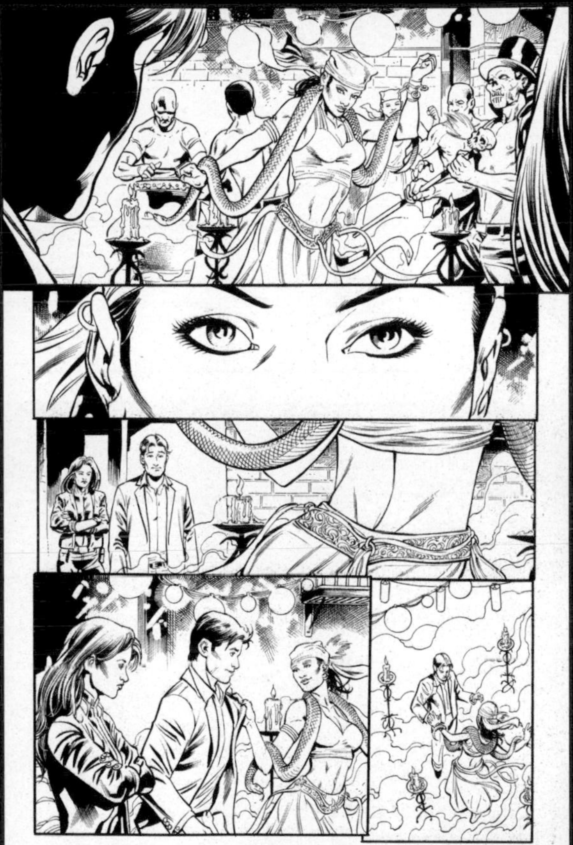

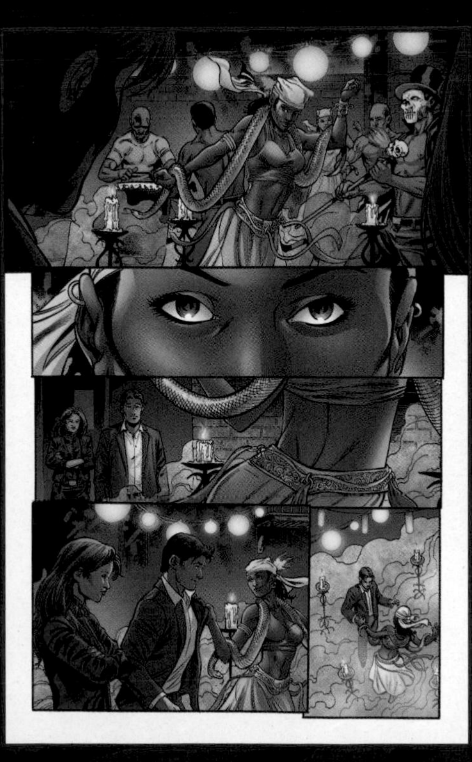

PAGE 28 ART PROCESS BY ROBERT ATKINS, SCOTT HANNA & CHRIS SOTOMAYOR

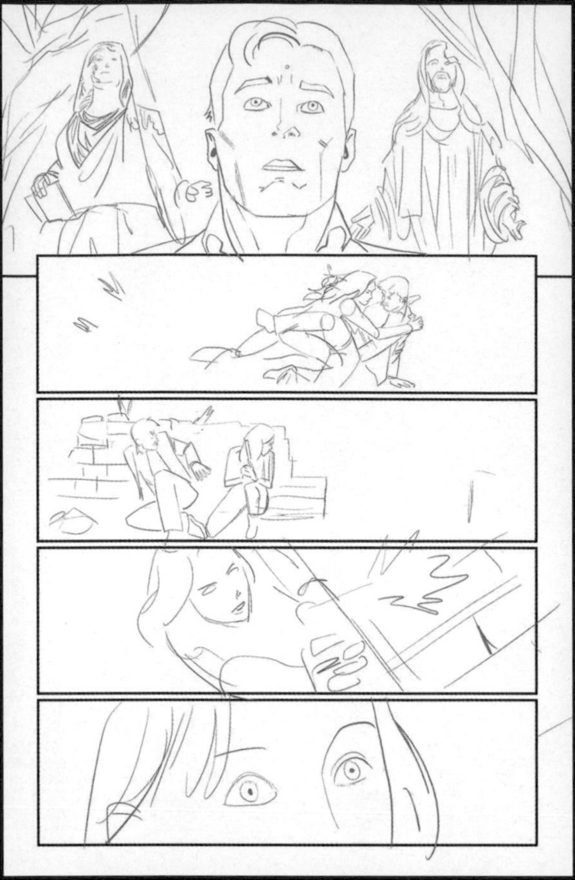

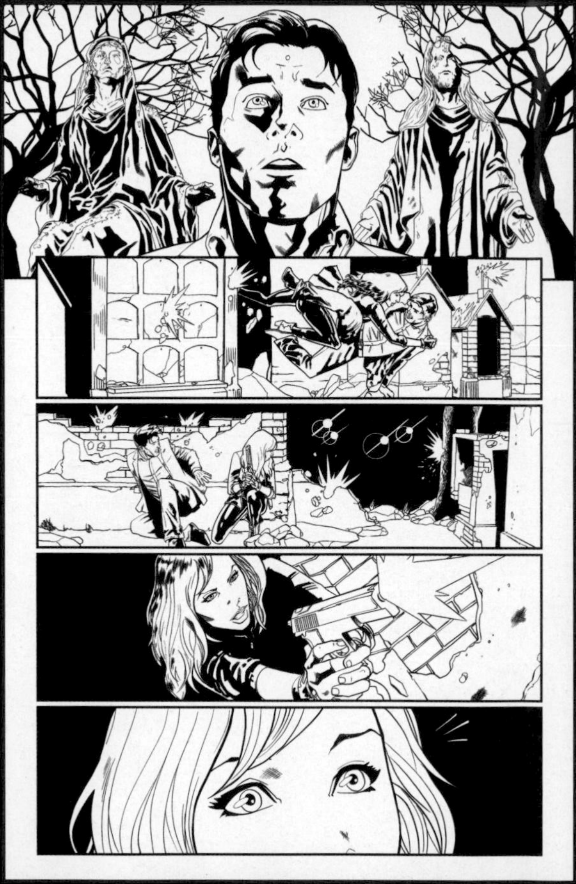

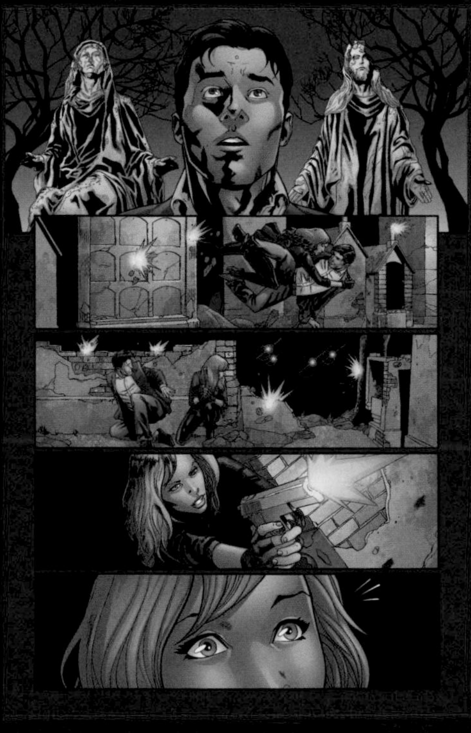

PAGE 41 ART PROCESS BY WILL SLINEY & CHRIS SOTOMAYOR

FOLLOW THE EXPLOITS OF DERRICK STORM

DEADLY STORM

While tracking down a missing husband for a desperate wife, private investigator Derrick Storm discovers there's a lot more to the job than he's been led to believe when he discovers the missing husband is actually a rogue CIA operative involved in selling national security secrets to enemy forces. He soon finds himself knee deep in international intrigue when he's recruited by the lovely and dangerous Clara Strike, a CIA agent with a penchant for trouble and adventure.

STORM SEASON

In Richard Castle's second Derrick Storm novel, the private investigator is hired to help a wealthy woman get back the money she lost to a con artist — but what should have been a routine mission quickly spirals out of control when the con artist reaches out to Storm seeking his help finding a missing woman. Haunted by a recording of the woman's scream for help, Storm investigates, and soon discovers an international conspiracy reaching further than he ever imagined — perhaps all the way to Clara Strike, a CIA agent the world thinks is dead.

A CALM BEFORE STORM

Derrick Storm is looking forward to finally getting out of the game — stocking up his cabin cruiser and heading out into the open Atlantic for good. But his plans are put on hold when, on the eve of a UN summit, the severed head of a Russian diplomat is found bobbing in the backwaters of the Hudson. Storm's CIA handler Clara Strike enlists him to crack a plot of global proportions, pitting the uncanny PI against a legion of eastern bloc mercenaries, and an ex-KGB hit man known simply as "The Fear."

STORM'S BREAK

A brutal cold snap has practically brought Manhattan to its knees, driving the island's denizens indoors. The city's homeless are driven down, into the bowels of ancient train tunnels and the concrete roots of skyscrapers. It's a world of predators and prey, and when runaway teenage girls start disappearing into this underworld, Derrick Storm isn't afraid to find out why. It doesn't take long before Storm trips to an international human trafficking ring headed by notorious Panama kingpin Marco Juarez. Teaming up with reliable and gutsy CIA agent Clara Strike, these two race to stop one of the world's most vile criminals before he destroys more innocent lives.

STORM WARNING

When Derrick Storm's close friend, attorney Sam Strummel, is murdered in cold blood in a cemetery outside of NYC, Storm launches his own investigation to bring the murderer to justice. While investigating Strummel's business dealings, Storm exposes a murder-for-hire syndicate that has just made him their next target.

UNHOLY STORM

When the daughters of four high-powered international businessmen are discovered dead in New York City, the NYPD scrambles to bring the murderer to justice. But when a fifth girl is found mutilated in a pool of her own blood, her prestigious French family hires Derrick Storm to run his own investigation and find the real killer. With limited access to evidence, Storm has only one lead — a strange symbol drawn in blood at each of the five crime scenes. While immersing himself in voodoo religion and rituals, Storm enlists the help of the beautiful and daring Clara Strike, his CIA handler. Together they uncover a deep web of deception under the guise of mysticism and devotion. And in a race against time, this most unlikely pair unlock the mystery behind a network of international assassins capable of creating a global catastrophe.

GATHERING STORM

While packing his bags for a much-needed vacation, Storm gets a call from CIA Agent Clara Strike with an urgent mission. Storm must help protect the Swiss Ambassador's daughter against a formidable foe: a former KGB officer who is known for killing his victims with undetectable poison. When the mission is compromised, Clara fears that there is a mole in the CIA. In a bold move, Clara decides to put Storm undercover at Langley in order to smoke out the guilty party. Unexpectedly, Storm does more than just that; he uncovers a conspiracy that goes to the top levels of the agency and threatens Clara's livelihood.

STORM RISING

On a quest to recover a rare sapphire stolen from one of Manhattan's elite, Derrick Storm comes face-to-face with Bentley Silver: notorious jewel thief and rival womanizer. As the two men compare their conquests, they form an unlikely union in order to bring down a Parisian thief who threatens to undermine Silver's livelihood and Storm's bank account. A trail of stolen jewels leads Storm and Bentley to an underground international society, which is shrouded in secrecy and has a deadly mission.

DRIVING STORM

Storm faces his toughest case to date when CIA Agent Clara Strike asks him to clear her sister Susan's name after she's accused of murdering her husband. Strike insists that it was police incompetence and tainted evidence that led to her sister's arrest. Storm takes the case, only to realize that the police conspiracy against Susan isn't just Clara's hunch, it's a stone wall of silence even he may not be able to get past. And the closer he gets to the truth, the more danger he puts Susan in, leading Storm to a terrible choice – prove her innocence or save her life.

STORM'S LAST STAND

An ex-con out for vengeance, an old lover looking for closure, and a hardened cop hoping to find peace of mind all come crashing into Storm's life when a man they all know jumps off the Brooklyn Bridge. Or was he pushed? Now these former foes must work together to solve a crime that brings up their complicated past history and some memories better left forgotten. Storm must protect his reputation, heart, and possibly his life while unlocking the mystery behind his friend's death. In the midst of this, CIA Agent Clara Strike calls on Storm to help with what she deems, an "easy" task. But when this mission leads to Clara's abduction by MI5 agents, Storm must balance his two identities and cases while trying to save Clara's life.

STORM FALL

Storm is finally feeling like he has his life back: a few open and shut PI cases that lack any danger or intrigue and no recent calls from CIA Agent Clara Strike. But when her lack of contact begins to concern him, Storm begins to search for the woman who he has begun to care for as more than just a colleague. But what Storm unravels quickly turns his world upside down. Is Clara the CIA agent she claimed to be or a rogue spy operating outside of the law? Just when he begins to scratch the surface of the truth, his bank account is drained and a murder of a rival PI is pinned on him. Storm must take on his most challenging client yet: himself. Is this the work of Clara or one of his many enemies? Storm has to comb through his entire career as a PI and as a secret CIA operative: every criminal he put away, every crime he solved, every life he affected, in order to find out who would do this to him. Will he find the culprit pulling the puppet strings or will this be the end of Derrick Storm?

STORM FRONT

From Tokyo, to London, to Johannesburg, high-level bankers are being gruesomely tortured and murdered. The killer, caught in a fleeting glimpse on a surveillance camera, has been described as a psychopath with an eye patch. And that means Gregor Volkov, Derrick Storm's old nemesis, has returned. Desperate to figure out who Volkov is working for and why, the CIA calls on the one man who can match Volkov's strength and cunning- Derrick Storm. With the help of a beautiful and mysterious foreign agent with whom Storm is becoming romantically and professionally entangled- he discovers that Volkov's treachery has embroiled a wealthy hedge-fund manager and a U.S. senator. In a heated race against time, Storm chases Volkov's shadow from Paris, to the lair of a computer genius in Iowa, to the streets of Manhattan, then through a bullet-ridden car chase on the New Jersey Turnpike. In the process, Storm uncovers a plot that could destroy the global economy, unleashing untold chaos which only he can stop.

OTHER BOOKS BY THE AUTHOR

HELL HATH NO FURY

Taking a sabbatical from his college teaching job, Adam Parel has moved his family to the remote Oregon town of Jessup to finish his first novel. At first, Jessup seems ideal. Adam's wife and sons make friends quickly and there's enough quiet for Adam to get his work done. But as he researches his new hometown, Adam becomes convinced there's something sinister going on beneath Jessup's peaceful façade. People have gone missing here for decades and Adam eventually discovers the horrifying reason why: an obsessive cult that will stop at nothing to keep their sacred region "pure." As Adam struggles to escape with his family, he soon finds himself hunted by bloodthirsty fanatics for whom killing is the only way of living.

FLOWERS FOR YOUR GRAVE

Four murders in and the NYPD are still desperate for a lead on the serial killer that the tabloids are calling "The Florist." Struggling journalist Leroy Fine knows if he cracked this story he could get back everything he's lost – his job, his wife, his self-respect. So when Leroy uncovers a piece of evidence the cops have overlooked, he begins his own private investigation into the twisted and deadly world of The Florist. But as Leroy gets closer to discovering the killer's identity, he soon realizes he's put himself and everyone he loves in mortal danger. Now Leroy must decipher the Florist's riddles and unmask his identity… or end up the latest flower-covered corpse on the Ledger's front page.

AT DUSK WE DIE

Still residing in the same tiny Texas town where he grew up, Ben Meltzer's life is a peaceful one. He runs the local drugstore and has a growing family with his high school sweetheart. So when the Satan's Creed motorcycle gang drive into town, he hardly pays them any mind. But after the entire town is ravaged by the Creed in a single night, he and his family are forced to flee for their lives and pray for the dawn. Because the Satan's Creed are no ordinary biker gang – they're ravenous vampires come to feed. As Ben attempts to keep his family safe, he quickly realizes that he must fight back – or watch as his family becomes fodder for nightmares come to life.

A SKULL AT SPRINGTIME

Looking for a way to pay for college after her father's death, Rachel Lyons is spending the summer planting trees in the clearcut forests of remote Washington. It's a lucrative but lonely job and Rachel soon finds the monotony draining. That is, until she stumbles upon a half-buried skeleton deep in the woods – a discovery that leads her to uncover an entire field of corpses. When Rachel's attempts to contact authorities are thwarted, it quickly becomes clear that she isn't alone out here. As she struggles to escape back to civilization, Rachel must struggle to stay alive or risk becoming yet another one of the skeletons beneath the dirt.

NEW YORK LEDGER #1 BESTSELLING AUTHOR
A ROSE FOR EVERAFTER

A ROSE FOR EVERAFTER

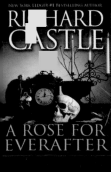

At the Blessed Sacrament School for Girls, Sister Mary Grace leads her young charges in daily Morning Prayer, asking the Lord their souls to keep. But the young women of Riverbend are starting to disappear, only to be found in shallow graves, wrapped in shrouds of white and grasping a red rose in their cold dead hands. Who could be killing the town's virgin daughters? And why is he burying them alive? When Sister Mary Grace starts investigating, she discovers a trail of evidence that leads from the local rectory to the upper echelons of the archdiocese – and ultimately to a secretive organization whose provenance may be very far from godly.

New York Ledger's #1 Best Seller
RICHARD CASTLE
WHEN IT COMES TO SLAUGHTER

WHEN IT COMES TO SLAUGHTER

The neo-hippie community of Fair Haven, Vermont, had never experienced a single murder in its nearly 40-year history – until one moonless night a week ago, when five members of the Akin family were brutally hacked to death and found hanging from meat hooks. Suddenly, the town's tiny two-man police force – Chief Derek Olson and Deputy Ana Ruiz – find themselves thrust into a nightmare world. They wrestle with a dearth of evidence and a populace becoming more paranoid by the second as rumors abound of a scarecrow-like creature with hatchets for hands prowling the countryside. When a second family is butchered in the same gruesome fashion, Olson and Ruiz begin to suspect that many of their townsfolk are not the radical peaceniks they claim to be – the majority, in fact, harbor dark, violent pasts that may finally be coming home to roost.

KISSED AND KILLED

KISSED AND KILLED

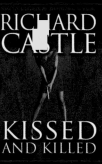

Rookie detective Alexandra Jones grew up fast on the mean streets of the Bronx. But nothing could prepare her for the spate of murders currently plaguing the five boroughs: Someone is killing the city's richest men by cutting off their tongues and – in a final coup de grace – lopping off their privates. Jones' street-smart investigative skills soon lead her to the dark underbelly of the fashion industry, where beauty is a commodity easily bought and sold. It becomes clear that the killer is amongst those tossed aside after their youth has been used and abused. But as she sinks deeper into the fashion underworld, Jones discovers she's become the latest target in the killer's quest. Can she uncover the murderer in time or will she end up as yet another victim of their lethal rage?

HEAT WAVE

HEAT WAVE

Mystery sensation Richard Castle introduces his newest character, NYPD Homicide Detective Nikki Heat. Tough, sexy, professional, Nikki Heat carries a passion for justice as she leads one of New York City's top homicide squads. She's hit with an unexpected challenge when the commissioner assigns superstar magazine journalist Jameson Rook to ride along with her to research an article on New York's Finest. Pulitzer Prize-winning Rook is as much a handful as he is handsome. His wise-cracking and meddling aren't her only problems. As she works to unravel the secrets of the murdered real estate tycoon, she must also confront the spark between them. The one called heat.

NAKED HEAT

CASTLE
NAKED

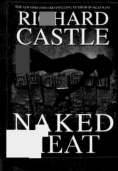

When New York's most vicious gossip columnist, Cassidy Towne, is found dead, Heat uncovers a gallery of high profile suspects, all with compelling motives for killing the most feared muckraker in Manhattan. Heat's investigation is complicated by her surprise reunion with superstar magazine journalist Jameson Rook. The residue of their unresolved romantic conflict and crackling sexual tension fills the air as Heat and Rook embark on a search for a killer among celebrities and mobsters, singers and hookers, pro athletes and shamed politicians. This new, explosive case brings on the heat in the glittery world of secrets, cover-ups, and scandals.

HEAT RISES

RICHARD
CASTLE
RISES

The bizarre murder of a parish priest at a New York bondage club is just the tip of an iceberg that leads Nikki Heat to a dark conspiracy that reaches all the way to the highest level of the NYPD. But when she gets too close to the truth, Nikki finds herself disgraced, stripped of her badge and out on her own with nobody she can trust. Except maybe the one man in her life who's not a cop. Reporter Jameson Rook. In the midst of New York's coldest winter in a hundred years, there's one thing Nikki is determined to prove. Heat Rises.

FROZEN HEAT

RICHARD
CASTLE

NYPD Homicide Detective Nikki Heat gets more mystery than she imagined when she arrives at her latest crime scene. The body of an unidentified woman has been found stabbed to death and stuffed inside a suitcase left sitting on a freezer truck. A startling enough death, but an even bigger shock comes when this new homicide surprisingly connects to the unsolved murder of Detective Heat's own mother. The gruesome killing of this Jane Doe launches Heat on a dangerous and emotional investigation, rekindling the cold case that has haunted her since she was nineteen. Paired once again with her romantic and investigative partner, top journalist Jameson Rook, Heat works to solve the mystery of the body in the suitcase while she also digs into unexplored areas of her mother's background. The question is, now that her mother's cold case has unexpectedly thawed, will Nikki Heat finally be able to solve the dark mystery that has been her demon for ten years?

DEADLY HEAT

CASTLE
DEADLY

Determined to find justice for her mother, top NYPD Homicide Detective Nikki Heat continues to pursue the elusive former CIA station chief who ordered her execution over a decade ago. For the hunt, Nikki teams once again with her romantic partner, Pulitzer Prize winning investigative journalist Jameson Rook, and their quest for the old spy and the motive behind the past murder unearths an alarming terror plot, which is anything but ancient history. It is lethal. It is now. And it has already entered its countdown phase. Complicating Heat's mission to bring the rogue spy to justice and thwart the looming terror event, a serial killer begins menacing the Twentieth Precinct, and her homicide squad is under pressure to stop him, and soon. Known for his chilling stealth, the diabolical murderer not only signals out to Nikki as the exclusive recipient of his taunting message, he names her as his next victim.

ABOUT THE AUTHOR

Richard Castle is the author of numerous bestsellers, including *Heat Wave*, *Naked Heat*, *Heat Rises*, *Frozen Heat*, *Deadly Heat* and *Storm Front*. When he's not writing bestsellers, Mr. Castle consults with the NYPD's 12th Precinct on New York's strangest homicides. For his contribution to law enforcement, he was recently honored by the Allonym Institute with their Brad Parks distinguished service award. Mr. Castle lives in Manhattan with his daughter and mother, both of whom infuse his life with humor and inspiration.

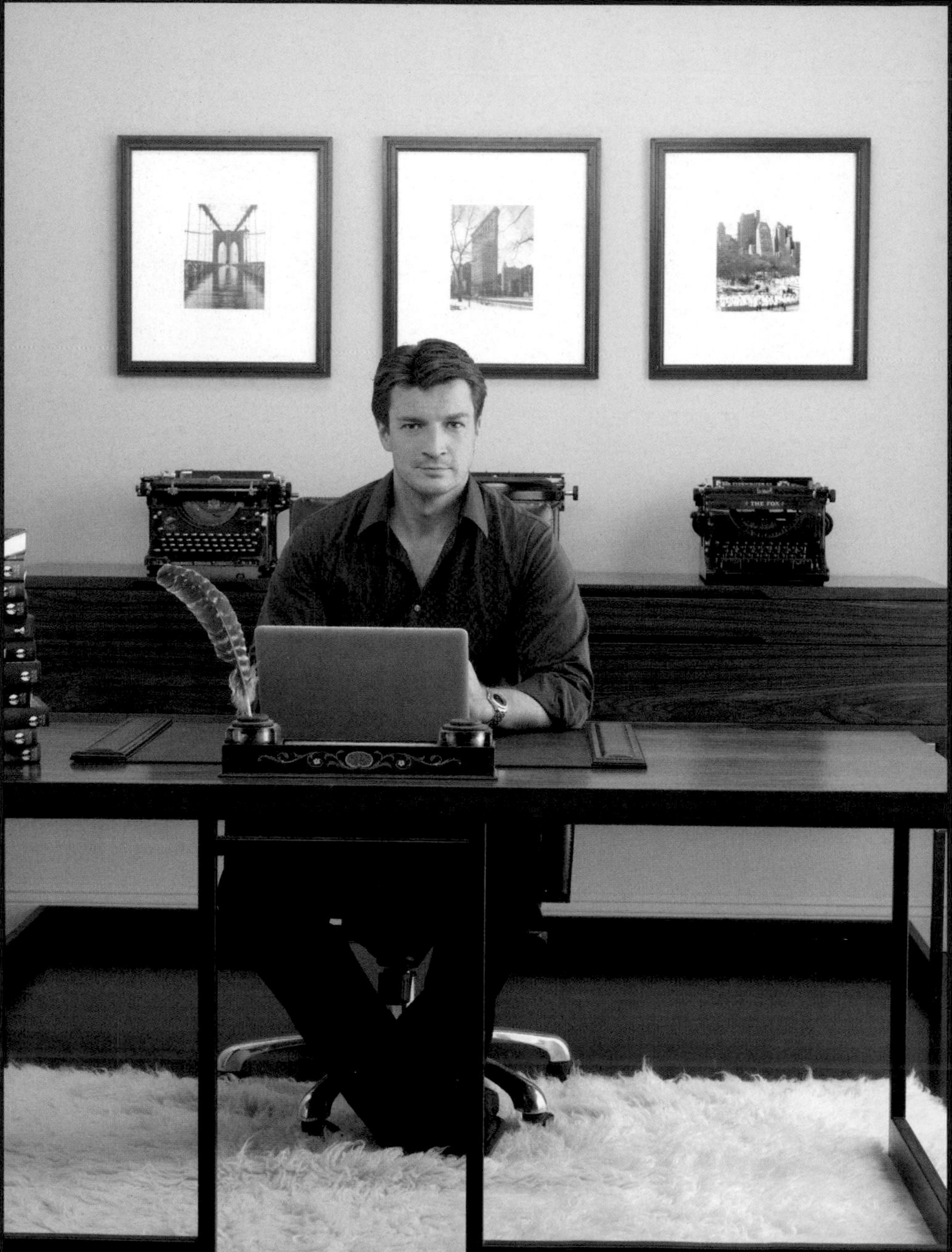